Ethnology and Empire

America and the Long 19th Century

GENERAL EDITORS
David Kazanjian, Elizabeth McHenry, and Priscilla Wald

Black Frankenstein: The Making of an American Metaphor
Elizabeth Young

Neither Fugitive nor Free: Atlantic Slavery, Freedom Suits, and the Legal Culture of Travel
Edlie L. Wong

Shadowing the White Man's Burden: U.S. Imperialism and the Problem of the Color Line
Gretchen Murphy

Bodies of Reform: The Rhetoric of Character in Gilded-Age America
James B. Salazar

Empire's Proxy: American Literature and U.S. Imperialism in the Philippines
Meg Wesling

Sites Unseen: Architecture, Race, and American Literature
William A. Gleason

Racial Innocence: Performing American Childhood from Slavery to Civil Rights
Robin Bernstein

American Arabesque: Arabs and Islam in the Nineteenth-Century Imaginary
Jacob Rama Berman

Racial Indigestion: Eating Bodies in the Nineteenth Century
Kyla Wazana Tompkins

Idle Threats: Men and the Limits of Productivity in Nineteenth-Century America
Andrew Lyndon Knighton

The Traumatic Colonel: The Founding Fathers, Slavery, and the Phantasmatic Aaron Burr
Michael J. Drexler and Ed White

Unsettled States: Nineteenth-Century American Literary Studies
Edited by Dana Luciano and Ivy G. Wilson

Sitting in Darkness: Mark Twain, Asia, and Comparative Racialization
Hsuan L. Hsu

Picture Freedom: Remaking Black Visuality in the Early Nineteenth Century
Jasmine Nichole Cobb

Stella
Émeric Bergeaud
Translated by Lesley Curtis and Christen Mucher

Racial Reconstruction: Black Inclusion, Chinese Exclusion, and the Fictions of Citizenship
Edlie L. Wong

Ethnology and Empire: Languages, Literature, and the Making of the North American Borderlands
Robert Lawrence Gunn

Ethnology and Empire

Languages, Literature, and the Making of the North American Borderlands

Robert Lawrence Gunn

NEW YORK UNIVERSITY PRESS
New York and London

NEW YORK UNIVERSITY PRESS
New York and London
www.nyupress.org

© 2015 by New York University

All rights reserved

ISBN: 978-1-4798-4258-2 (hardback)
ISBN: 978-1-4798-4905-5 (paperback)

For Library of Congress Cataloging-in-Publication data, please contact the Library of Congress.

References to Internet websites (URLs) were accurate at the time of writing.

Neither the author nor New York University Press is responsible for URLs that may have expired or changed since the manuscript was prepared.

New York University Press books are printed on acid-free paper, and their binding materials are chosen for strength and durability. We strive to use environmentally responsible suppliers and materials to the greatest extent possible in publishing our books.

Manufactured in the United States of America

10 9 8 7 6 5 4 3 2 1

Also available as an ebook

A book in the American Literatures Initiative (ALI), a collaborative publishing project of NYU Press, Fordham University Press, Rutgers University Press, Temple University Press, and the University of Virginia Press. The Initiative is supported by The Andrew W. Mellon Foundation. For more information, please visit www.americanliteratures.org.

Contents

	Acknowledgments	ix
	Introduction	1
1	Philologies of Race: Ethnological Linguistics and Novelistic Representation	17
2	Empire, Sign Languages, and the Long Expedition, 1819–1821	52
3	John Dunn Hunter, Tecumseh, and the Linguistic Politics of Pan-Indianism	83
4	Connecting Borderlands: Native Networks and the Fredonian Rebellion	114
5	John Russell Bartlett's Literary Borderlands: Ethnology, the U.S-Mexico War, and the United States Boundary Survey	145
	Indian Passports	177
	Notes	187
	Index	229
	About the Author	242

Acknowledgments

Although the idea for this book began for me after graduate school, my deepest intellectual debts extend to my graduate mentors at New York University: Cyrus R. K. Patell, Elizabeth McHenry, Nancy Ruttenburg, Ross Posnock, and Bryan Waterman. My warmest gratitude to all for teaching me to read, think, and write as an academic professional. My deepest thanks are to my advisor, Cyrus Patell, for his inspiring example, professional guidance, and ongoing discussions about work and ideas over the years.

This book would not have been possible without the financial and fellowship support of a number of entities and institutions. For supporting this book, my thanks to the American Antiquarian Society, the American Philosophical Society, the John Carter Brown Library, and the University Research Institute at the University of Texas at El Paso. A version of chapter 5, "John Russell Bartlett's Literary Borderlands," appeared previously in *Western American Literature* 48.4 (Winter 2012): 349–80. I am grateful to Melody Graulich, Sabine Barcatta, and to the University of Nebraska Press for permission to republish here. A few phrases from my article "The Ethnologists' Bookshop: Bartlett & Welford in 1840s New York," *Wordsworth Circle* 41.3 (Summer 2010): 159–63, are incorporated here also; I am warmly grateful to Marilyn Gaull for her permission to republish this work.

At UTEP, I have been lucky to work in a warm departmental community filled with dedicated colleagues and wonderful students. I am grateful to the chairs of the English Department who have supported my work during the writing of this book: Evelyn Posey, David Ruiter, and Maggy Smith. In the Literature Program, I am thankful for the support of my colleagues Meredith Abarca, Ezra Cappell, Ruben Espinosa, Mimi Gladstein, Maryse Jayasuriya, Deane Mansfield-Kelley, Lois Marchino, Joe Ortiz, Marion Rohrleitner, Tom Schmid, Tony Stafford, Brian Yothers, and Barbara Zimbalist. Elsewhere at UTEP, I have been grateful for the friendship and intellectual stimulation of a number of valued colleagues during the writing of this book, and I wish to thank especially Chuck Ambler, Adam Arenson, Ernie Chavez, Sandra McGee Deutsch, Lawry Martin, and Sandra Garabano. Special thanks here to Chuck, for the valuable feedback that stemmed from his invitation to present an early portion of this book during the History Department's Interdisciplinary Seminar Series, and to Sandra for her invitation to give a talk at the Center for Inter-American and Border Studies. I am especially grateful to those colleagues who have read and responded to portions of this book: Adam Arenson, Brad Cartwright, Jonna Perrillo, Tom Schmid, and Brian Yothers. Warm thanks to J. Sam Moore for his gift of books about J. R. Bartlett. My humble thanks to all of my students at UTEP, both undergraduate and graduate, for engaging with many of the ideas and texts explored here with diligence and enthusiasm.

I was immensely fortunate to meet Paul Erickson, Director of Academic Programs at the American Antiquarian Society, at an early formative stage of this project. During my time as a Peterson Fellow at AAS, Paul was my first sounding board for some of the major ideas in this book before I was sure if it was even going to be a book, or, if so, what kind of book it was going to be. Since that time, I have continued to find great pleasure and profit in his deep knowledge, unstinting support and advocacy of my work, incredible sense of humor, and uncanny gifts of quality restaurant detection. I am also grateful to the library staff at AAS, who have been extremely generous with their time and expertise during my visits, particularly Thomas G. Knoles, Elizabeth Pope, and Jackie Penny. My thanks to David Whitesell for answering my queries about dictionaries and nineteenth-century book-binding practices. At the American Philosophical Society, I took immense pleasure in my daily interactions with Roy Goodman and am very grateful for his kindness and generosity in opening up the Society's collections, and their histories, to my understanding. I owe many debts to the courtesy, friendliness, and professionalism of the staff at the John Carter Brown Library and am particularly thankful to Kim Nuscoe, Ken Ward, and Ted Widmer. Many thanks, too, to the staffs of the Rhode Island Historical Society, the Providence Athenaeum, and the Providence Public Library. I am particularly grateful to Kate Wodehouse and to Rick Ring for sharing their wonderful knowledge of John Russell Bartlett with me. Warm thanks also to the staff at the Manuscripts and Archives Division at the New York Public Library, to the staff of the New-York Historical Society Library, and to the staff of the

Southwestern Collections at the University of Texas at El Paso. A special word of thanks to Mike Kelly, Head of Archives and Special Collections at Amherst, who quite literally first ushered me into the joys of archival research at Fales Library, and whose energy, intelligence, and generosity continue to inspire.

I want to thank my many friends and connections in the wider profession who have engaged with my work in various ways, in conversations at conferences and seminars and via email, in responses to my papers at sessions, and as fellow scholars in residence at different libraries and archives. Some are old friends, some new, and some I know only very slightly, but all listed here have offered me something I didn't see before that made my thinking sharper, my knowledge deeper, and this book better: Rachel Adams, Juliane Braun, Lisa Brooks, Stuart Burrows, Jeffrey Davis, Nicholas Dew, Elizabeth Dillon, Ben Fagan, Erin Forbes, Wayne Franklin, John Funchion, Marilyn Gaull, Naomi Greyser, Sean Goudie, Sandra Gustafson, Keri Holt, Alex Hunt, Jesse Johnson, Julie Kim, Rebecca Lush, Rachel Mazique, Dennis Moore, Laura Murray, Dana Nelson, Cyrus Patell, Matthew Rebhorn, Peter Reed, Mark Rifkin, Phillip Round, Lisa Schilz, Carolyn Sorisio, Scott Manning Stevens, Mac Test, Ned Watts, and Jon Zimmerman. Additional and heartfelt thanks to Brian DeLay for his encouragement and support of my work. I offer my special thanks here to Sean Harvey and Sarah Rivett for their deep knowledge and warm spirit of cooperation during our work to organize a roundtable on Native American languages at C19 in Berkeley. I also want extend my deep gratitude to Lindsay Reckson for her work to bring me to the University of Texas at Austin English Department in the fall of 2012 for a talk on Plains Indian Sign Language and to visit her remarkable class on gesture; I am also very grateful to Matt Cohen for his cosponsorship of that visit through the Native American and Indigenous Studies Program at UT-Austin, and for his and Coleman Hutchinson's warm reception of me and my work. My deepest thanks also to Colin Calloway, Dave Edmunds, Donald Fixico, and Stephen Warren for sharing their expertise in responding to my speculations about Tecumseh's possible knowledge of American Indian Sign Language. Their knowledge and generosity was invaluable to me; any errors of judgment on that score are my own and exist in spite of the insight they provided.

My deepest gratitude to Eric Zinner at NYU Press and to the series editors of "America and the Long 19th Century": David Kazanjian, Elizabeth McHenry, and Priscilla Wald. Their commitment to me, and to this project, over the course of its stages of development exemplified a standard of professional generosity, patience, and scholarly validation it is the dream of every junior scholar to know firsthand. I am forever grateful for their support of my work. As a reader for NYU Press, Kirsten Silva Gruesz read and commented on multiple drafts of this book; her remarkable insights and recommendations, and those of another anonymous reader, helped transform the character and scope of this project at a crucial early juncture, and vastly improved it at every stage. Ciara McLaughlin, and later Alicia Nadkarni, have been wonderful to work with throughout the process—responsive, detail-oriented, and conscientious in their work with me to make this project better whenever possible. I am grateful for their kindness and professionalism. My thanks to Tim Roberts at the American Literatures Initiative for shepherding the manuscript through the production process. Very special thanks to the copyediting prowess of Susan Murray, who worked through the manuscript with respectful and impressive attention to detail.

To the many wonderful friends who have offered hospitality—in the form of meals, office space, places to rest, and ever-inspiring and salubrious discussions about work and ideas—during my research trips back east, eternal thanks: Tom Jacobs, Carley Moore, Matt Longabucco, Nicole Wallack, Bob Petty, Liz Camp, Dmitri Tymoczko, John Zeman, Nicole Beland, Heather Alumbaugh, and Dave Rippon.

Cristobal Silva deserves special mention—a pathbreaking scholar who has been, luckily for me, a perspicacious reader of my work since grad school; he is a warm, extremely funny, and incredibly generous friend besides. I am deeply grateful for his friendship inside the profession, and for his and Elizabeth Ronan's friendship outside of it.

My warmest thanks and deepest esteem to those cherished friends who have done so much to make El Paso become a real home to us: Rosa Alcalá, Jeff Sirkin, Stacey Sowards, Marion Rohrleitner, Richard Piñeda, Deane Mansfield-Kelley, Tom Schmid and Joanie Ericson, and Amy and Beto O'Rourke.

My family has always been a source of strength, pride, deep encouragement and support, and shared joy. To my parents, Ann and Larry Gunn, I thank you for a lifetime built of people, places, and things I love and have learned to value through your enduring example—I hope this book reflects back to you some of the excitement about ideas, literature, history, and conversation you have always embodied for me and have nurtured in me since I was young. Fondest love to my sister, Sara G. Wilhelm, and to Stephen Wilhelm. My love and gratitude also to Bob and Johanna Perrillo, who, like my own parents, are wonderful sources of support and joy in our lives. My very great thanks to Johanna, too, for the special trips and babysitting help she has offered to me and Jonna so often over the years. Much love also to Fredericka Bell-Berti, Kerry Perrillo Childress, Tim Childress, and to the cousins, Kenzie, Cooper, and Grant.

To Jonna Perrillo, my colleague, wife, and partner in all things: all that words can say and all they cannot. Without you, this book simply would not have been possible; with you, everything, including this book, is. I take inspiration from your brilliant scholarship, strength from your strength, heart from your heart. For all of the times I have leaned on you for time and support, when I could not find enough hours in the days or nights to get this book written, I can never thank you enough. To our children, Frances and Henry, for whom the persistent claims of this project on my attention were often unwelcome, but somehow understood: all of my love. You make the hard things easier, and everything worthwhile. This book is for you.

Introduction

During the early months of the U.S.-Mexico War, fueled by the writings of "The Pathfinder," John C. Frémont, a sickly but adventurous seventeen-year-old from Cincinnati named Hector Lewis Garrard found employment with a shipping company in Missouri run by Céran St. Vrain and headed west on the Taos Trail. Garrard published a lively account of his experiences in his book *Wah-to-Yah and the Taos Trail; Or Prairie Travel and Scalp Dances, with a Look at Los Rancheros from Muleback and the Rocky Mountain Campfire* (1850). Recorded in its pages is a remarkable succession of intercultural bewilderments, including one episode that commences with the arrival of the mule train at a Southern Cheyenne village in the western foothills of the Rocky Mountains, in November 1846. Fashioning himself as both an explorer and cultural documentarian, Garrard undertakes a glossary of the Cheyenne language, an endeavor that provokes considerable amusement among his Cheyenne hosts.

> Thinking me a queer customer (*mah-son-ne*—"a fool"—as they were pleased to denominate me and my vocabularic efforts), [they] replied willingly to my inquiries of *"Ten-o-wast?"*—"What is it?"—at the same time pointing to any object whose name I wished to know. The squaws of our lodge gave me words, purposely, not easily articulated or written; my attempts at correct enunciation were greeted with lively sallies of laughter. Our conversation was carried on in broken, very broken sentences; and, I must say, the part that they too ably sustained was not of the most refined character.[1]

As Garrard further relates, what these Cheyenne women found so entertaining about Garrard's "vocabularic efforts" was the novelty that they were undertaken by one so young. Yet, Garrard's youthful pantomime of the role of anthropological linguist invites the recognition that he, and the Cheyenne women who humored him, were participating in a highly conventionalized scenario of white-Indian contact—one that, by virtue of its familiarity, was open to playful subversion of its informally scripted parts. In her influential book *The Archive and the Repertoire*, the Latin American performance theorist Diana Taylor invites us to recognize such scenarios, alongside more common objects of colonial study such as texts and narratives, as "meaning-making paradigms that structure social environments, behaviors, and potential outcomes."[2] Such scenarios, and the paradigms they reflect and contingently reproduce, are at the heart of this book. Prototypically, the colonial scenario of linguistic collection in Native North America (whether undertaken for purposes of trade, missionary activity, treaty making, or ethnological inquiry) relies on certain epistemological and representational assumptions: American Indian words have the status of unitary artifacts, which may be collected in the manner of physical specimens; European and Indian languages fundamentally correspond in content and structure, with interchangeable words for common objects that combine to produce parallel meanings according to common laws; and, finally, the expectation that a successful written representation of Indian phonemes will provide a neutral and reliable basis for future communication.

Although Garrard's disorienting experience suggests that such assumptions are highly unstable fictions, he seems unable to recognize that their underlying premise of fundamental symmetry between languages may be flawed. Garrard assumes that Cheyenne must bear an essential (if only teasingly withheld) relationship to writing and suspects that the Cheyenne women knowingly offered words that would be particularly difficult to transcribe. Succeeding only at "broken, very broken sentences," Garrard is yet capable of supposing that the apparent absence of refinement in their manner, which they "too ably sustained," revealed likewise a willful departure from a social etiquette that must be shared. More disorienting still was his subsequent discovery that any transcription of oral speech could, at best, offer only a partial image of the full spectrum of Cheyenne communication practices. Immediately following this scene, he writes: "So complete and comprehensive is their mode of communication by signs that they can understand each other without a word being said, and with more facility than with the lips."[3] In this slippage of the colonizing frame, Taylor's conception of the scenario invites us to recognize and "take seriously the repertoire of embodied practices as an important system of knowing and transmitting knowledge."[4] Indeed, as the sudden and belated revelation of Plains Indian Sign Language in Garrard's narrative demonstrates, the scenario of linguistic exchange in which he understood himself to be participating was, in fact, false. Attempted as an earnest effort to possess Cheyenne speech according to established practices, Garrard's linguistic scenario returns as farce. As Garrard acknowledges in ironic and self-deprecating fashion, the most definitive act of naming produced by this linguistic exchange was the Cheyenne denomination of him as "*mah-son-ne*—'a fool.'"

Such scenarios of troubled linguistic exchange and communicative misrecognition echo routinely across the shifting borderlands and contact zones of American history.[5] As Garrard's example suggests, the practice of lexical collection as a text-based paradigm for the documentation of Native speech is highly susceptible to incompletion, but it also reveals the signifying copresence of Native bodies within the performative scenarios of multilingual borderlands encounter in an indigenous space that is, in this instance, both sovereign to the Cheyenne and nevertheless shifting in its geopolitical assignment in the context of the U.S.-Mexico War. As Taylor's fellow performance theorist Joseph Roach has argued: "Genealogies of performance also attend to 'counter-memories,' or the disparities between history as it is discursively transmitted and memory as it is publicly enacted by the bodies that bear its consequences."[6] Like every scenario of colonial performance, there are several actors here. On one hand, Garrard's awkward approximation of the actions of frontier vocabulary collectors (such as William Emory in Frémont's narrative) speaks to a degree of cultural saturation with U.S. scientific and linguistic discourse that is perhaps surprising, a penetration of esoteric research and collection practices into popular consciousness such that a teenager might roughly perform a role that was commonly understood. On the other are the Cheyenne women themselves, unnamed here on land indigenous to them, whose ludic if haunting presence should remind us of the geopolitics reflected in those Native expressive practices and embodied textualities that lie on or beyond the margins of documentation and historical recoverability. Indeed, among the intellectual elite who developed the research practices pantomimed by Garrard, within the hallowed precincts of learned societies in Philadelphia, New York, and Worcester, Massachusetts, American Indian Sign Language, the most widely shared linguistic system practiced in Native North America, was not recognized as a developed form of human speech—and would not be classified by linguists as a language until the 1960s.

In its broadest outlines, this book explores colonial language scenarios in the contested national, indigenous, and cultural spaces of the nineteenth-century western North American borderlands in an effort to contextualize the emergence of ethnological linguistics as both a professionalized research discipline and popular imaginative concern of American literary culture prior to the U.S.-Mexico War.[7] Dating to seventeenth-century New England missionaries like John Eliot and Roger Williams but reframed through monumental works of naturalism by such Enlightenment figures as the Comte de Buffon and the Baron Alexander von Humboldt, ethnological linguistic study in United States in the early decades of the nineteenth century was transitioning from an amateur field led disparately by gentlemen travelers, missionaries, military explorers, and armchair speculators into a more specialized discipline of knowledge production. Not yet established as the formal academic field of anthropology in American colleges and universities, the developing methodologies of what was known as ethnology instead coalesced through ad hoc constellations of state historical and antiquarian societies, athenaeums, networks of personal acquaintance, and the traffic of print commodities through bookshops and private libraries. By the 1840s, prominent ethnologists such E. G. Squier had begun to promote ethnology as a uniquely totalizing discipline of human knowledge that matched the aspirations of American empire; ethnology was "the science of the age," in Squier's words, that "begins where the rest stop" and "neglects no subject of inquiry."[8] Such boundless conceptions of ethnological practice were at the heart of the philosophy and mission of the new American Ethnological Society (AES), founded in New York in 1842. Announcing "the promotion of a most important and interesting branch of knowledge, that of Man and the Globe he inhabits," the inaugurating "Preface" printed in the first volume of the AES *Transactions* is presented in a stream of manifest-destinarian rhetoric, finding the global importance of ethnological investigation "to be of daily increasing moment in relation to the commercial and maritime interests of the nation" and proclaiming that "the artificial barriers that have hitherto divided nations and kept them from a knowledge of each other, are every where seen falling the advance of commerce, and its attendant, civilization."[9] *Ethnology and Empire* undertakes an archival survey of the ensemble of cultural, scientific, and government practices that gave rise to this coordination of scientific and national agendas in the first half of the nineteenth century. Throughout, I argue that relays between developing theories of Native American languages, works of fiction, travel and captivity narratives, and the political and communication networks of Native peoples gave imaginative shape to U.S. expansionist activity and federal policy in the western borderlands, even as the exigencies of imperial activity contributed to the consolidation of ethnological practices through the research programs of institutions with an avowedly national sense of mission, such as the AES, the American Philosophical Society, and the American Antiquarian Society.

More intimately, *Ethnology and Empire* tells stories about the traffic of words and ideas, and of ideas about words, and the interanimating networks of peoples, spaces, and communication practices that carried them across western borderlands regions and metropolitan centers of knowledge production and power. Those locations span from New York and Philadelphia to Washington and Mexico City, across, in Robert Warrior's term, the "intellectual trade routes" that connect the Great Lakes region of Tecumseh's Pan-Indian Confederacy to the Muskogee peoples of Florida, the diaspora of displaced Native peoples who emigrated to Texas in the 1820s, and the U.S. and Mexican officials, surveyors, and soldiers who sought to clarify and inscribe lasting boundaries of national geopolitical difference.[10] Exemplifying one such story is the life and career of John Russell Bartlett (1805–1886)—antiquarian bookshop owner, amateur ethnologist, talented sketch artist, accomplished lexicographer and bibliographer—whose unlikely appointment as the U.S. boundary commissioner charged with establishing the U.S./Mexico border pursuant to the Treaty of Guadalupe-Hidalgo closes an important chapter in the collaboration of amateur learned societies with the War Department in the work of westward expansion. Cofounder, with Albert Gallatin, of the American Ethnological Society in New York, Bartlett sought out his appointment to the Boundary Commission as an opportunity to conduct the linguistic fieldwork necessary to make his own lasting contribution to the field of ethnology, predicting boldly to his friend Evert Duyckinck, "If I can carry out a scheme which is now on the carpet, I shall be able to do more for American Ethnology, than has been done by any one, not even excepting Humboldt or Squier."[11] However, following his controversial in-field decision to concede back to Mexico a substantial portion of New Mexico claimed by the United States following the U.S.-Mexico War (which prompted the Gadsden Purchase of 1854), Bartlett was ousted from his post, and his ambition to publish the full results of his researches under the imprimatur of the United States Congress was unrealized. Nevertheless, Bartlett wrote and published his *Personal Narrative of Explorations and Incidents in Texas, New Mexico, California, Sonora, and Chihuahua* (1854), a rich though rarely discussed first-person account of his experiences that, as I discuss in chapter 5, represents a key literary consolidation of the agendas of ethnology and empire along the U.S./Mexico borderlands.

John Russell Bartlett's interest in Native American linguistics grew out of an earlier research project rooted in popular culture, newspapers, and cosmopolitan sociality—his *Dictionary of Americanisms*, widely regarded as the most significant glossary of nonstandard American English produced during the nineteenth century. In his *Autobiography*, Bartlett recounts the origins of his *Dictionary* on an Erie Canal boat, headed west from Utica, New York, in the early 1840s. Reading a "late work in which the vulgar language of the United States abounded," Bartlett amused himself by marking its "strange words and expressions" in the margins of the text; upon his return to New York City, he copied these words, along with a greater sampling of unconventional speech gleaned from several popular works attributed to David Crockett, in his personally customized copy of John Pickering's 1816 *Vocabulary; Or, Collection of Words and Phrases which have been supposed to be peculiar to the United States*. The particular copy of Pickering's *Vocabulary* in his possession had been altered to become, in essence, an amateur lexicographer's field kit. Disbound, and then rebound with interleaved blank pages, Bartlett used it to supplement Pickering's *Vocabulary* by recording alphabetically new specimens of American dialect he encountered on any occasion—in newspapers and magazines, from the lips of cosmopolitan New Yorkers, from conversations overheard aboard the canal boats he took on his regular journeys to Cape Vincent, and primarily from the literary texts that circulated through his famous bookshop on the ground floor of the Astor House Hotel in New York.

What is perhaps most striking in Bartlett's brief reminiscence is the assemblage of conditions and material circumstances it brings into relation: the development of an innovative technique of linguistic collection; the practice of that technique as a form of nonstandard ethnographic survey; its ready enlistment of literary sources of dubious historical authenticity; and, finally, its execution on a new transportation network that refashioned relations of national space through the circulation of persons, texts, and commodities from New York to distant western geographies. Although he could not have known it at the time, Bartlett's self-fashioned field dictionary replicated an identical research technique used by American Philosophical Society's Peter Stephen Du Ponceau, the most important scholar of Native American languages in the United States, who, in the 1810s, had disbound and intercalated with blank leaves Benjamin Smith Barton's important 1797 work on Indian languages, *New Views of the Origin of the Tribes and Nations of America*.[12] While patterns of connection between the developing research practices of figures like Bartlett and Du Ponceau shed light on one kind of story about the relationship of lexicography to literature and transforming conceptions of western spaces in North America, the content of their ideas tells another. Du Ponceau's pioneering work in comparative grammar at the American Philosophical Society, and particularly his development of the concept of polysynthesis to describe the combinative qualities of Algonquian languages, are foundational to the development of ethnological linguistics. A major story line in the chapters that follow addresses the impacts of his model of comparative philology on early anthropological research, military and topographical expeditions, exploration and captivity narratives, and literary form. Drawing new energy from recent developments in German linguistics and studies of human anatomy, the early-nineteenth-century practice of Native linguistic comparison constitutes an important, though seldom discussed, paradigm for the construction of racial difference—an emergent philology of race that is not simply reducible to familiar discourses of embodiment. Comparative philology is thus a major topic of my book, but it is also the grounds for developing techniques of interpretation that foreground the linguistic and literary encoding of race, national and borderlands spaces, and human networks in a transnational, scientific, and indigenous archive.

Rooted in the interpretive practices of literary studies but positioned at the conjunction of Native American and indigenous studies, borderlands history, performance studies, and the history of ideas, *Ethnology and Empire* aims to build on a range of important recent disciplinary efforts to reimagine the cultural practices of nineteenth-century North America, while emphasizing the geographically, politically, and culturally transformative impacts of western expansionism and Indian Removal for future conceptions of hemispheric American literatures.[13] Implicitly and often explicitly, these elements highlight the appeal of thinking about the early work of U.S. imperialism in terms of the concept of "the network"—an approach that tends to recognize institutionalized networks as vehicles of power, instruments of conquest. Such a formulation casts institutional actions as the material and logical precursor of ideological completion, the groundwork and scaffolding upon which national narratives and official story lines are made. This implicitly sequential logic has a familiar ring in Americanist historiography and frontier histories, even as that logic always risks passively reproducing, rather than interrogating and reimagining, the structural vantage point of historical projects of imperialism. For example, this logic underwrites the projections of a writer for the *New York Globe* heralding the 1819 Long Expedition into the southwestern borderlands (which is the topic of chapter 2), who suggested that Lewis and Clark "were the pioneers to establish the practicability of a safe journey," but who posited their goals and gains as merely a national prolegomena: "Their journal is an outline of a scheme to be yet filled up—the present expedition bids fair to add some splendid touches, if not to complete the work."[14] To "complete the work" of expeditionary design is to figure national expansion and empire formation as a kind of representational enterprise, a "scheme to be filled up" in, perhaps, much the same manner that a blank topography awaited the inscription of geopolitical boundaries, or that skeletal vocabulary forms awaited only the incorporation of linguistic data. While this book examines the relays between expeditionary frameworks and the imperial story lines to which they have given rise historically, what interests me primarily are the forms of linguistic slippage between the two, in a manner suggested by the following passage from Foucault's *The Order of Things*:

> Having become a dense and consistent historical reality, language forms the locus of tradition, of the unspoken habits of thoughts in a people's minds; it accumulates an ineluctable memory which does not even know itself as memory. Expressing their thoughts in words of which they are not the masters, enclosing them in verbal forms whose historical dimensions they are unaware of, men believe that their speech is their servant and do not realize that they are submitting to its demands. The grammatical arrangements of a language are the *a priori* of what can be expressed in it. The truth of discourse is caught in the trap of philology.[15]

There is powerful and enduring irony at play here. Philology was, in Foucault's estimation, one of the signature disciplines that constituted the emergence of taxonomic discourse and its modern regimes of power. To suggest that the hidden truth of that discourse is subject ultimately to its own genealogical procedures—caught in its own trap, as it were—is to recognize that truth as constituted both by its internal necessities and by its unconscious externalities, and by implication that the transformation of words into objects of study realizes power that is neither stable nor unidirectional, but recursive and circular. In this view of the unspoken, unconscious, and unmemorialized historical dimensions at the heart of the philological tree, Foucault anticipates the rhizomatic figure imagined by Deleuze and Guattari as a rejoinder to the prototypical tree of knowledge and opens critical thinking to reflexive strategies of deterritorialization, and new assemblages of knowledge and power.[16] In a famous passage from *A Thousand Plateaus*, Deleuze and Guattari suggest the explanatory power at stake in this metaphorical reconfiguration: "Unlike trees or their roots, the rhizome connects any point to any other point, and its traits are not necessarily linked to traits of the same nature; it brings into play very different regimes of signs, and even nonsign states."[17] Deleuze and Guattari's rhizomatic figure asks for a fundamental reorientation of critical assumptions and procedures of interpretation; even so, as the Chickasaw theorist Jodi A. Byrd suggests in her own trenchant reading of their work, this reorientation should provoke the recognition of more fundamental truths: "The maps of settler colonialism were always proliferative, the nation-state's borders were always perforated, and the U.S. lines of flight across treaties with indigenous nations were always rhizomatic and fluid rather than hierarchical, linear, and coherent."[18] As a practical matter, a type of literary and historical study informed by this recognition is and must be, in part, a speculative exercise of intellectual, disciplinary, ideological, institutional, and biographical documentation—but one that must assemble, as Bruno Latour has argued in *Reassembling the Social*, a "*tracing of associations*" that reveals and incorporates "*a type of connection between things that are not themselves social.*"[19] The promise of such a paradigm is a different kind of explanatory and critical utility—one that does not rely on intentionality as such or posit an ideological center that entails a fictitious reduction of the reach of empire to the narrative elements of a coherent (if decentered) nationalist paradigm, such as "manifest destiny."

In this, I take insight from Mark Rifkin's rejection of traditional portrayals of manifest destiny as "a monolith, an unstoppable force" and his understanding of the U.S. appropriation of Native lands in the West as "a shifting matrix in which national territoriality remains haunted by geopolitical formations absorbed but not entirely eliminated."[20] Rifkin's formulation of an expansionist national territoriality as a haunted, shifting matrix relative to Native America offers a compelling model of *reassembly* that anticipates the future promise of an emergent project of borderlands history that is, in the benchmark assessment of Pekka Hämäläinen and

Samuel Truett from the *Journal of American History*, "anchored in spatial mobility, situational identity, local contingency, and the ambiguities of power." Hämäläinen and Truett characterize this trend in relation to traditional histories of the western borderlands in the following way:

> These are not traditional frontier histories, where empires and settler colonists prepare the stage for nations, national expansion, and a transcontinental future. The open-ended horizons of borderlands history cut against that grain. If frontiers were the places where we once told our master American narratives, then borderlands are the places where those narratives come unraveled. They are ambiguous and often-unstable realms where boundaries are also crossroads, peripheries are also central places, homelands are also passing-through places, and the end points of empire are also forks in the road. If frontiers are spaces of narrative closure, then borderlands are places where stories take unpredictable turns and rarely end as expected.

Whereas the emergence of borderlands history began preponderantly with "mostly small-scale tales, privileging local description over large-scale conceptualization," Hämäläinen and Truett identify the future challenge of borderlands work in incorporating "the very real power of empires and nations without missing the field's central insight: that history pivoted not only on a succession of state-centered polities but also on other turning points anchored in vast stretches of America where the visions of empires and nations often foundered and the future was far from certain."[21] As I take up the challenge posed collectively by these thinkers, my broad strategy here is to foreground not only theories of language and scenarios of encounter but also seemingly dry imperial matters of bureaucracy, law, and policy, as reflexive conditions of legibility for literatures of encounter on an unstable, shifting borderlands—mirroring in that literature, and also reflecting from it, relations that are inescapably both local and national, individual and systemic, firmly terrestrial yet deeply vested in the cultural imaginary of nineteenth-century U.S. imperialism.

In work that spans more than twenty years, Walter D. Mignolo has developed a more specific model for the style of "border thinking" I have in mind here, grounded in a process he has termed "colonial semiosis." Conceived as a corrective to "the tyranny of the alphabet-oriented notions of text and discourse," Mignolo's approach to colonial semiosis introduces philological procedures and comparative hermeneutics to "indicate a network of semiotic processes in which signs from different cultural systems interact" and highlights the production of subaltern knowledge (or gnosis), "conceived from the exterior borders of the modern/colonial system."[22] Mignolo's work is highly abstract and relies to an unusual degree on theoretical neologisms. But in substituting such terms as *gnosis* for knowledge, *gnoseology* for epistemology, Mignolo thematizes in his use of critical language a potent decolonizing agenda of hegemonic displacement that anticipates an emergent language of subaltern resistance to legacy forms of colonial and imperial action. In contrast to the concept of transculturation, Mignolo's work in this vein emphasizes neither syncretism nor hybridity; it delimits, rather, "an intense battlefield in the long history of colonial subalternization of knowledge and legitimation of the colonial difference."[23] In this sense, the aim of Mignolo's work is not the excavation of "pristine" forms of indigenous knowledge in an ahistorical moment prior to their encounter with colonial power (and the regime of Occidental reason), but rather the illumination of indigenous knowledge in historical contest with those colonizing procedures through which subalternity itself is created and the colonial difference inscribed. Although it remains debatable whether postcolonial theory is truly apposite to the context of Indian Removal in the early-nineteenth-century United States, I am attracted to this paradigm (despite its imposing theoretical threshold) both for its expansive approach to semiotics in historical borderlands charged with power and for his interest in discerning the "loci of enunciation" of indigenous resistance. What Mignolo has in mind with "loci of enunciation" are primarily new and future possibilities of cultural and political engagement in the postcolonial scenario, a point of inception from which subalternized forms of knowledge may be creatively reimagined and transformed. But I am more interested in what this concept might offer as a means of reorienting an extant historical archive of Native expressive practice, and in exploring that possibility I will take Mignolo literally at his word: to imagine "loci of enunciation" as the locations (bodies, contact zones, and in networks that transcend them) and manners of speaking (signed, embodied, written, oral, and through signifying objects) of Native peoples in an effort to highlight a linguistic network of intertribal pathways through which acts of Native resistance might be reimagined historically and projected spatially.[24]

* * *

Within and against this backdrop of shifting borderlands, intellectual currents, and schemes of representation, chapter 1 of this book begins in a cultural world in which the generic boundaries of literature were far more fluid than they are today to explore the cross-pollination and consensus building of emergent ideas about Native American languages in relation to James Fenimore Cooper's developing program for American fiction. In his 1826 "Preface" to *The Last of the Mohicans,* Cooper voices regret over the disjuncture between his fictional project of romantic realism and what he describes as a scientific state of "utter confusion" pervading Native American languages. Cooper's concerns offer a major cultural touchstone for a widespread transformation in practices of philological ethnology that paradoxically seemed to generate and multiply the kind of linguistic confusion it was designed to clarify. In this chapter, I explore the influence of Friedrich Schlegel's and Sir William Jones's pioneering work in comparative grammar on U.S. debates concerning Native American origins as an early turning point for the emergent practice of ethnology in North America in the 1810s and 1820s. Even as Schlegel's comparative techniques promised a standardization of method that was seen to usher in new era of philological research, I argue that the subsequent projects of figures like Peter Du Ponceau, Henry Rowe Schoolcraft, and Albert Gallatin to map the linguistic families of North America entailed the establishment of an epistemological framework that was itself highly unstable. Comparative grammar operates on the assumption that, while surface-level linguistic phenomena may be highly variable, foundational grammatical structures (like skeletal architecture) are fixed over time and therefore expressive of ancient patterns of human kinship and difference. Adjunct to this emerging philology of race, the actual practice of linguistic mapping as advanced by such figures as Gallatin (who provided the first consolidated map of the linguistic families of North America in 1826) proceeded through the collection and comparison of relatively small lexical samples in isolated conditions. Lacking a standardized orthography across languages and, frequently, a common lexical basis of comparison, small language samples tend to exhibit patterns of linguistic exchange between groups and lexical variability between individuals more readily than deep structures of enduring similarity or difference. For some, the consequent image of widespread linguistic promiscuity between groups produced by this knowledge project amplified widespread cultural anxieties about racial mixing between whites and Native Americans—a paradoxical phenomenon I document with what I call "interracial speech acts" in Cooper's *Mohicans* and *The Pioneers.*

Chapter 2 explores early written documentation of Plains Indian Sign Language (PISL)—often referred to as Plains Sign Talk, or Hand Talk—a widely practiced Native American linguistic system noted pervasively across nineteenth-century literatures of encounter. Misrecognized routinely as a form of sublinguistic pantomime prior to the 1960s, and almost preponderantly overlooked in nineteenth-century Americanist literary study to date, PISL yet represents a central mode of expressive discourse across the Great Plains with important implications for questions of language, embodiment, race, disability, and politics across a range of critical horizons. My attention to PISL focuses on key shortcomings in developing theories of Indian languages and explores PISL's semiotics of embodiment in racial theories of Indian oratory and an emergent U.S. discourse on disability. In my reading, I emphasize the hidden or misrepresented linguistic content of a transnational expansionist literature that failed to recognize PISL for what it was and is: a rule-based grammatical language with important ritual, oratorical, and intertribal communication functions. This discussion begins with a review of the Long Expedition along the Red and Arkansas Rivers (1819–21), organized by the War Department to survey the new international boundary negotiated with Spain in the Adams-Onís Treaty. Outfitted with highly detailed philological instructions by the Historical and Literary Committee of the American Philosophical Society, the Long Expedition was intended to realize a concert of imperial and scientific interests. What they found was a highly developed manual linguistic system that existing theories of Indian languages were ill-equipped to assess but that demonstrated a largely unrecognized network of linguistic communication across the territorial horizons of the "Great American Desert" and beyond. Examining PISL documentation first in scenarios of expeditionary encounter, this chapter also explores a broad intellectual climate of literary reception in which the findings of the Long Expedition concerning PISL were taken up eagerly by a host of figures like Thomas Gallaudet and Samuel Akerly, who theorized in Native sign language practice a suggestive analogue to a developing program of manual instruction for deaf students in the United States.

Chapters 3 and 4 revisit the famous case of John Dunn Hunter as a means of reading comparatively the Shawnee leader Tecumseh's Pan-Indian movement in the Old Northwest and the ill-fated Red and White Republic of Fredonia spearheaded by Hunter near Nacogdoches, Texas, in the 1820s. An internationally famous author of a popular captivity narrative and ethnographic treatise on Plains Indians, Hunter championed Tecumseh's Pan-Indian politics and published the only record of the latter's speech before the Osage—only to be denounced by such figures as Lewis Cass and William Clark as an imposter, his writings fabrications. The historical record has largely vindicated Hunter. Revisiting his case here, and the vehemence with which he was attacked in the 1820s, reveals the degree to which the ideological struggle to shape an emergent national narrative concerning Indian Removal in the 1820s was impacted by nineteenth-century Indian linguistics (and, more to the point, the limitations of that discourse in regard to sign language), even as it underscores the challenges of working with ambiguous sources of oral and manual evidence that exist on the margins of historical recoverability and verifiability. In reading Hunter's popular *Memoirs* and ethnographic writings, I pay particular attention to the relationship between Indian languages, embodied speech, and literary representation, and emphasize the manner in which slippages between these expressive registers complicate (both for Hunter and his readers) his status as a racial and national outlier.

Chapters 3 and 4 also explore the level of threat that intertribal Native resistance, and the nonoral and nonprinted communication systems upon which they relied, were perceived to represent by the U.S. government within the public dialogue surrounding Indian Removal and to contextualize Hunter's revolutionary actions in Texas in the 1820s. In this work, I consider evidence that Tecumseh, enduring emblem of Pan-Indian resistance, knew American Indian Sign Language and may have incorporated elements of it into his transnational diplomatic oratory—a previously unexplored possibility that has significant implications for the linguistic and cultural histories of intertribal resistance movements and the politics of Pan-Indianism, even as it highlights the existence of a largely unacknowledged linguistic system that enabled Native political organization and insurgent military action in a range of historical settings from Canada to Mexico. Chapter 4 closes with a discussion of the Fredonian Rebellion and the response of the Mexican government to it in the wake of the Colonization Laws and the widespread displacement of Native peoples from U.S. territories and highlights the shifting national and racial loyalties of a U.S./Mexico borderlands region undergoing processes of major political and demographic upheaval.

As a closing case study, chapter 5 historicizes Bartlett's controversial tenure as boundary commissioner in terms of previous acts of scientific collaboration between the American Ethnological Society and the War Department, and exposes the degree to which the ethnological project participated in the larger national and imperial enterprise of the U.S.-Mexico War and international boundary creation. At the same time,

I explore in depth the complex manner in which ethnological prerogatives shape the techniques of Bartlett's literary representation. This work focuses on two contrasting dramatic episodes in which Bartlett acts on the authority of the Treaty of Guadalupe-Hidalgo to liberate Indian captives, examples that illustrate the legal problematics of intercultural negotiation on an area of land not yet officially within American jurisdiction. While committing to ethnological techniques of representation that cast the Apache encountered by the Boundary Commission both as political adversaries and objects of scientific speculation, Bartlett deploys the midcentury romantic conventions of literary sentiment to represent the plight of his liberated Mexican captives. As I suggest, the literary boundaries between Bartlett's oscillating styles of representation correspond powerfully to the troubled efforts of the commission to establish stable boundaries in their survey of the international border.

The completion of the post-1848 U.S.-Mexico Boundary Survey brings to a close an important early chapter of the interlocking institutional and literary histories of ethnology in the United States and thus concludes this book. Spurred by American efforts to map and politically incorporate large areas of western North America, the ad hoc pattern of coordination between the War Department and the Department of Interior and private learned societies led by figures such as Du Ponceau, Gallatin, and Bartlett was displaced by the official establishment of the Smithsonian Institution in 1846 and the Bureau of Ethnology in 1879; by the turn of the century, Franz Boas's establishment of the Ph.D. in anthropology at Columbia University signaled the consolidation of disciplinary authority for the field of anthropology as an academically credentialed enterprise. For Bartlett, the beginnings of this tectonic shift were experienced with remarkable rapidity. In November 1849, the editor Evert Duyckinck wrote from New York to Bartlett in Washington, who was then angling for his appointment as boundary commissioner, inquiring about the date of his return and congratulating him on the burgeoning scientific and literary culture Bartlett had helped to create: "Are not the ethnologists accumulating in Manhattan?" he asked.[25] This question was, of course, rhetorical; its obvious and affirmative answer was intended as a tribute to its recipient. As the senior partner of Bartlett & Welford, a bookstore that, throughout the decade, was one of the nation's premier locations for the collection and sale of ethnological and antiquarian research titles, and as Gallatin's cofounder of the American Ethnological Society, Bartlett stood near the center of a broad intellectual and commercial project. But less than two years after Duyckinck spoke so brightly of the wealth of ethnologists converging on New York, the Yale linguist William Wadden Turner wrote to Bartlett in New Mexico to inform him that the internationally famous Ethnological Society Bartlett cofounded had "come almost to a stand still" and at best "dragged out a prosaic humdrum sort of existence."[26] With Gallatin's death in 1849 and Bartlett's absence in the Southwest, there was little to hold the center; the intellectual community Bartlett had helped to cultivate in New York had become moribund. Moreover, Bartlett's national reputation was badly damaged upon his return in 1853, and the dissolution of his business partnership with Charles Welford was not to be renewed. Partly as a consequence, their shared vision of a centralized program for the advancement of American ethnology in New York, and the commercial and scientific networks upon which this vision materially relied, passed into obsolescence.

1

Philologies of Race: Ethnological Linguistics and Novelistic Representation

> The idioms of conquering nations have been generalized, and have survived the national preponderance; where they have not been substituted altogether for the native languages, they have left insulated words on their passage, which have been mixed, incorporated, *agglomerated* [original italics] to languages entirely different. Those words, recognized by the dissimilarity of the sounds, are in barbarous countries the sole monuments of the antique revolutions of the human race. They have often a singular form, and in a country destitute of traditions, present themselves to the imagination like the vestiges of the animals of the primitive world, and which buried in the earth, are in contrast with the forms of the animals of our days.
> —Alexander von Humboldt, *Personal Narrative*, passage copied by Peter S. Du Ponceau in his philological notebooks

Documenting Language and Race

In the spring of 1851, Brevet Major S. P. Heintzelman, while stationed at Ft. Yuma near the junction of the Gila and Colorado Rivers, attempted to collect a vocabulary of the Coco-Maricopas at the request of John Russell Bartlett, who had enlisted Heintzelman in his project of collecting Indian vocabularies during his survey of the U.S-Mexico border as commissioner of the United States Boundary Survey.[1] Heintzelman met with little success: "I find the same Indian will on different days give different names for the same things."[2] Such confusion often resulted from the fundamental asymmetry of English and Native words and syntactical construction, as the linguist John Trumbull pointed out in 1869: "It is nearly impossible to find an Indian name or verb which admits of exact translation by an English name or verb. But the standard vocabularies which have been most largely used in the collection and exhibition of materials are framed on the hypothesis that such translation *is* generally possible." Given his description to Bartlett, Heintzelman likely fell prey to what Trumbull identified as the principal blunder committed in the production of faulty Indian vocabularies, in which it is erroneously assumed that "equivalents of English *generic* names may be found among Indian *specific* and *individual* names,—that English analysis may be adequately represented, word for word, by Indian synthesis."[3] Had he been aware of them, Heintzelman might have taken some small consolation in the experiences of the important linguist and Moravian missionary John Heckewelder, whose initial efforts to obtain the vocabulary of the Lenni Lenape resulted in "a dozen names for 'tree,' as many for 'fish,' and so on with other things and yet I had not a single generic name. What was still worse, when I pointed to something, repeating the name or one of the names by which I had been taught to call it, I was sure to excite a laugh." This roadblock prompted for him the dispiriting conclusion "that every thing was not as it should be, and that I was not in the right way to learn the Indian language."[4]

But what did it mean to be in "the right way"—methodologically, philosophically—to study American Indian languages? And what forms of knowledge might accurate vocabularies of Native American languages be expected to produce? Such questions were at the heart of an emergent ethnological project in the United States in the first half of the nineteenth century, one that was gaining significant traction and momentum by virtue of recent theoretical breakthroughs in the field of comparative linguistics. This chapter charts the traffic and transformation of those developments across a range of cultural locations—from landmark works in Native American linguistics orchestrated by learned institutions such as the American Philosophical Society and the American Antiquarian Society, to popular works of literary fiction by James Fenimore Cooper. Common to each of these locations is an abiding preoccupation with questions of racial difference and a tantalizing sense that race and language corresponded in ways that were fundamental, if frustratingly opaque. These concerns converge in what I call here "philologies of race," a loose set of theoretical propositions and analytical practices for the comparison of Indian vocabularies and grammars that was informed by the methods of comparative anatomy and touted by its proponents as a scholarly method that promised unprecedented insight into questions concerning Native American origins and the phenomenon of human diversity more broadly. The scope of this ethnological agenda had profound cultural and historical implications that carried well beyond the esoteric transactions of learned societies. In the cultural environment of the 1820s United States, the literary genre of the historical romance emerged as a particularly resonant and productive field for the reception and complication of theories of language and race. In the first two novels of James Fenimore Cooper's Leather-Stocking series, the basis of that interaction centers on the abiding problem of nonuniform orthographies in printed representations of oral Indian languages—the problem, that is, of rendering the phonology of Native American spoken languages in the form of Latin alphabetic writing in the absence of a common standard for representing sounds within, or across, various European languages. Linguistics matter in these novels as problems of racial expression, embodiment, and documentation, but because novels are, in a sense, linguistic matters themselves, questions of language vis-à-vis race resonate with unusual force as problems of representation. In the final section of this chapter, I explore these linked issues of racial epistemology and literary representation in the phenomenon of interracial speech acts, instances of troubled oral expression that frustrate desires for transparent racial attributions according to the conventions of narrative form.

Philologies of Novelistic Representation: Confusion and Synthesis

In his 1826 "Preface" to *The Last of the Mohicans*, the second of the Leather-Stocking Tales in both order of composition and chronological sequence, James Fenimore Cooper speaks ambivalently about the slippage between his fictional project of romantic realism and the "utter confusion" he finds to pervade knowledge of American Indian languages, which he acknowledges to be "the greatest difficulty with which the student of Indian history has to contend."[5] Having already offered the challenging assertion that the general ignorance of the public cautions against trusting too much to the imagination of his readers, and that, "therefore, nothing which can well be explained, should be left a mystery," Cooper is forced to acknowledge that the complicated and conflicting record of Indian languages in his novel is a mystery that may not admit of easy explanation: "When, however, it is recollected, that the Dutch, the English, and the

French, each took a conqueror's liberty in this particular; that the natives themselves not only speak different languages, and even dialects of those languages, but that they are also fond of multiplying their appellations, the difficulty is more a matter of regret than of surprise. It is hoped, that whatever other faults may exist in the following pages, their obscurity will be thought to arise from this fact" (1). Thereafter, as readers familiar with the novel will remember, Cooper embarks on a lengthy and detailed discussion of the respective origins, geographical ranges, relations of kinship, and multiple appellations belonging to the two principal Indian nations depicted in the novel: the Lenni Lenape, or Delaware (from whom are derived the Mohicans of the novel's title); and the six nations of the Iroquois (the Mohawks, Oneidas, Senecas, Cayugas, Onondagas, and Tuscarora), whom he and his protagonists epithetically group together with the Hurons under the label "Mingoes." This move on Cooper's part is both a flaunting of his exacting verisimilitude and, where languages are concerned, an ironic advertisement of the futility of that project with respect to American Indians.[6] On one hand, his commitment to historical fidelity is so rigorous and complete that he will refuse to soften for his reader the experience of "so many unintelligible words" at the threshold of his narrative; on the other, his insistence on reproducing the "utter confusion" that pervades Western ethnologies with respect to competing translations and orthographies of Indian language betrays the truth that he is yoking himself to a knowledge project that scatters and distorts the objects of cultural history it purports to represent (1).

As a counterpoint to this scene of confusion, Cooper offers a much-noted sentence of praise to John Heckewelder, the recently deceased Moravian missionary and accomplished linguist of the Lenni Lenape. Heckewelder's 1819 *History, Manners, and Customs of the Indian Nations* is well known to Cooper scholars as the source material for much of Cooper's novel, and in particular for the names of Chingachgook and Uncas, but he is perhaps more widely known to intellectual historians and cultural anthropologists for his association with the research program on Indian languages advanced by the American Philosophical Society of Philadelphia.[7] A generation prior to the efforts of Albert Gallatin and John Russell Bartlett to centralize the ad hoc network of research practices carried out by missionaries, military explorers, travelers, physicians, and armchair theorists under the professional banner of the American Ethnological Society in New York, comparative linguistics had emerged in the early decades of the nineteenth century as the most prominent, and promising, research practice of Indian ethnology—one that enjoyed national prestige by virtue of its strong identification with the American Philosophical Society and its president, Thomas Jefferson. As corresponding secretary of the society (he would later serve as its president), the gifted Swiss linguist Peter Stephen Du Ponceau stood at the forefront of this research agenda. His correspondence with Heckewelder on the language of the Lenni Lenape, published in the first volume of the APS *Transactions* along with the results of his own grammatical research, and Heckewelder's *History, Manners, and Customs of the Indian Nations* in 1819, stands as an early high-water mark for the advancement and promotion of American Indian linguistics as a disinterested disciplinary project. Cooper does not reference Du Ponceau here, lamenting instead the passing of "the pious, the venerable, and the experienced Heckewelder," whose lost knowledge echoes the evanishment of his own last Mohicans and represents "a fund of information . . . which, it is feared, can never again be collected in one individual" (3). In this elegiac gesture to the loss of civilizations and to the embodiments of knowledge that cannot forever sustain their memory, Cooper foreshadows the novel that is to come. But this gesture is also a repetition of sorts, a meta-fictional signal that he intends to develop further the equation of nostalgia to linguistic confusion that he explores at the end of *The Pioneers* (1823).

At the close of that novel, following the ritualized death of an elderly Chingachgook amid a blazing forest fire that had consumed the mountain above Templeton, Cooper depicts the erection of funeral stones to mark the graves of Chingachgook and Major Oliver Effingham—one the cultural grandfather, and the other the biological grandfather, to the racially ambiguous character of Edward Oliver Effingham (who is disguised by the alias Oliver Edwards for the majority of the novel). When Natty Bumppo, who is illiterate, asks Edwards/Effingham to read the inscription chiseled on Chingachgook's headstone, this white cultural heir to the last of the Mohicans cannot pronounce the language it records. Reading aloud the multiple names by which Chingachgook was known, Edwards/Effingham falters over the word "Mohican" and is corrected by Natty; he then reads aloud the name "Chingagook," which he has transcribed erroneously onto the gravestone. At this point, Natty interrupts him again: "Gach, boy;—gach-gook; Chingachgook; which, intarpreted, means Big-sarpent. The name should be set down right, for an Indian's name has always some meaning in it."[8] Cooper's phonetic depiction of Natty Bumppo's unusual speech patterns is sustained throughout the Leather-Stocking novels. But here, juxtaposed with the failure of Edwards/Effingham both to record and pronounce properly words from the Delaware language, Natty's odd inflections underscore the disjunction between cultures of orality and literacy and emphasize the unreliability of written representations to reproduce faithfully the depths of meaning embedded in oral cultures. Natty's etymological lesson on the meaning of Chingachgook's name, and of Indian names more broadly, only deepens the sense of loss produced by this contrast. Although Edwards/Effingham promises to see the name altered on the headstone so that "Chingachgook" will survive in phonetic correctness, its meaning of "Big-sarpent" will be lost to all who, in the novel's imagined future, may one day encounter the monument. More emphatically, the lines that conclude Chingachgook's gravestone inscription suggest that the nature of this loss corresponds to the erasure of Indian identity: "He was the last of his people who continued to inhabit this country; and it may be said of him, that his faults were those of an Indian, and his virtues those of a man" (452). Cleaving racial and cultural particularity from Chingachgook's legacy under a shallow pretense of universalism, this statement asserts that the most appropriate tribute to the merits of extinguished Indian cultures is one in which all signs of difference are elided. Natty Bumppo enthusiastically endorses this assessment ("You never said a truer word, Mr. Oliver; ah's me!"), but he also fundamentally misunderstands the racial politics it expresses. Embracing for Chingachgook this posthumous title of "man," Natty reveals that his own definition of manly virtue is hardly universalistic but is modeled instead on an ideal of warrior prowess that is specifically Indian. In a spontaneous recollection of Chingachgook's deadly skill with the tomahawk and knife in battle, Natty declares: "He did lay about him like a man! I met him as I was coming home from the trail, with eleven Mingo scalps on his pole" (452). But, much as "Big-sarpent" is destined to be severed from the phoneme "Chingachgook" on the gravestone of the last of the Mohicans, Natty's and Chingachgook's culturally distinct definition of "man" shall likewise be invisible to educated white readers of the monument.

Such, at least, is the destiny of Indian cultural meanings at the end of *The Pioneers*, though of course this represents a fate that it is the project of the subsequent four Leather-Stocking novels fictively to counteract. As I shall discuss in greater depth later in this chapter, this intertextual relay between the first two Leather-Stocking novels advances an equation of nostalgia to the loss of Indian languages, emblematized in their confusion by a white culture ill-adept at recording their subtle meanings within systems of writing. This theme amounts to a powerful fictional statement about the nature of human cultural extinction, even if Cooper finds that extinction to be inevitable, and necessary to the progress of white American civilization. Yet that statement is connected ambiguously to another ongoing preoccupation of Cooper's, with answers less clear, about the relationship of language to race. An important clue into this preoccupation for Cooper is to be found in another metatextual setting, in the "Introduction" to the 1831 Bentley Standard Novels edition of *The Last of the Mohicans*. Here, Cooper returns again to the theme of linguistic confusion he had addressed five years prior, but he now extrapolates from this complicated image of linguistic diversity to offer a speculative prototype of Indian racial attributes. Drawing on a by then common (but by no means unanimous) view that Native Americans migrated to the North American continent from Asia, Cooper reflects that observable differences of complexion and physiology from Asian peoples may be attributable to environmental factors such as climate. But the proof of this origin, he finds, is to be discovered in language.

> The imagery of the Indian, both in his poetry and his oratory, is Oriental—chastened, and perhaps improved, by the limited range of his practical knowledge. He draws his metaphors from the clouds, the seasons, the birds, the beasts, and the vegetable world. In this, perhaps, he does no more than any other energetic and imaginative race would do, being compelled to set bounds to fancy by experience; but the North American Indian clothes his ideas in a dress that is so different from that of the African, and is Oriental in itself. His language has the richness and sententious fullness of the Chinese. He will express a phrase in a word, and he will qualify the meaning of an entire sentence by a syllable; he will even convey different significations by the simplest inflexions of the voice. (5)[9]

In his assertion that Native American language "will express a phrase in a word, and . . . will qualify the meaning of an entire sentence by a syllable," Cooper reflects important recent findings by several contemporary philologists, including Heckewelder and Wilhelm von Humboldt, and most notably Peter Stephen Du Ponceau of the American Philosophical Society. What Humboldt termed the "agglutinative" tendency of American Indian languages to form syntactically complete expressions in compound words and syllables, Du Ponceau famously named "polysynthesis." In contrast to Humboldt (who doubted that Indian languages had "real grammatical forms"), Du Ponceau found the phenomenon of polysynthesis to be a general grammatical principle of all American Indian languages and evidence of an extraordinary semantic and expressive richness unique among the recorded languages of the world.[10] "That they deserve to make a class by themselves cannot be doubted," he wrote.[11] Having availed himself of every available source material of Indian vocabularies and grammars (in addition to printed vocabularies, grammars, and dictionaries, he relied on missionary accounts, personal interviews, and extensive correspondence with other linguists), Du Ponceau announced after two years of study that the phenomenon of polysynthesis expressed two modes of linguistic construction: first, "by interweaving together the most significant sounds or syllables of each simple word, so as to form a compound that will awaken in the mind at once all the ideas singly expressed by the words from which they are taken"; and, second, "by an analogous combination of the various parts of speech, particularly by means of the verb, so that its various forms and inflections will express not only the principal action, but the greatest possible number of the moral ideas and physical objects constructed with it."[12] Du Ponceau expressed open astonishment at these findings, not only for the poetic economy polysynthesis appeared to express and its novel awakening of a virtually limitless host of words, associations, and moral ideas to the mind, but for the radical structural contrast this principle offered to grammars derived from the languages of Europe, Asia, and Africa[13]

For Cooper, this general characteristic of Indian languages to synthesize diverse and subtle meanings in compound expressions seemed to offer a potent analogy to inherent traits of Indian character: "Few men exhibit greater diversity, or, if we may so express it, greater antithesis of character, than the native warrior of North America" (5). Moving from the plural of "men" to the singular of "the native warrior," Cooper offers an embodied view of this "antithesis of character": "In war, he is daring, boastful, cunning, ruthless, self-denying, and self-devoted; in peace, just, generous, hospitable, revengeful, superstitious, modest and commonly chaste. These are qualities, it is true, which do not distinguish all alike; but they are so far the predominating traits of these remarkable people, as to be characteristic" (5). Other commentators echoed this view of Indian character as a prototypical melding of opposed attributes for which language was a unique prism. In an unattributed paean to Indian eloquence that appeared in the *Knickerbocker* in 1836, the author espouses Native oratory as "the most perfect emblem of their character" in a manner that strongly echoes Cooper's view of Indian "antithesis of character": "We perceive in him fine emotions of feeling and delicacy, and unrestrained, systematic cruelty, grandeur of spirit and hypocritical cunning, genuine courage and fiendish treachery."[14] To be clear, Cooper does not go so far here as to assert that Indian racial characteristics are grounded in Indian linguistic characteristics (or vice versa), nor does the writer of "Indian Eloquence" directly correlate Native oratory with the morphology of Native languages. Instead, the mutual tendencies of character, oratory, and language itself to embody antithetical qualities in singular forms reside here in metonymic parallel, in a resonant if causatively indistinct correspondence.

What is most interesting and consequential here is the very ambiguity of that correspondence, an ambiguity that indexes a critical set of cultural and scientific anxieties in the early nineteenth century about the respective natures of language and race. In contrast to Cooper, Edward Gray has suggested that, for Du Ponceau, "the distinctive qualities of American Indian societies bore no immediate relation to the distinct character of American Indian languages.... [L]anguage was distinct from mind; the speaker, distinct from the spoken."[15] Du Ponceau's insistence on differentiating these questions nevertheless carried powerful implications for those more explicitly concerned with a developing discourse of racial differentiation. In this light, it is important to consider that Du Ponceau's position reflected a cultural climate in which invidious assumptions about Native American racial and civilizational limitations had impaired neutral inquiry into the nature and function of Indian languages—a pattern of derogatory thinking advanced most vigorously by Lewis Cass in the following decade.[16] Du Ponceau's rigorous compartmentalization of linguistic questions from philosophical theories about the racial origins and attributes of Native peoples was thus calculated to rescue Indian philology from common forms of racial reductionism, but he also imagined his work to be complementary to those broader concerns, if ultimately very different in disposition and philosophical intent. Rather than disallow those questions altogether, Du Ponceau sought to defer them to a more solid evidentiary basis.

As corresponding secretary of the American Philosophical Society, Du Ponceau had been charged in 1817 by the Historical Committee of the society to initiate a correspondence with Heckewelder in the service of conducting a comprehensive investigation into the structural and grammatical forms of the indigenous languages of America. Divesting himself of any "favourite hypothesis or theory to support," in particular, "whether the Indian population of this country took its origin from the Tartars, or from any other race of men; whether America was peopled from any of the countries of the old hemisphere, or those from America," Du Ponceau announces his method as assuming "an abstract point of view, unmixed and unconnected with those more important subjects on which their results, when fully ascertained, may, perhaps, ultimately throw light." Even from this abstract point of view, "unmixed and unconnected," as it were, from questions of Indian racial origins and human kinship, Du Ponceau anticipates (correctly, as it would turn out) the kinds of objections his findings were likely to generate: "It has been said, and will be said again, that 'Savages having but few ideas, can want few words, and therefore that their languages must necessarily be poor.'" To this predicted objection, Du Ponceau initially avers that this question is "not my province to determine," but after presenting an example of polysynthesis in Iroquois, he has difficulty maintaining this neutral posture: "For my part, I confess that I am lost in astonishment at the copiousness and admirable structure of their languages, for which I can only account by looking up to the GREAT FIRST CAUSE."[17] The implications were clear: however unique their grammatical system from the rest of the world's languages, Indian languages expressed an order of genius that made their consignment to a separate order of creation within the human family impossible.

Comparative Linguistics and the Philology of Race

The 1819 first volume of the *Transactions of the American Philosophical Society*, showcasing Du Ponceau's "Report," Heckewelder's *History, Manners, and Customs of the Indian Nations*, and the lengthy correspondence between the two on the Lenni Lenape (Delaware) language family, culminates an important early chapter in the consolidation of a general program for ethnological linguistics, one that begins with the emergence of a global consciousness in European linguistics in the closing decades of the eighteenth century. In May 1785, Catherine the Great of Russia undertook a project of acquiring vocabularies of all the known languages of the world, beginning with a list she compiled of two hundred to three hundred radical words from the Russian, and which she had "translated into every tongue and jargon that I could hear of; the number of which already exceeds two hundred."[18] At her subsequent request, this project was taken up by the linguist Peter Pallas, who sent, on her instructions, vocabulary lists to the seats of power in Europe, Asia, and America—a request met in the United States by George Washington, who (unlike many) honored her request by furnishing it to government agents working in Ohio.[19] With Catherine's project commenced a new age of vocabulary collection; following Pallas, an active cohort of German philologists, most prominently Johann Vater and Johann and Frederick Adelung, assembled a series of glossaries and comparative vocabularies intended to reach a global scale.[20] In the United States, these efforts resonated powerfully with the lifelong interests of Thomas Jefferson to collect and preserve Indian vocabularies, a project that began as a personal hobby that he elevated to the status of compelling national interest, offering specific instructions to Lewis and Clark to collect detailed linguistic specimens from the tribes they encountered in their expedition to scout the Louisiana Purchase.[21]

This broad development in the collection of languages worldwide reflected important Enlightenment values about the susceptibility of the natural world (of which language might be conceived to form a part), to new revelations proceeding from application of systematic scientific methods. In 1786, within this active intellectual environment, Sir William Jones presented his findings—much heralded on both sides of the Atlantic—that Sanskrit, Latin, and Greek belonged to the same Indo-European language family.[22] If mutually unintelligible languages might be demonstrated through techniques of linguistic comparison to be cognate to a preexisting, possibly extinct language, a full mapping of the known languages of the world promised to offer a fundamental record of human kinship—a look back in time to the origins of human beings and, crucially, a monogenetic origin consistent with Genesis and mosaic chronology, or a polygenetic origin that might point to a natural racial hierarchy.[23]

Central to the question of single or multiple human origins was, of course, the primary origins of indigenous American peoples—and thus the field of American Indian languages offered to many the most eligible field in which to pursue the new philology of race. As John Pickering would write in a letter to Jeremiah N. Reynolds in 1836, this ambition remained urgent, and its realization tantalizingly close, for much of the first half of the nineteenth century: "In short, the affinities of the different people of the globe, and their migrations in ages prior to authentic history, can be traced only by means of language; and among the problems which are ultimately to be solved by these is one of the highest interest to Americans—that of the affinity between the original nations of this continent and those of the old world."[24] Building on Jones's influential arguments, Friedrich Schlegel published *Über die Sprache und Weisheit der Indianer* in 1808, a work cited at midcentury by Samuel F. Haven, librarian of the American Antiquarian Society, as having revolutionized the system of inquiry into the indigenous languages of the Americas, providing "the true key to the origin and connection of the varieties of human speech."[25] Schlegel's key innovation proceeded from an imaginative proposition: that the abstract structures of language are analogous to the physical structures of animal bodies, proclaiming that "the structure of comparative grammar of the language furnishes as certain a key to their general analogy, as the study of comparative anatomy has done to the loftiest branch of natural science."[26] In essence, Schlegel's modeling of comparative grammar on the biological techniques of comparative anatomy asserts that, while surface-level linguistic phenomena (such as vocabulary, as sampled by the lexical inventories of individuals) may be highly variable, the foundational grammatical structures they manifest are, like skeletal architecture, deeply enduring over time and therefore expressive of basic patterns of human kinship and difference. Writing to Jefferson in February 1817, Du Ponceau announced that the introduction of the comparative method had defined a new direction for linguistic research for the Historical and Literary Committee, noting that "the Study of languages has been too long confined to mere 'word hunting' for the sake of finding affinities of sound."[27]

As the Prussian intellectual Christian C. J. Bunsen (the Prussian minister to London, and an intimate of Alexander von Humboldt) reflected in 1854, this methodological shift to a surface-depth model of comparative analysis was "epoch-making": "It fully established the decisive importance and precedence which grammatical forms ought to have over single words in proving the affinities of languages. He based this claim on the primeval and indestructible nature, and the unmistakeable [sic] evidence, of the grammatical system as to the original formative principles of language."[28] Bunsen's appraisal offers a useful touchstone for mapping the historical implications of this development of philological method. Key here is the opposition Bunsen posits between "grammatical forms" and "single words." The latter, as embodied in the vocabularies compiled from the lexica of individual speakers of nonwritten languages, formed the primary linguistic evidence of etymological linguistics. Du Ponceau had criticized this as "mere word hunting," but the etymological method had characterized the comparative work of Pallas, which had first been advanced systematically on American shores by Benjamin Smith Barton's *New Views on the Origins of the Tribes and Nations of America* (1797).[29] Although it would continue to represent an important line of ethnological research long after Du Ponceau's groundbreaking case for the superior merits of grammatical comparison—most fruitfully, in the works of Albert Gallatin, whose monumental "Synopsis," supported and published by the American Antiquarian Society, offered the first comprehensive survey of the language families east of the Rockies in 1836 and relied primarily on lexical comparison—the etymological method was notoriously prone to errors of misconstruction. Basic characteristics of language presented etymologists of Native languages with two primary obstacles: diversity (spoken languages are mutable and evolve unpredictably); and variability (lexical samples tend to differ among individuals). These challenges were made even more imposing by the fact that, in the collection and analysis of nonwritten languages, documentation of historical linguistic development is incredibly scarce, if not nonexistent. Thus Gallatin, in addition to those lexical sources whose collection he had directed himself (through the dissemination of his linguistic surveys throughout the 1820s and 1830s, and the language samples collected by contemporary missionaries, Indian agents, and military personnel), was forced to rely on vocabularies of extinct languages that dated to the seventeenth century, including those of John Eliot (Massachusett) and Roger Williams (Narragansett). Such dated sources placed obvious practical limits for Gallatin on the project of assembling a common inventory of words for lexical comparison across languages (if a given word was not recorded to begin with, it cannot be supplied after the fact),[30] even as they represent the ghostly survival of colonial forms of cultural domination in a theoretically neutral project of knowledge production.[31] Although insensitive to the latter consideration, Gallatin was able to traverse the methodological risks entailed by working with nonstandard forms of lexical evidence through sheer volume and by being alert to its inherent limitations.[32]

Nevertheless, the uneven nature of lexical samples offered an evidentiary field from which inferences were, for many, perilous at best. Perhaps the most famous illustration of the risks entailed in working from a collection of diverse linguistic samples was the etymological comparison presented by Thomas Jefferson in *Notes on the State of Virginia*. Arguing that evidence of the derivation of languages "is the best proof of the affinity of nations which can ever be referred to," Jefferson asserted that the proportion of "radical languages" in America to those of Asia was perhaps twenty to one. Languages that he classified as "radical" were those which, "if they were ever the same, they have lost all resemblance to one another. A separation into dialects may be the work of a few ages only, but for two dialects to recede from one another till they have lost all vestiges of their common origin, must require an immense course of time; perhaps not less than many people give to the age of the earth."[33] On this basis, he inferred that: (*a*) the origins of Native Americans were ancient; and, (*b*) they predated (and, indeed, were the ancestors of) Asian peoples. In fact, as most nineteenth-century philologists would come to recognize, Jefferson mistook "dialects" for "languages" (which, as Du Ponceau, Pickering, and Gallatin would demonstrate conclusively, were structurally very similar).[34] Indeed, so familiar had the hazards associated with the etymological study of Indian languages become by the mid-1820s that they were considered a fit subject for eye-rolling literary parody. In 1826, Henry Rowe Schoolcraft and his wife, Jane Johnston Schoolcraft, the Irish-Ojibwe writer and poet, produced together at Sault Ste. Marie, in the Upper Peninsula of Michigan, a small magazine called the *Literary Voyager; Or, Muzzenigun*, which is sometimes cited as the first ethnological magazine in the United States. In it is contained a short send-up of ethnological linguistics called "An Etymological Lucubration," which purports to be a reflection on the origin of the tribal name of Chippewa/Ojibwe, made by a figure identified as "William Word Catcher":

> The subject of Indian etymologies, has occupied some of the brightest minds in the land. I cannot aspire to be very bright, but at the same time, think it may not be uninteresting to advance something on the subject. Writers and travelers have puzzled their ingenuity to learn the true meaning of this word. Some write it, with an O, as if it were a tribe of O'Neil's, or O'Donnels. Some put the letter y, to the final a, while all the modern writers insist that the true orthography is Ojibway. This may be food for the learned, who are often wrong, and dine their fancies on very slender food. To me, it is a gratification to find, that this tribe has not felt above drawing some of its names from our own noble English language. Thus it is easy enough to perceive that the first syllable *Chip*, is a plain derivative from our vocabulary, as if they had been thought as light as chips. By adding the term *away* to this, this idea is still further strenthened [*sic*] as if their lives, were at all times to be thrown away like chips. The moralist & etymologist must coincide in this conclusion at any rate, I am truly yours,[35]

In contrast to Jefferson's failure to perceive etymological commonalities within the Algonquian languages that comprised his study, the

Schoolcrafts' parody of "William Word Catcher" focuses on the production of false etymologies that stemmed from the ill-informed study of single words. Yet both illustrate the intellectual danger of ethnological study in which "the moralist & etymologist must coincide." Jefferson's theory of a North American origin for the migration of Asian peoples across the Bering Strait reflected his investment in refuting Buffon's theory of American degeneracy; for the "William Word Catchers" of the world, an investment in the romantic "Cult of the Vanishing Indian" (to borrow Lora Romero's phrase) and his voluntary surrender of land and culture to the superior claims of Anglo-American civilization might lead to linguistic conclusions as faulty as they were ideologically transparent.

In contrast to the pitfalls associated with the etymological work of comparative vocabulary, the structural method of comparative grammar, as pioneered by Schlegel and realized by Du Ponceau, promised a more reliable and unwavering basis upon which to advance the work of linguistic study. Handled judiciously, with the concerns of "the moralist" held at arm's length (as Du Ponceau took pains to emphasize), the analysis of adequate grammatical specimens promised to organize language into broader classifications akin to those of genus and class, as would proceed from a Linnaean system of taxonomy. In his review of the first volume of the APS *Transactions*, the Massachusetts linguist John Pickering (himself a pioneer in the development of a standard orthography for Indian languages) cast the scale of Du Ponceau's achievement as a Newtonian revolution in Native American linguistics:

> Every body who reads of the Indian languages in our old historians, becomes perplexed and confounded with the numerous distinctions of tribes and dialects, and naturally receives the impression, that those dialects are so many essentially different languages, and that it would be a fruitless labour to attempt to master them. Just as an untaught spectator, who beholds the endless variety of flowers that adorn the earth, or the innumerable stars that glitter in the heavens, is lost in the irregularity and confusion which seem to pervade the whole; and is appalled at the very thought of attempting to attain to the knowledge of them. But when, under the guidance of his Newton and Linnæus he is enabled to class and systematize the one and the other, the perplexity and confusion are dissipated, order reigns through the chaos, and each object settles into its place in the general arrangement; while the light of science, like the sun, discloses the wonders of the scene in all the beauty and harmony in which they came from the hand of their author.[36]

Pickering's remarkable vision, in which all "perplexity and confusion are dissipated, order reigns through the chaos, and each object settles into its place in the general arrangement," is more than a bold projection of a golden age in linguistics; it is a romantic fantasy of restored unity in which all contingency is extinguished in a true knowledge of heavenly design, and in which the previously misaligned work of the Schoolcrafts' "moralist & etymologist" shall again become one. Leaving to one side the theological dimensions of Pickering's age-to-come, the dream of perfect order promised by a Linnaean classification of grammars was more elusive than the proponents of an anatomical analogy for grammar might have anticipated.

To be sure, the technique of comparative grammar was capable of affording real insight into higher ranks of linguistic classification (like Linnaeus's genus and class), but this order of knowledge did not necessarily amount to a comprehensively stable epistemology in which "each object settles into its place in the general arrangement." However fruitful the assertion of analogy between them might be, languages are not biological entities, and a too-rigid imaginative effort to conform the properties of the former to those of the latter is liable to fallacy. Simply put, as Linda F. Wiener has pointed out, "Languages do not adapt in the way in which organisms can be said to adapt."[37] While languages and biological systems "are both characterized by descent with modification through time," evolutionary genealogies express split lines of descent that tend to become isolated in separate reproductive groups (within which advantageous traits are reproduced selectively).[38] By contrast, while linguistic genealogies mark points of divergence and may reflect periods of isolation, they are forever open-ended in their susceptibility to transformation by other languages and sources of social and cultural influence. Consider further that anatomical taxonomies (however accurate they may be in designations of higher rank) tend to reify incidences of variability into seemingly stable classifications in positions of lower rank, such as species or subspecies. On this end of the spectrum, the general analogy of anatomy to language breaks down. Because vertebrate evolution by natural selection is relatively slow in terms of human lifetimes, classifications of species and subspecies persist as stable points of reference within scientific communities (even if those species and subspecies are, in fact, constantly undergoing evolutionary processes). By contrast, linguistic evolution is sometimes slow and sometimes extremely abrupt, but on the main it is incommensurably rapid when contrasted to the timelines necessary for species-differentiating innovations of biological evolution by natural selection. More importantly, the variability between lexica possessed by individual speakers of the same language (let us imagine lexical specimens, typically obtained from individuals, to occupy the lowest rank in a linguistic taxonomy) may be far more pronounced than consequential differences of biological variation between specimens of the same identifiable species or subspecies. Here, a simple truth avails: a person may possess his or her own lexicon, but language itself belongs properly to no one. Given these conditions, a taxonomy of languages that extends to the lower rank of the lexicon may be, despite Pickering's anticipations to the contrary, especially prone to error—serving to freeze arbitrarily an unending cultural process of linguistic transformation into seemingly permanent images of divergent types and subtypes.[39] The resultant image of linguistic diversity produced by such a system may paradoxically thus be too rigid *and* too weak—too rigid in the sense of constructing an artificial image of enduring linguistic difference (giving rise to the sort of error to which Jefferson fell prey), but too weak in undervaluing the meanings of cultural transformation in favor of a reduction to overriding type.

In the case of comparative grammar as applied to American Indian languages, the limitation imposed by variable lexical samples among individuals may frustrate an accurate "typing" of the given language studied—an obstacle that may be overcome by a rigorous analysis of its underlying grammatical structure in the service of establishing its position in larger language families. Yet the explanatory power attributed to grammatical structures has the converse effect of lending to mutable lexical phenomena a semblance of formal order that either affirmed illusory forms of enduring racial difference or abolished culturally significant forms of ethnic and tribal difference. By way of illustration, let me turn once again to the example of Henry Rowe Schoolcraft, who disdained etymological linguistics, but who advocated grammatical study as a more eligible ground for ethnological research. In 1839, the year he was appointed the superintendant of Indian Affairs for the Northern Territories, he published his *Algic Researches*, the first record of his observations of the "mythology, distinctive opinions, and intellectual character of the aborigines."[40] "Algic" was Schoolcraft's coinage, a root-term derived from the words "Allegheny" and "Atlantic," with which he encompassed a vast range of tribes originally situated in these regions but since the seventeenth century having migrated extensively to the north and west. To these he contrasted the "tribes of the Ostic stock," comprising the Iroquois and the Wyandotte, which he classed as a separate "race." Within the tribes of the "Algic" family, Schoolcraft notes the following:

> They were marked by peculiarities and shades of language and customs deemed to be quite striking among themselves. They were separated by large areas of territory, differing considerably in their climate and productions. They had forgotten the general points in their history, and each tribe and sub-tribe was prone to regard itself as independent of all others, if not the leading or parent tribe. Their languages exhibited diversities of sound, where there was none whatever in its syntax. Changes of accent and interchanges of consonants had almost entirely altered the aspect of words, and obscured their etymology. Some of the derivates were local, and not understood beyond a few hundred miles, and all the roots of the language were buried, as we find them at this day, beneath a load of superadded verbiage. The identity of the stock is, however, to be readily traced amid these discrepancies. They are assimilated by peculiar traits of a common physical resemblance; by general coincidence of manners, customs, and opinions; by the rude rites of a worship of spirits, everywhere the same; by a few points of general tradition; and by the peculiar and strongly-marked features of a transpositive language identified by its grammar, alike in its primitive words, and absolutely fixed in the number and mode of modification of its radical sounds.[41]

One might take stock of this inventory of characteristics to note that it represents an image of wide cultural diversity: tribes with independent identities and unique histories, separated culturally by distinct and insulated linguistic codes and dialects. But for Schoolcraft, such discrepancies amount to false understandings and "superadded verbiage" that it is the proper business of ethnology to pare away. In addition to noting shared qualities of ritual worship and a few isolated points of "general tradition," he does so by recourse to two explanatory categories: physical racial characteristics and grammatical form ("transpositive" being Schoolcraft's version of Du Ponceau's "polysynthetic"), each affirming the other, and both combining to verify the classification of "Algic" in a manner that elides the cultural significance of ethnic and tribal difference.

In this context, perhaps a more pertinent and illustrative prototype for surface-depth models of linguistic analysis is not Linnaean classification as such, but its specific application to human anatomies by such figures as Linnaeus, Blumenbach, and Cuvier in the development of biological racism. Widely regarded as the "father" of craniology, Johann Gottfried von Blumenbach devised a system of five racial types within the human species (the Caucasian, Asiatic, American, Ethiopian, and Malay) for which he perceived the Caucasian as the historical prototype and the four others its degenerate, yet stable categorical subtypes. The results of his analysis of human skulls suggested that cranial structure exhibited patterns of predictable regularity that conformed to preconceived categories of racial type and thus offered a more reliable index of racial difference than the more variable phenomenon of skin color: "There is in them a constancy of characteristics that cannot be denied, and is indeed remarkable, which has a great deal to do with the racial habit, and which answers most accurately to the nations and their peculiar physiognomy" (i.e., of pre-identified racial type).[42] Expressed here in Blumenbach is an almost circular logic: although he defines race categorically according to externally visible physical characteristics, the median of the true racial type may not be present in any given individual; but in his reasoning, the greater regularity of cranial structure affirms the truth of the preconceived, outward physical type. This is precisely the logic employed by the French physician and ethnologist Louis Ferdinand Alfred Maury, secretary-general of the Société de Géographie de Paris, in his chapter on languages that opens the now-infamous polygenist volume *Indigenous Races of the Earth* (1857). "Languages," Maury writes,

> are organisms that are all conceived upon the same plan,—one might say, upon the same *skeleton*, which, in their development and their composition, follow fixed laws: inasmuch as these laws are the consequence of this organism itself. But, alongside of this identity in the procedure, each family of tongues has its own special evolution, and its own destinies.... In brief, the specific characters of languages are like those of animals; no characteristic taken singly possesses an absolute value, being merely a true indication of lineage or relationship.[43]

Relying on the metaphor of grammar-as-skeleton, Maury asserts linguistic variation from classed type to be a phenomenon analogous to biological variation from organismal type. Constructing linguistics and anatomy as mirrors of one another, Maury uses them, in effect, to cancel out incidences of variation in each as epiphenomena, meaningless anomalies that serve only to prove the rule of permanent underlying type. Thus, even as he notes with evident distaste the promiscuous borrowings, analogies, and echoes that are evident across the language families of the globe throughout history in a manner suggestive of miscegenation, Maury is yet able to conclude that "the crossing of languages, like that of races, has really not been very deep." Rejecting the "slavish interpreters of Genesis" and their misreading of the Tower of Babel as literal, Maury finds "the constitution of the tongues of each family appears as a primitive fact, of which we can no more pierce the origins than we can seize those of the animal species."[44] For polygenists like Maury, mapping global linguistic diversity onto the supposedly fixed anatomical boundaries of racial difference serves not only to evidence the underlying truth of separate racial constitution but to racialize linguistics, and hence language, itself.

This is not to suggest that what follows from these overlapping models of surface-depth anatomical comparison is that grammatical structure expressed racial essence, per se, but rather something like its opposite: that anatomies and racialized bodies expressed linguistic essence. This underlying theoretical orientation was widespread—often explicit for writers like Maury with an avowed polygenist agenda but present among many monogenist thinkers as well, though here it was often implicit or mentioned only in passing. For example, Jefferson's famous vocabulary form of 282 radical words was referred to routinely as a "skeleton," another fixed structure (though, of course, not a grammatical one) upon which words—variable, impermanent, and imprecise—could be made flesh (see figures 1.1 and 1.2).[45] Another example is found in a letter Du Ponceau wrote to Jefferson about his examination of a Nottoway vocabulary, in which he notes casually that he was struck by "its decided Iroquois physiognomy, which habit has taught me easily to descriminate [sic]".[46] This latter metaphor had been used by Du Ponceau in the 1819 "Report" as well: one need only become "tolerably conversant with Indian languages, and familiarised, as it were, with their physiognomy," in order to "judge with more or less certainty, sometimes by a single insulated word, of their general construction and grammatical forms."[47] The phrase "as it were, with their physiognomy" echoes a much-quoted passage from Alexander von Humboldt's *Personal Narrative* in which he writes: "From the country of the Eskimoes to the banks of the Oroonoko, and again from these torrid banks to the frozen climates of the Straits of Magellan, mother tongues, entirely different with regards to their roots, have, if we may use the expression, the same physiognomy."[48] Du Ponceau copied a similar passage from Humboldt in his philological notebooks that speaks even more concretely to the idea, equating the notion of linguistic diversity to a physiognomy of national difference: "If the multiplicity of

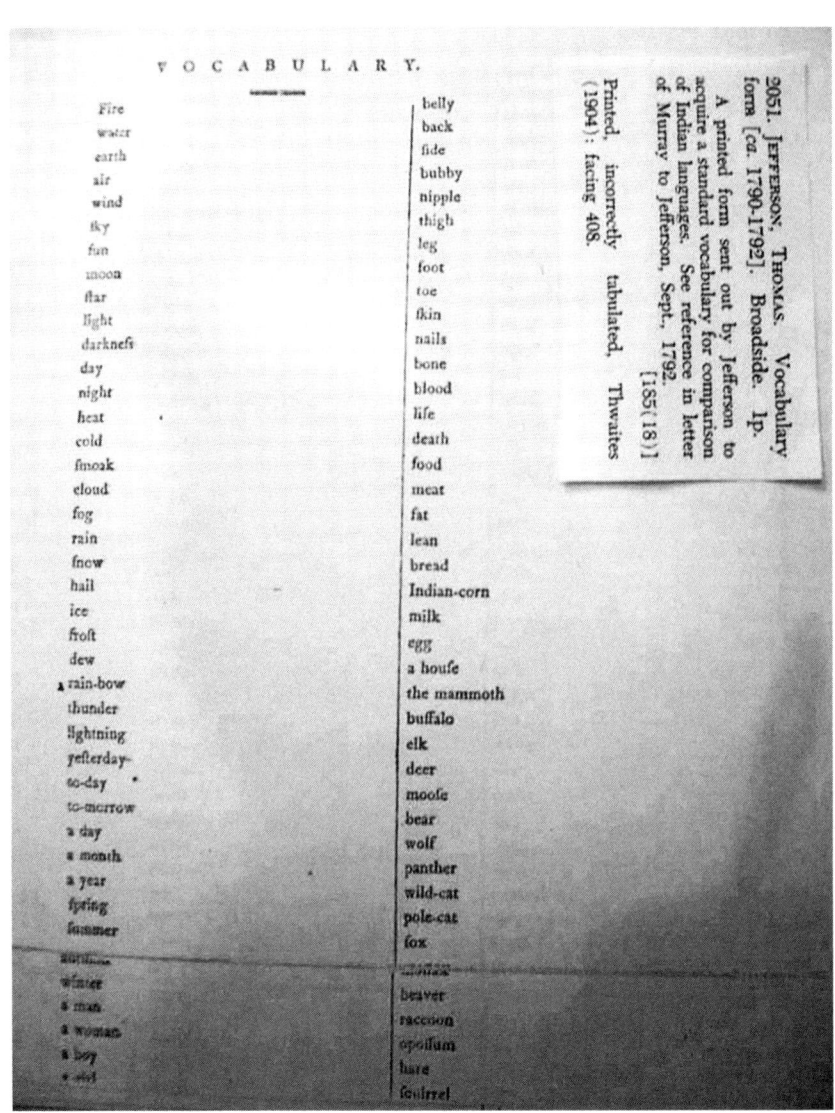

Figure 1.1. Blank Jefferson vocabulary form, often referred to as a "skeleton," ca. 1790–92. Image courtesy of the American Philosophical Society. Photograph by the author.

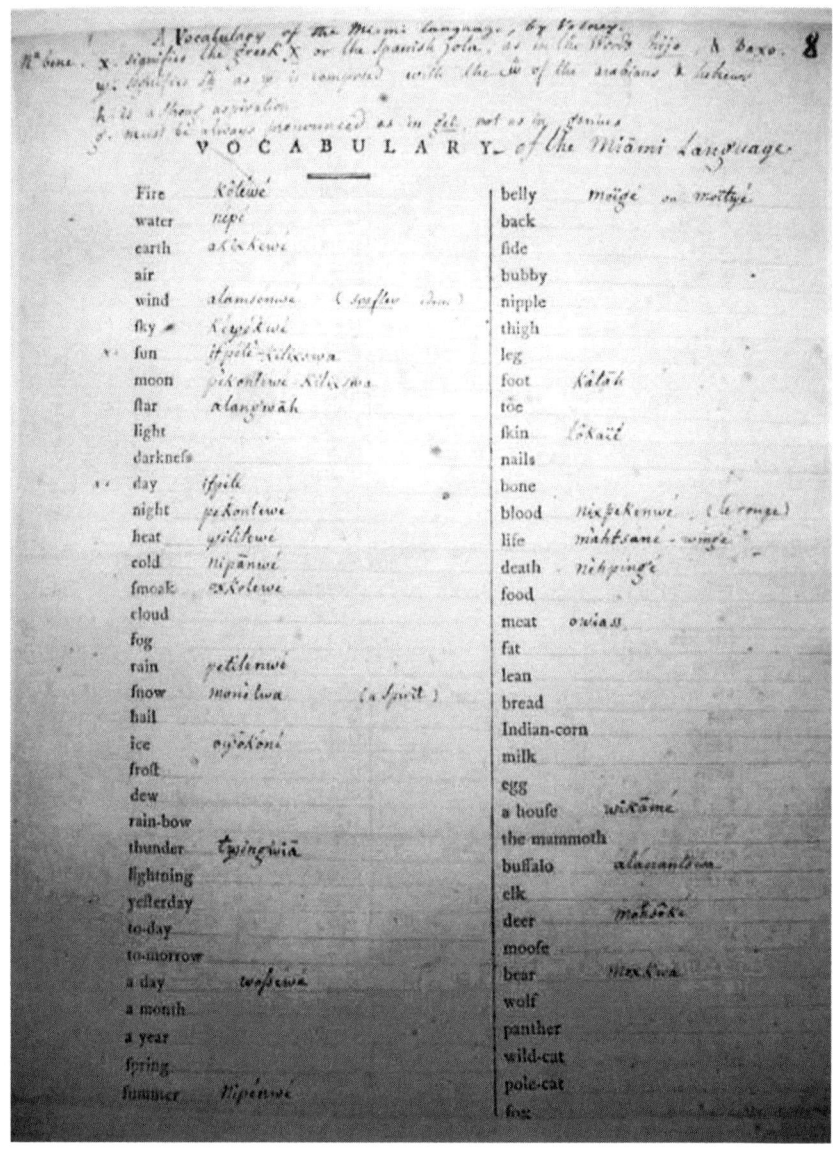

Figure 1.2. "A Vocabulary of the Miami Language, by Volney." Words made flesh. This example of a partially completed vocabulary of the Miami language, using Jefferson's "skeleton" form, was one of several supplied by Jefferson to Heckewelder and Du Ponceau. Image courtesy of the American Philosophical Society. Photograph by the author.

languages existing on a small space, opposes great obstacles to the communication of different tribes, it gives them the advantage of preserving the character of individuality, without which all that belongs to national physiognomy is effaced."[49]

Such equations were not short-lived. Acknowledging Du Ponceau's principle of polysynthesis but rejecting his appraisal of it as evidence of expressive richness, the English explorer Sir Richard Burton suggested that the complexity of Dakota grammar was evidence of primitive inelegance: "Savages, who have no mental exercise but the cultivation of speech, and semi-barbarous people, who still retain the habit, employ complicated and highly elaborate tongues.... With time these become more simple; the *modus operandi* appears to be admixture of race."[50] By citing these examples, I do not mean to suggest that such racialized assumptions were universal but rather to indicate a disposition toward anatomical metaphor within a diverse and influential intellectual genealogy. Far from being inevitable, this figurative style of thinking about language instead reflects a paradigmatic cast of mind. In this light, one might compare the reflexive interpretive framework of Albert Gallatin, whose long and brilliant career in international finance preceded his work on Indian languages. As William Wadden Turner reported following a meeting with Gallatin at the end of his life: "Mr. Gallatin says that he is puzzled to describe the principle of agglomeration which pervades all the Indian languages to a greater or less[er] degree. He says that he *feels* the peculiarities which characterize these tongues & make them differ from others somewhat in the same way as a bank teller distinguishes good from bad bills without always being able to specify the differences between them."[51] Looking at polysynthetic languages, Burton sees race; by contrast, Gallatin sees money.

It is a point of considerable irony that, despite the influence of comparative anatomy on the linguistic study of Native America in the first half of the nineteenth century, ethnologists and race theorists who themselves relied on comparative human anatomy to devise theories of racial difference that encompassed American Indians consistently rejected the work of philologists as unscientific. One aspect of this repudiation was competitive. Prior to the efforts of Gallatin, Bartlett, and Schoolcraft to synthesize ethnological study into a coordinated program of research into the natural history of humankind at midcentury, ethnology was a fragmented field of study carried out by enthusiastic amateurs lacking a common sense of disciplinary bearing. In this environment, rival methods were strongly associated in personal terms with the individuals who were most visible in developing and advancing them (for comparative grammar, Du Ponceau; comparative vocabulary, Jefferson and Gallatin; comparative anatomy, Samuel George Morton; the hybrid study of mythology, language, and race, Schoolcraft). But underlying these personally identified research programs lay a deeper philosophical debate: whether the phenomenon of human diversity had a common origin (the monogenetic school); or whether human beings had multiple and separate origins (the polygenetic school). The philologists tended to be monogenists (Maury being a notable exception), believing that deep structures of grammatical conformity across a wide range of languages suggested strongly a common primordial linguistic root structure for all peoples of the world; and many, like Gallatin, undertook their linguistic researches at least in part to vindicate personally held views of universal human equality. By contrast, the comparative anatomists—that group of physicians, biologists, and phrenologists who rallied around the leading voice of the Philadelphia physician Samuel George Morton, and who have gone down in the historiography as the "American School of ethnology"— were deeply invested in the polygenetic account and managed their pursuit of physical evidence to produce findings of permanent racial difference.

In this light, it is somewhat less than surprising that Louis Agassiz, a champion of Morton's, in a special letter prefixed to the 1857 edition of Josiah C. Nott and George Gliddon's invidious *Types of Mankind*, should take special pains to offer ridicule to the program of ethnological philology. Lumping the methods of comparative vocabulary and comparative grammar together, Agassiz suggested that altogether too much is attached to the affinity of languages by those who insist upon the unity of humankind. The whole of his remarks are worth reprinting here:

> The very same thing might be shown of any natural family of animals,— even of such families as contain a large number of distinct genera and species. Let any one follow upon a map exhibiting the geographical distribution of the bears, the cats, the hollow-horned ruminants, the gallinaceous birds, the ducks, or of any other families, and he may trace, as satisfactorily as any philological evidence can prove it for the human language, and upon a much larger scale, that the brumming of the bears of Kamtschatka is akin to that of the bears of Thibet, of the East Indies, of the Sunda islands, of Nepal, of Syria, of Europe, of Siberia, of the United states, of the Rocky mountains, and of the Andes; though all these bears are considered as distinct species, who have not anymore inherited their voice one from the other, than the different races of men. The same may be said of

the roaring and miawing of the cats of Europe, Asia, Africa, and America; or of the lowing of the bulls, the species of which are so widely distributed nearly over the whole globe. The same is true of the gackeling of the gallinaceous birds, and of the quacking of the ducks, as well as of the song of the thrushes,—all of which pour forth their gay and harmonious notes in a distinct and independent dialect, neither derived nor inherited one from the other, even though all sing thrush*ish*. Let any philologist study these facts, and learn, at the same time, how independent the animals are, one from the other, which utter such closely allied systems of intonations, and, if he be not altogether blind to the significance of analogies in nature, he must begin himself to question the reliability of philological evidence as proving genetic derivation.[52]

As a rejoinder, a philologist might meekly protest this misrepresentation of method and point out that the analogy of isolated phonemes, exclusive of lexical or grammatical considerations, would comprise a sorrowfully incomplete basis of linguistic comparison. But argument on the merits was not the point. Diminishment was, and the message was clear: philologists were not scientists and did not understand the nature of embodied analogies in nature. This point had been made, more gently but no less dismissively, by Samuel George Morton in a letter to John Russell Bartlett, ten years prior, in which he had noted off-handedly that the island of Madagascar contained three races—"Mongols, Hindoos, and Negroes—two of which were "exotic" to the island: "Mere proximity, the necessity of the case,—has fused their totally diverse tongues into a single language which is understood by the inhabitants of every part of the island. Will any one venture to surmise in explanation that all these people are of one race? You may rely upon it Philology, however important in Ethnography, is not unfrequently a broken reed."[53] Philology as a "broken reed"—Morton here offers an allusion to the January Eclogue of Spenser's *Shepheardes Calender*, in which a despairing Colin breaks his reed pipe for having failed to summon the Muse that would win Rosalind:

> Wherefore my pype, albee rude Pan thou please,
> Yet for thou pleasest not, where most I would:
> And thou vnlucky Muse, that wontst to ease
> My musing mynd, yet canst not, when thou should:
> Both pype and Muse, shall sore the while abye.
> So broke his oaten pype, and downe dyd lye.[54]

In Morton's view, philology is most kindly thought of as a relic of the pastoral imagination, a plaything appropriately broken and discarded in the recognition of hard reality.[55] From one point of view, at least, Morton is certainly correct that the commonality of a single language across populations in Madagascar is not evidence of a common race according to his own definition. Yet this trumped-up charge against philology reveals his more fundamental anxiety: that the impulse to assert racial commonality upon linguistic commonality muddies lines of racial difference it was the business of proper ethnological science to distinguish and brightly maintain.

Philologies of Novelistic Representation (II): Interracial Speech Acts

Despite such challenges to its fundamental methods and assumptions, the emergence of comparative philology represents a key moment of disciplinary consolidation for the research practices of ethnology in North America in the 1810s and 1820s. Touted by its proponents as a scholarly enterprise that opened unprecedented vistas into questions concerning Native American origins and the historical basis of human difference, the philological study of Native America was transformative with respect to the emergence of ethnology as a forwardly thinking scientific, rather than antiquarian, enterprise. By 1820, three primary methods for the development of what Du Ponceau called a "Universal Philology" devoted to broad ethnographic questions had begun to coalesce: phonology, an inquiry into sound patterns of Native speech, with comparative attention paid to their qualities of differentiation and pronunciation, and a focus on adequate standard orthographies for rendering sound patterns accurately in print; the etymological comparison of collected lexical specimens across language groups (an evidentiary model that might point to patterns of cultural exchange and historical bases of kinship between groups on the basis of common word origins); and comparative grammar (what Du Ponceau called "ideology," a structural inquiry into the governing rules of syntax and morphology that might point to still deeper histories of commonality across distinct linguistic families and also afford more immediate insight into the linguistic processes through which spoken human discourse creates meaning).[56] Ambiguously, across each of these methods circulated unresolved questions about the nature and legibility of American Indian racial identity. One might find it virtually anywhere one looked:

in the extraordinary eloquence and expressive power of polysynthetic root structures, as championed by Du Ponceau, Gallatin, and Pickering; or in the degenerated qualities of Schoolcraft's "Algic" tribes, whose confused cultural practices failed any longer to recall their own common ancestry.

Thus, even as the coordination of overlapping comparative techniques promised a unification of method that was seen to usher in new era of philological research, the subsequent project of figures like Du Ponceau, Schoolcraft, Pickering, and Gallatin to survey and accurately represent the linguistic families of North America entailed the establishment of an epistemological framework that was itself highly unstable. It is a point that bears repeating that linguistic comparison of any sort—phonological, etymological, or grammatical—must be made on the basis of spoken lexical samples, which alters fundamentally the evidentiary model of classical philology. Classical philology works from the basis of written historical documentation, that is, texts intentionally composed as written artifacts that may be compared across time; by contrast, the comparison of Native American linguistic specimens must proceed from the basis of transcriptions of speech, collected by different people from usually unknown individuals, at different times, and in different places. Although the vocabularies collected by such people as Jefferson, Heckewelder, Du Ponceau, Gallatin, and Bartlett tended to be fairly small in size (usually two hundred or fewer words) and comprise fairly standard words, small language samples nevertheless exhibit surprising levels of variation between individual lexica and often exhibit the limitations of the linguistic collector more prominently than anything else. As John Pickering noted in his 1820 essay for the American Academy of Arts and Sciences proposing a standard orthographic system for the representation of Indian languages, differences of representation of *the same words* of nonwritten languages at times offered extraordinary obstacles. No less frustrating was the lack of a nonstandard orthographic system in the face of the linguistic diversity of the linguistic collectors themselves. As Pickering pointed out, "unless a reader is conversant with the several languages of the authors, whose remarks upon the Indian dialects may fall within his observation (which remarks too are often rendered still further unintelligible by being read in a translation) he will be very likely to imagine, that the words of a single dialect, as he sees them written by a German, a Frenchman, or an Englishman, belong to languages as widely different as those of his several authors."[57] More exasperating to Du Ponceau were those variations of pattern that seemed to obey no linguistic convention whatsoever. Material limitations at the scene of print production, wholly separate from the scene of the language encounter, might add a layer of additional distortion to the linguistic exchange a vocabulary purported to represent. As explained by Heckewelder to Du Ponceau upon his inquiries concerning Zeisberger's vocabulary of the Lenni Lenape, in a letter from June 1818: "Sometimes the letters *c* or *g*, are used in writing the Delaware language instead of *k*, to shew that this consonant is not pronounced too hard; but in general *c* and *g* have been used as substitutes for *k*, because our printers had not a sufficient supply of types for that character."[58] Any of these factors might frustrate a would-be language scholar; taken together, the knotted complexities such conditions imposed consistently confounded the desire of linguistic ethnologists for clear and stable taxonomies. Where taxonomical lines are blurred, anxieties concerning race tend to become heightened as well.

For early-nineteenth-century American linguists, this host of practical challenges and unresolved theoretical questions distilled into three primary sets of issues. The first were epistemological: What forms of knowledge are embedded in collected vocabularies? Grammatical structures? How do specimens of either bear on questions of race and human origins? Second were methodological issues: How are languages to be sampled for study? Upon what basis are the synthetic and specific words of Indian languages to be translated into the generic and analytical words of English? Third, and finally, were issues of representation: What orthographies should prevail? Upon what basis might the establishment of a standard orthography for the transcription of Indian languages solve the issue of received vocabularies, rendered in writing by persons long dead, of languages long extinct?

The literary form of the historical romance emerged in the 1820s as a site in which these difficulties resonated with a peculiar and compounded force and reveal—in a way that the scientific reports do not—the manner in which such linguistic questions are, inevitably, racially valenced. The problem of nonstandard orthography, in particular, represents an unstable site of epistemological representation that has specific bearing on the novelistic practice of representing racial difference. In what follows I want to return to Cooper to illustrate these issues in what I call *interracial speech acts*, moments of linguistic encounter in which the representational conventions of narrative discourse seem to buckle under the pressures of ambiguous racial attribution.

In Cooper's *The Pioneers*, a great deal of narrative suspense builds over the course of the novel with respect to the racial identity of Oliver

Edwards—the character I discussed briefly in the opening pages of this chapter, whose faltering attempt to pronounce Chingachgook's name reveals his ultimate inability to inhabit and appreciate Indian speech codes fully. Oliver's reputation of biracial identity serves, among other things, as a plot device that enables his successful disguise. As the son of Edward Effingham, Oliver believes that his patrimony—fully half of the enormous land grant controlled by Marmaduke Temple, the patriarch of the novel for whom the town Templeton is named—was in fact stolen from him by Judge Temple. Effingham, an English Royalist, army officer, and trusted business partner of Judge Temple prior to the Revolutionary War, had entrusted his title to the land to him for the duration of the conflict to forestall the possibility of its confiscation, and had thereafter died in battle. By the time the novel commences, in 1793, Judge Temple had richly developed their previously shared holdings into the town of Templeton without advertising the terms of his prior arrangement with Effingham—tacit proof, from Oliver's point of view, that Temple had capitalized opportunistically on Effingham's death and had no intention of restoring Effingham's pre-Revolutionary land patent to its rightful claimant. For the majority of the novel, the racially disguised Oliver Edwards seethes in volatile if mysterious resentment at the Judge, a posture awkwardly though graciously accepted by the Judge in light of the fact that (in the opening scene of the novel) an errant ball from Temple's musket had struck an unseen Oliver in the arm during a deer hunt.

Phenotypically white, Edwards is repeatedly identified as having Indian blood by several different characters—Chingachgook (or, John Mohegan), Natty Bumppo, and Edwards himself (all of whom are presumably in a position to know the details of his family history); these claims are echoed credulously by several characters in Templeton as well, including Marmaduke Temple, Elizabeth Temple, Richard Jones, the Reverend Grant, and his daughter Louisa. The most striking interracial speech acts in this novel occur when Oliver's racial identity is first introduced as a topic of discussion in chapter 12, in which, following the Christmas Eve sermon of Reverend Grant, Oliver and Chingachgook accompany Grant and his daughter Louisa homeward. Following a short conversation about the service, Grant remarks on the refined and unusual qualities of Oliver's speech and surmises that he had enjoyed the benefits of some education. Asking him what state he is from, Oliver replies, "Of this—," an answer that shocks Grant, as Oliver's speech patterns fail to match up to the "peculiarities" of any local dialect. Oliver is, for the moment, a taxonomical

46   *Philologies of Race*

outlier—a figure who violates the observed parameters of regional linguistic identity. As if to discipline him for this linguistic nonconformity, Grant then reproaches Oliver for his ill-mannered and excessive display of bitterness toward Judge Temple earlier in the evening (Grant believing the source of his rage still to be rooted in his minor accidental gunshot wound). To this, Chingachgook replies, "The white man may do as his fathers have told him; but the 'Young Eagle' [Oliver's Delaware name] has the blood of a Delaware chief in his veins: it is red, and the stain it makes, can only be washed out with the blood of a Mingo*" (138). For this asterisk, Cooper supplies the footnote, "His enemy." Three significant ambiguities are embedded here; each of them veiling whiteness under cover of Indianness. First, the "Young Eagle" does, in fact, have the blood of a Delaware chief in his veins, given the high status accorded to his grandfather, who, as Oliver puts it later, "was once master of these noble hills, these beautiful vales, and of this water, over which we tread" (206). This hidden reference is reinforced by the second ambiguity Cooper introduces here: Chingachgook's claim that the blood of the "Young Eagle" is "red"—a statement that is of course perfectly true, in one sense, but that here seems to carry the unmistakable connotation that the "Young Eagle" is a "red man." Finally, the term "Mingo," despite Cooper's footnote, is not synonymous in his oeuvre with the neutral word "enemy"; instead, it is an epithet reserved for the Iroquois, the sworn and irremediable tribal enemies of Chingachgook's Delaware.

At the opening of chapter 7, the term "Mingo" is introduced as part of a narrative digression into the history of the Delaware and the Iroquois, who were "generally called, by the Anglo-Americans, Iroquois, or the Six nations, and sometimes Mingoes. Their appellation, among their rivals," that is, the Delaware, "seems generally to have been the Mengwe, or Maqua," an associative practice reaffirmed shortly thereafter in mention of the Delaware's "old enemies, the Iroquois, or Mingoes" (83, 84). Notably, Cooper identifies "Mingo" as a term for the Iroquois employed by "Anglo-Americans"; in his remarks to Reverend Grant in chapter 12, Chingachgook is, in this sense, ventriloquizing an English approximation of "Mengwe, or Maqua" (and he uses these terms interchangeably throughout the novel). Nowhere in the book, with the exception of Chingachgook's remarks concerning Oliver to Reverend Grant above, is the term employed to designate anyone other than the Iroquois. That Chingachgook could be using this term figuratively at this moment to designate Judge Temple, in other words, is a possibility that an uninitiated reader could not possibly suspect. Cooper's choice to insert a misleading footnote here constitutes an explicit narratorial participation in this extended interracial speech act, further reinforcing the fact this sequence of racial misrecognitions turns on problems of language, on the slipperiness of translation. Indeed, the nature of the "mistranslation" here precisely mirrors the common error previously noted by J. H. Trumbull in the production of faulty Indian vocabularies, which assumes that "equivalents of English *generic* names [in this case, "enemy"] may be found among Indian *specific* and *individual* names [i.e., "Mingo/Mengwe," here],—that English analysis may be adequately represented, word for word, by Indian synthesis."[59]

Thereafter in this chapter, the building question of Oliver's racial background is connected even more closely with matters of language, but now Oliver's own speech takes center stage—oscillating unpredictably between the epitome of genteel English refinement and the volatile yet poetic emotionalism Cooper employs to characterize the directness and eloquence of Indian speech. Consider the following two specimens of Oliver's speech. Louisa, obviously alarmed by Chingachgook's vivid testimony of his own motive for revenge, has slowed her pace behind the others; Oliver pauses to offer his assistance: "'You are fatigued, Miss Grant,' he said: 'the snow yields to the foot, and you are unequal to the strides of us men. Step on the crust, I entreat you, and take the help of my arm. Yonder light is, I believe, the house off your father; but it seems yet at some distance'" (139). Oliver's diction here is gentlemanly, decorous, and precise, embodying in speech a style of upper-class manner and courtesy that puts Louisa instantly at ease. Confessing at first that she was "startled by the manner of that Indian," she regains her composure: "I forget, sir; he is your friend, and by his language, may be your relative; and yet, of you I do not feel afraid" (139). Following this restoration of social confidence, Grant once again counsels Oliver to forgive Temple for the gunshot wound—adding that, if he were to do so, the consequent restoration of him to the good graces of Temple would all but be assured. Thereafter, he might wander the Judge's lands freely, with "the lightest conscience" (142). Offered as reassurance, Grant's remark is in fact an outrage to Oliver, but once again Chingachgook steps in to speak for him. Without stating outright the nature of his grievance against Temple, Chingachgook affirms once more that Oliver does possess Delaware blood and submits this fact as the foundation of his own claim of being the rightful possessor of all of the land around Templeton.

But he goes further here as well, predicting that the Judge himself will eventually see justice served in recognition of this older truth and divide his dominion in two to share with the mysterious young man (143). What follows is a surprising and volatile eruption of language, one that initially frustrates the reader's ability to locate its source: "'Never!' exclaimed the young hunter, with the vehemence that destroyed the rapt attention with which the divine and his daughter were listening to the Indian—'The wolf of the forest is not more rapacious for his prey, than that man is greedy of gold; and yet his gildings into wealth are subtle as the movements of a serpent'" (142). Who, in the second quoted passage of dialogue, is speaking? Following Oliver's exclamation of, "Never!" the passage would seem to present Oliver's elaboration of his objection. And yet, following disruption of the "rapt attention with which the divine and his daughter were listening to the Indian—," the second quotation might, as easily, signify the resumption of Chingachgook's speech, a highly plausible readerly inference given the fact that Chingachgook has already made a regular practice of speaking for Oliver in this chapter when Judge Temple is discussed. Moreover, the content of that second utterance conforms precisely to the syntactical conventions Cooper uses to model the poetic typicality of Indian speech. It is highly figurative, achieving meaning through the conjunction of two similes drawn from natural predators. Only with the onset of the succeeding paragraph, in which Grant urges Oliver to forebear in this sentiment, do we know with certainty that this stylized instance of violent emotional expressivism belongs to Oliver. As a moment of ungovernable and uncensored anger, the obvious sincerity of Oliver's imprecations seem to give voice to a more authentic version of himself than was revealed by his solicitous and well-modulated entreaties to Louisa just moments earlier. Such a conclusion, even if only provisional in light of later revelations about Oliver's identity, is suggested by Cooper through the figure of Grant: "'It is the hereditary violence of a native's passion, my child,' said Mr. Grant, in a low tone, to his affrighted daughter, who was clinging, in terror, to his arm. 'He is mixed with the blood of the Indians, you have heard; and neither the refinements of education, nor the advantages of our excellent liturgy, have been able entirely to eradicate the evil'" (143). Through the character of Oliver, Cooper deliberately troubles the nature of heredity on an axis of race, calling into question the nature of those categories by which identity and virtue are generated. But on the most literal level, at least, Oliver's claim of Indian "blood" is false; both of his parents were white, and the genealogy that connects him to the Delaware tribe is through his white paternal grandfather, Oliver Effingham, who was an adopted member of the tribe.

In *The Last of the Mohicans*, Cooper further develops themes of race in light of language, and language in light of race. In one famous sequence, like the preceding scene from *The Pioneers*, Cooper models the cultural attributes of racialized forms of identity in light of contrasting educational traditions. This episode takes place in chapter 3 of the novel, in which Cooper reintroduces the characters of Natty Bumppo (known principally as "Hawk-eye" here) and Chingachgook (not yet known as "Indian John") to his readers. Stepping back in time from their more aged incarnations in *The Pioneers*, they are now, in 1757, formidable prototypes of young manhood. Cooper introduces their first spoken words in the novel under a linguistic veil, of sorts. Alone together, they speak in Delaware, "of which we shall give a free translation for the benefit of the reader, endeavouring, at the same time, to preserve some of the peculiarities, both of the individual and of the language" (30). Clearly intended to enhance the impression of verisimilitude, this conceit carries the irony that Cooper, of course, did not speak Delaware; somewhat more puzzling to readers familiar with Cooper's works is that this careful qualification ("a free translation" that yet attempts to "preserve some of the peculiarities") seems barely, if at all, to alter Natty Bumppo's distinctive English speech patterns. At one point in their conversation, Natty exclaims, "I am not a prejudiced man, nor one who vaunts himself on his natural privileges, though the worst enemy I have on earth, and he is an Iroquois, daren't deny that I am genuine white"—a statement that, though ostensibly offered here in translated Delaware, is seamlessly interchangeable with numerous other instances of the English voicing of Natty's racial pride.

The topic of their discourse here is tradition, and they exchange back and forth the inherited versions of the origins and values of their respective cultures. Central to their spirited debate is the nature of writing, and their agreement that writing is an unreliable mode of cultural transmission when contrasted to the social conventions proper to speech. In one much-discussed passage, Natty concedes this point to Chingachgook:

> I am willing to own that my people have many ways, of which, as an honest man, I can't approve. It is one of their customs to write in books what they have done and seen, instead of telling them in their villages, where the lie can be given to the face of a cowardly boaster, and the brave soldier can call

on his comrades to witness for the truth of his words. In consequence of this bad fashion, a man who is too conscientious to misspend his days among the women, in learning the names of black marks, may never hear of the deeds of his fathers, nor feel a pride in striving to outdo them. For myself, I conclude that all the Bumppos could shoot; for I have a natural turn with a rifle, which must have been handed down from generation to generation, as our holy commandments tell us, all good and evil gifts are bestowed; though I should be loth to answer for other people in such a matter. (31)

Gendering writing as both feminine and deceptive, Hawk-eye equates masculine virtue with honesty and action in idealized settings in which oral speech is joined to the performance of heroic deeds. Locating true manhood in an embodied warrior ethic belonging properly to the wilderness, Hawk-eye's speech rejects the confines of domesticity as enervating, and, as Lora Romero argued, "free of books, Hawk-eye liberates himself from the power that nineteenth-century domesticity gave to women."[60] Presumably, of course, such a critique would extend to the novel at hand—a point of metacommentary already anticipated by the 1826 "Preface," in which he advises three classes of readers who uncannily resemble major characters of the novel ("young ladies," like, perhaps, Alice and Cora; "single gentlemen, of a certain age, who are under the influence of the wind," like Heyward; and "clergymen," like the psalmodist David Gamut) to "abandon the design" of reading it.

What risks being overlooked in discussions of Cooper's charged gender and literary commentary is the fact that Hawk-eye and Chingachgook are also having a philosophical debate about the nature of heredity. Although Cooper was almost certainly ignorant of Schlegel's model of comparative grammar, Hawk-eye's remarks here take seriously the idea that anatomical endowment (his well-developed physicality) is analogous to cultural endowment (religious belief). In this regard, however, it is telling to observe that Cooper does not bestow Hawk-eye with much in the way of logical competence. Hawk-eye erroneously conflates theological concepts of innate goodness and depravity with genetically determined physical traits (that is, in supposing that his powers of marksmanship belong to the moral category of "good and evil gifts," and must be eternally present for all generations of Bumppos in a neo-Lamarckian version of soft inheritance). Hawk-eye's fallacious reasoning presents a conspicuous dramatic irony at this key early moment of the novel, introducing a slippage between Hawk-eye's understanding of heredity, race, and culture, and a broader narrative consciousness of the novel that laments the illogic and immorality of exclusionary models of racial difference even as it expresses resignation to their ideological dominance.

If there is slippage on this score here, Cooper, Hawk-eye, and Chingachgook all seem to affirm the superiority of oral culture to written—a view that resonates strongly with the linguistic discourse of Cooper's period. In the "Preface" to his translation of Zeisberger's vocabulary of the Delaware, Du Ponceau affirms unambiguously the superiority of speech to writing as evidence for the investigation of the character of the human mind: "For it is by audible sounds that the ideas of mankind are embodied, and acquire outward form to the ear and an inward form to the mind; while writing is but a secondary mode of communication, much more limited in its objects and use, and which is in necessary connection with the oral signs of ideas. It seems idle at this day to talk of a written language, entirely independent of speech, and unconnected with it."[61] In this assessment, once more, the philological models of Cooper and Du Ponceau are in accord: oral languages do provide a reliable field of evidence for inquiring into questions of human origins, even as they provide a powerful index for discerning cultural values and intrinsic qualities of mind. From another point of view, Cooper and Du Ponceau reify what already was a primary structuring dichotomy of American Indian linguistics: the binary between orality and print. In the following chapter, I explore the imperial and territorial contexts in which that philological paradigm was put to a major early test in the United States: the Exploring Expedition headed by Stephen Harriman Long, launched to survey the new international boundary between the United States and New Spain in 1819, which was outfitted with instructions by Du Ponceau and his colleagues at the American Philosophical Society to document exhaustively the languages and lifeways of the Indian tribes of the southern Great Plains. That expedition brought, in most historical assessments, uneven returns. But in their documentation of Plains Indian Sign Language, the Long Expedition provided material of lasting significance to linguists—even as the nature of their documentation throws deeply into question a linguistic model that oscillated in its imagination between orality and print and failed largely to consider the embodied medium of Native expressive culture in territory that ranged from Canada to Mexico.

2

Empire, Sign Languages, and the Long Expedition, 1819–1821

> The new cultural and creative consciousness lives in an actively polyglot world. The world becomes polyglot, once and for all and irreversibly. The period of national languages, coexisting but closed and deaf to each other, comes to an end. Languages throw light on each other: one language can, after all, see itself only in the light of another language.
> —Mikhail Bakhtin, *The Dialogic Imagination*

Empire and Network

On May 4, 1819, the assembled members of the scientific expedition headed by Major Stephen Harriman Long steamed west on the Ohio River from Pittsburgh aboard the *Western Engineer*, a fearsome-looking vessel painted to resemble a scaly sea monster, from which steam poured out of a forward-facing vent carved to evoke the creature's serpentine neck and open jaws. As Titian Ramsay Peale, the expedition's young draughtsman and assistant naturalist, mused in his diary, the, "gapping mouth ... will give no doubt to the Indians an Idea that the boat is pulled along by this monster."[1] High above the two rear-mounted wheels, upon which were emblazoned the names of James Monroe and J. C. Calhoun, waved a flag that, echoing but pointedly revising the image on Lewis and Clark's peace medallions, bore a double-edged message: an image of a white man and a Native American shaking hands, against a backdrop depicting a calumet crossed with a sword (see figure 2.1). The geographical objectives of this expedition, authored by Secretary of War John C. Calhoun and copied to Robert Walsh of the American Philosophical Society (APS) in March

Figure 2.1. Titian Ramsay Peale, *Western Engineer* (1819). Titian Ramsay Peale Sketches, Mss.B.P31.15d, American Philosophical Society, Philadelphia. For one observer who witnessed the arrival of the *Western Engineer* in St. Louis, the message it embodied for Native peoples was unmistakable: "Objects pleasing and terrifying are at once placed before him—artillery, the flag of the Republic, portraits of the white man and the Indian shaking hands, the calumet of peace, a sword, then the apparent monster with a painted vessel on his back, the sides gaping with portholes and bristling with guns. Taken together, and without intelligence of her composition and design, it would require a daring savage to approach and accost her with Hamlet's speech: 'Be thou a spirit of health or goblin damned'" (qtd. in Hiram Martin Chittenden, *The American Fur Trade of the Far West*, vol. 2 [Lincoln: University of Nebraska Press, 1986], 568). This conjuration of the scenario of contact as a moment of high drama underscores the theatricality of the Long Expedition's calculated outward display, even as it figures that moment as a prelude to tragedy. For this observer, the encounter itself would be dramatically transforming, converting people into conventionalized roles on a western stage: Native peoples, in their awe and terror, could only recognize themselves as passive children of the United States, the Great Father possessed of supernatural and irresistible power.

1819, were twofold: first, to explore and survey the upper Missouri and Platte Rivers to the foothills of the Rocky Mountains; and, second, to survey and map the new international boundary negotiated between the United States and Spain in the Adams-Onís Transcontinental Treaty, along the Arkansas and Red Rivers.[2] Complementing the steamboat's foreboding iconography of conquest, its six cannons installed on the boat's deck, and the surveyor's tools employed by the expedition's topographical specialists, was another set of imperial tools—these were research instruments, compiled by the Historical and Literary Committee of the American Philosophical Society, which, like the cannons above-decks, were designed to promote American interests in these little-explored western territories. These consisted of a detailed questionnaire about Native American culture, politics, health and physiology, and social relations, and blank forms assembled for the collection of Indian vocabularies. Included also were three imprints: Benjamin Smith Barton's *New Views of the Origins of Tribes of the United States* (1797); Jonathan Carver's *Travels through the Interior Parts of North America* (1778); and the recently published first volume of the new series of the APS *Transactions*, which featured John Heckewelder's *History, Manners, and Customs of the Indians*, and Peter Du Ponceau's landmark study of Indian grammars.[3]

Expeditionary surveys of the territories and peoples bordering New Spain had been a national priority beginning with Andrew Ellicott's 1796–1800 survey of the Florida border; following the Louisiana Purchase in 1803, that emphasis shifted to the regions bordering the Arkansas and Red Rivers.[4] The two expeditions that followed, though—the Freeman-Custis Expedition of 1806, and the Zebulon Pike Expedition of 1806–7—were diplomatic embarrassments. Both were intercepted by Spanish forces: the Freeman-Custis Expedition was turned back early on, in Texas; and Pike, far off course, was captured in New Mexico and marched to Mexico City.[5] The Long Expedition signaled a renewal of approach. As a tangible symbol of American military force, the menacing aspect of the *Western Engineer* expressed a more robust model of expansionist power projected through riverine networks connecting the commercial waterways of the eastern seaboard to the continental interior and the southern territories of New Spain. Even the revision to the Lewis and Clark peace medallions for the Long Expedition flag betokened a significant shift of imperial posture: where the Lewis and Clark peace medallions depicted a tomahawk crossed with a calumet, the flag's substitution of sword for tomahawk transformed a nominal semiotics of peaceful and autonomous coexistence into an explicit portent of Anglo domination and Indian capitulation.

Informed by the record of previous expeditions, the Long Expedition marked also the threshold of a new era of collaboration between the War Department and the American Philosophical Society, a paradigmatic revamping of the model of natural and cultural data collection exemplified by the earlier Lewis and Clark Expedition. A key index of this shift is the emphasis accorded in the Long questionnaire to questions relating to Indian languages. Thomas Jefferson was, of course, a devoted student of Indian languages, and the collection of new vocabularies was emphasized to Meriwether Lewis during his training prior to the expedition, but Lewis's official instructions, written by Jefferson in April 1803, lacked important instructional detail, directing Lewis simply to "make yourself acquainted, as far as a diligent pursuit of your journey shall admit, with . . . their languages, traditions and monuments."[6] By contrast, the Long Expedition questionnaire includes detailed instructions with respect to standardizing orthography in the work of lexical collection (German, rather than English, diphthongs were to be employed, following John Pickering's new orthography), in addition to specific grammatical queries concerning verb conjugation, compound word forms (what Du Ponceau famously termed "polysynthesis"), and the gendering of syntax (all supplemented extensively by the linguistic findings of the accompanying imprints and vocabulary forms).[7] These more detailed instructions reflect, in the first order, the pioneering linguistic research of Du Ponceau over the previous decade—a program motivated by the monumental goal of developing a full map of the world's languages as a means of uncovering the origins, relations of kinship, and paths of migration for human beings worldwide.

Such a project in the Americas depended on an extensive network of willing research collaborators across vast geographical spaces: agents who, with carefully designed instruments of linguistic collection, might document the enormous variety of Native American oral languages according to standardized conventions. Capitalizing on the developing capillary apparatus of a War Department invested heavily in a project of territorial expansion (which shared a complementary interest in collecting data on Native Americans in the interest of managing indigenous spaces and peoples), the leadership of the APS committed its intellectual resources to the work of American empire, a collaboration that in turn gave shape to the developing field of ethnology in the early nineteenth century. Hopes, then, were high for a new overland expedition outfitted with unprecedented care and expense in documenting the topography, geology, flora and fauna of a new international border—along with the languages, bodies, and lifeways of a host of Indian nations and tribes, including the Cherokee, Osage, Omaha, Pawnee, Konza, Oto, Kiowa, and Comanche peoples. In this sense, the carefully crafted research agenda of a private learned society coincided with public anticipations of the national meanings of a western expeditionary project. The *New York Globe*, for example, compared the expedition expectantly with Napoleon's 1799 incursion into Egypt, and its iconic joining of modern empire to the monuments of the ancient world, adding that "undertakings of this kind do honour to a government—at the same time that they extend her own influence, the cause of universal science is advanced."[8]

The coordinated aims of this national, ethnological, and natural historical project illustrate a broad scenario of "networking" and "empire" in a conventionally accepted sense: the intentional and coordinated actions of individuals and institutions toward specific ends, here a developing epistemological project in concert with a campaign of territorial expansion that replaced the Pacific with the landlocked West as the object of focus. In a broader sense, though, it represents a bold externalization of the romantic scientific imagination. Embodied in its prototypical exemplar, the Baron Alexander von Humboldt, that imagination entails a form of heroic self-fashioning that is implicitly superhuman: "I have conceived the mad notion of representing, in a graphic and attractive manner, the whole of the physical aspect of the universe in one work, which is to include all that is at present known of celestial and terrestrial phenomena, from the nature of the nebula down to the geography of the mosses clinging to a granite rock."[9] As Humboldt avers with ironic humility, the grandiosity of such a notion is "mad," yet it is also logically necessary. Even the most modest act of natural history classification entails a logic of completion (however implied, however distant), a projection of totality through which the constituent parts of classification may eventually achieve the full range of their systemic meanings. Recast from the romantic individual as an institutional, networked, and open-ended enterprise, natural historical enactment was, for the early United States, both a vehicle for generating power and a project of national fulfillment.

One aim of this chapter is to explore the historical interplay of the different forms of network that the U.S. national endeavor of the Long Expedition brings into relation, beginning with the institutional collaboration of prominent scientists and linguists at the APS with the War Department in the formation of a national scientific network, and more extensively in the Long Party's documentation of Plains Indian Sign Language in contradistinction to its documentation of oral languages, linguistic networks, and social practices. Contextualizing the Long Expedition's approach to Plains Indian Sign Language within a network of standing philosophical, oratorical, and linguistic assumptions about race and disability underscores what is politically at stake in the semiotics of Indian embodiment and gesture and reveals how an impoverished image of Native communication networks contributed to spatial understandings of the land the Long Expedition famously termed "The Great American Desert." In what follows, I focus on the linguistic agenda of the Long Expedition and the challenges of representation that "different regimes of signs"—specifically, Plains Indian Sign Language—presented for an evolving knowledge project and will suggest that Indian linguistics is haunted by Indian sign language both as a matter of linguistic classification and in the performative scenarios of social and scientific encounter in the western borderlands. As Victor Turner once advised, "We will know one another better by entering one another's performances and learning their grammars and vocabularies."[10]

With Turner's suggestion in mind, my approach in this and the following chapter might be thought of as a form of literary cryptolinguistics, in the first place as a critical examination of texts that include unrecognized linguistic content—as, most prominently, in early American documentations of Plains Indian Sign Language, which was not classified by linguists *as a language*, with distinctive attributes of grammar, syntax, and morphology, until the second half of the twentieth century. But a "literary cryptolinguistics" also serves as a fair description of the kind of assemblage I want to sketch here, one that rethinks traditional understandings of the network by resituating literary and manual discourses in reference to emergent philosophies of racial hierarchy and Native systems of communication that encode culturally specific conventions and political histories, along what might be thought of as the hidden grammatical axes of a shifting borderlands.

Sign Language and Indian Linguistics

In her excellent study of the territorial fictions that gave imaginative shape to the deserts of the North American West in the early nineteenth century, Stephanie LeMenager characterizes Edwin James's record of the Long Expedition, *Account of an Expedition from Pittsburgh to the Rocky Mountains*, as an "anti-exploration narrative." It "is unique in the genre of expedition narrative for its consistently sheepish tone and its frequent admissions of failure," she writes, adding that its record of physical suffering evokes a "landscape worthy of Edgar Allan Poe or Hieronymus Bosch [that] defies exploration and makes a mockery of the explorer's map." LeMenager's vivid characterization captures the sense of a literary and territorial space in representational dissonance.[11] In another sense, her emphasis on expeditionary failure echoes a long history of negative assessments in which the real scientific and strategic gains of the Long Expedition have been overshadowed almost entirely by a conspicuous record of shortcomings in other areas, a tally that must include the failure of their object to discover the headwaters of the Red River (and Long's embarrassing misidentification of the Canadian River for the Red River on the return trek), the near-starvation of an advance party on the Arkansas, and the unevenness of the quality of the researches into natural history conducted by the expedition.[12] In the area of linguistics, however, their results were highly significant, though these, too, were received skeptically when the results appeared as part of the expeditionary narrative compiled by Edwin James and published by Carey & Lea in 1823. In an unfortunate echo of the fate of the vocabularies collected by Lewis and Clark, much of the Long Expedition's linguistic materials were lost to theft in the vicinity of Fort Smith, Arkansas; and, of what remained, the four incomplete vocabularies and lists of "promiscuous words" collected by Thomas Say did not answer adequately to the level of syntactical detail required by Du Ponceau for complex grammatical analysis.[13] But included with the oral vocabularies in a special addendum was something unique: a compendium of 104 discrete manual expressions of Plains Indian Sign Language (PISL)—what is sometimes called Plains Sign Talk or Hand Talk—making it by far the most extensive Indian sign language vocabulary collected and published to that point in American history.[14] Each is described in prose in exacting detail, comprising data accurate enough still to be useful to linguists today (the same confidence often does not apply to oral vocabularies collected prior to recognized standardizations of orthography).[15]

Documentation of the use of sign language in mainland North America dates to Cabeza de Vaca's 1542 *Relación*, in which he first reported communication by sign with the Apalache in Florida prior to his capture, and later extensively with various groups in the interior of what would become

Texas, Coahuila, Chihuahua, Tamaulipas, and Nueva León. For Cabeza de Vaca, the efficacy of sign language was evidence of heavenly favor: "We passed through a great number and diversity of languages. With all of them God our Lord favored us, because they always understood us and we understood them. And thus we asked and they responded by signs as if they spoke our language and we theirs."[16] Subtracting the element of divine intercession from Cabeza de Vaca's account, the assessment of sign language as a commonplace and stable means of communication across oral linguistic barriers is a common theme of North American contact literature. Perhaps the most famous example of sign language documentation is contained in the journals of Lewis and Clark. As Meriwether Lewis reported in his journal for August 14, 1805: "The means I had of communication with [the Shoshone] was by way of Drewyer [George Drouillard] who understood perfectly the common language of jesticulation or signs which seems to be universally understood by all the Nations we have yet seen." Acknowledging that "it is true that this language is imperfect and liable to error but is much less so than would be expected," Lewis affirms that "the strong parts of the ideas are seldom mistaken."[17] Lewis expresses confidence here in the fundamental transparency of PISL, but he dispensed with sign language as the principal mode of communication with the Shoshone following the arrival of Sacagawea on August 17, writing that "by means of her I hoped to explain myself more fully tha [sic] I could do by signs" (185). That the expedition thus preferred an attenuated translation chain that went through four oral languages—from English to French (which Labiche spoke and conveyed to Charbonneau), then from French to Hidatsa (which Sacagawea spoke), with Sacagawea finally translating from Hidatsa to Shoshone—may speak to Lewis's reflection that sign language, despite its demonstrated efficacy on the expedition in a host of contexts, "is imperfect and liable to error."[18] As Larzer Ziff astutely observed in his reading of another episode of linguistic exchange on the expedition, "the message of imperialism was sent and received only when principal reliance could be placed upon words."[19] But Lewis's discomfort in using sign language in his official communications with the Shoshone Chief Cameahwait also suggests that Lewis held the common view that sign language was intrinsically inferior to oral speech, that it was an informal substitute for "real" language when oral communication was not possible; this likelihood is further corroborated by his neglect of recording manual signs alongside the other Indian vocabularies the expedition was mandated to collect.

Yet despite the abundant record of sign language use across literatures of contact and its role in signal episodes of imperial exchange such as those documented by Lewis and Clark, scholarly discussion of American Indian Sign Language is surprisingly scant in American literary and cultural studies. An exception to the historiography is Ziff, who idealizes sign language as an elementary medium that promotes exchanges of cross-cultural equality, a vision that rests on his assertion of sign language's pantomimic simplicity and emotional paucity. "Each recognizes that he has left the stronghold of his native tongue to meet on neutral ground where neither can impose his thoughts upon the other or sway him emotionally," he writes. "When sign language gave way to interpreted speech, even as the recorded facts and unmediated impressions of the travelers gave way to the written history, so cultural equality gave way to dominance and the process of literary annihilation."[20] Ziff's idealization of signed exchange as a lost "neutral ground" significantly underestimates PISL's grammatical complexity and semantic richness, as well as its deep integration into the expressive spectrum and exchange practices of Native peoples.[21] Nevertheless, his recognition of the significance of signed discourse in the contact scenario invites us to think deeply about the bodily interface of linguistic exchange, both for Native peoples independently and in scenarios of Euro-American contact, in conjunction with the ideological and material processes whereby "cultural equality gave way to dominance and the process of literary annihilation."

In contrast to the above, let me turn to another perspective nearly a half century after the Lewis and Clark Expedition: that of the English explorer George A. F. Ruxton, who traveled extensively from Mexico north along the Santa Fe Trail into the Rockies in 1846, and who found Plains Indian Sign Language to bear open-ended possibilities:

> The language of signs is so perfectly understood in the western country, and the Indians themselves are such admirable pantomimists, that, after a little use, no difficulty whatever exists in carrying on a conversation by such a channel; and there are few mountain-men who are at a loss in thoroughly understanding and making themselves intelligible by signs alone, although they neither speak nor understand a word of the Indian tongue.[22]

A member of the Ethnological Society of London who achieved early fame for a bold attempt to cross Africa on foot along the Tropic of Capricorn, Ruxton was, like Lewis and Clark, a dedicated observer of Native

American cultural practices. His expansive claim that Indian sign language was widely used by white traders who spoke no Indian oral language anticipates Ziff's conception of a "neutral ground" available impartially to all and deserves to be taken seriously as indication of the broad incidence of signed linguistic practice. Elsewhere, Ruxton documented the incorporation of PISL into English among trappers in the Rocky Mountains, which yet survive in the colloquial expressions, "to rub out" (for "kill") and "go under" (for "die").[23] Nevertheless, Ruxton, like Lewis before him and Ziff after him, also seems to have misrecognized the nature of the linguistic system he described.[24] In suggesting that "the Indians themselves are such admirable pantomimists, that, after a little use, no difficulty whatever exists in carrying on a conversation by such a channel," Ruxton fashions Indian Sign Language as a style of improvisatory performance, a pseudotheatrical *technique* to be mastered rather than a language with a large conventionalized vocabulary governed by grammatical rules.

Contemporary reaction to the Long Expedition's documentation of PISL was often dismissive upon its publication in 1823 and likewise reflects commonly held misunderstandings about the nature of sign language practice. Edward Everett found the expedition's pathbreaking documentation of Indian Sign Language dubious, writing that "the extremely arbitrary character of many of these signs makes us ... skeptical, as to the extent to which they are used."[25] Ironically, Everett's skepticism about the sign language vocabulary was that it suggested something rather too much like a language to be plausible. Lewis Cass, in a long and famous denunciation of several recent works in the field of ethnology in the *North American Review*, acknowledged that "the statistical facts" compiled by the expedition "are highly valuable, and will be hereafter referred to, as important data in all general and comprehensive views," but he also suggested that the expedition plainly felt "the inconvenience of pursuing these speculations ... without the aid of persons competent to interchange ideas between the red and the white man."[26] Although Cass did not comment on the Long Expedition's "Indian Language of Signs" explicitly, he recognized the prevalence of manual sign language as well as its intimate connection to oral speech but found its existence to evidence the poverty of Indian languages more broadly. In the same review quoted above, Cass asserts that "gesticulation only" conferred prepositional clarity on the "many useless variations" of the Delaware language and that "no man has ever seen an Indian in conversation, without being sensible, that the head, and the hands, and the body, are all put in requisition to aid the tongue in the performance of its appropriate duty" (79). For Cass, "the tongue" is both member and metaphor, either too lazy or constitutionally weak to fulfill linguistic purpose; from his perspective, sign language is a disorganized bodily reflex that cannot compensate for, but only advertise physically, an oral language that lacks expressive self-adequacy. Cass's remarks here were part of a scathing criticism of Heckewelder's positive account of Indian cultures and languages, which (as discussed in chapter 1) the latter found to express subtlety and sophistication on par with the languages of Europe. For his part, Heckewelder had recognized earlier the wide practice of Indian sign languages but firmly rejected its linguistic significance. "It is true that the Indians have a language of signs," Heckewelder writes, "by which they communicate with each other on occasions when speaking is not prudent or proper.... It is also, in many cases, a saving of words which the Indians are much intent on, believing that too much talking disgraces a man. When, therefore, they will relate something extraordinary in a few words, they make use of corresponding signs, which is very entertaining to those who listen and attend to them, and who are acquainted both with the language and the signs, being very much as if somebody were to explain a picture set before them."[27]

Observing that sign language has, at times, a unique social purpose that does not merely substitute for speech but comparatively resignifies the intent of speech, provides reflexive linguistic commentary, and modifies the social character of speech acts, Heckewelder provides evidence of real cultural significance. Yet he concludes by saying that sign language expresses nothing that oral speech does not convey on its own—"they never make use of signs to supply any deficiency of language, as they have words and phrases sufficient to express every thing."—voicing implicitly a zero-sum logic that suggests that any estimation of the importance of sign language would detract from the fullness and legitimacy of the oral languages he sought to publicize and celebrate.[28] These assessments were new but flawed hypotheses about the nature of American Indian sign languages by persons associated with the American Philosophical Society were not. Indeed, the decision by the Long Expedition to collect a sign language vocabulary reflected a standing interest in Indian Sign Language on the part of the APS, Thomas Jefferson having presented the research of William Dunbar into Indian sign language to the APS in 1801. Dunbar speculated that the iconic character of much of Indian Sign Language (Dunbar had submitted some fifty examples) suggested linguistic analogy to Chinese written characters because of the latter's apparent traits of iconicity. His emphasis on iconicity was a mischaracterization of both Indian sign language and Chinese written script, but it was a hypothesis that accorded with Jefferson's earlier assertions of a primordial connection of descent between Asian and Native American peoples.[29]

This pattern of misrecognition hints at a largely uncontemplated truth of the contact scenario: the early American field practice of Indian linguistics is haunted by Indian Sign Language and is significantly complicated by its misrecognition of it. In the first place, the wide diffusion and use of PISL ensured that the familiar colonial scenario of oral linguistic collection was often at least partially governed by manual sign language, even if this fact is seldom acknowledged explicitly on vocabulary forms themselves. Because language collectors routinely mistook PISL as a spontaneous form of sublinguistic gesture, manual signs were rarely transcribed. Yet the presence of Indian Sign Language is noted pervasively across many texts of encounter that feature oral linguistic collection, suggesting that the prototypical scenario of Euro-American language collection on the Great Plains was one that failed to document (or even fully perceive) the multiform linguistic reality of Native Americans.[30] One common misconception about PISL (and signed languages in general) is that they are surrogates for speech; in fact, the manual signs of PISL are not derivative of spoken words, and the grammatical system that governs the physical syntax of manual gesture is distinct from those of oral languages.[31] Moreover, the fact that PISL was employed widely as a lingua franca—the emerging consensus among linguists is that it predates Columbus and probably began on the Gulf Coast, spread northwesterly, and accelerated in its diffusion with the rise of mobile horse cultures following the Spanish Conquest—led many nineteenth-century observers to conclude that it was merely a pidgin-of-convenience, a simple code useful only in passing for purposes of trade. This, too, is incorrect, but even in this erroneously restricted context, PISL encodes ethnogenetic patterns of contact, lexical borrowing, social and economic traffic, and axes of political coordination between Indian nations on a different temporal scheme than the geographical patterning and migration of Native peoples suggested by the classification of oral language families.[32] Finally, vocabularies of signed languages illuminate the embodied contexts of social interaction in a manner that oral vocabularies do not and cannot. Indeed, the complex linguistic modalities of physical performance in Native American cultures are largely elided in vocabularies that document only phonetic events. But as Brenda Farnell has argued, although PISL and other spoken languages are discrete linguistic systems, they operate on a continuum of expressive culture for which lines of separation are not always clear. In fact, the practice of Indian sign language is deeply integrated into other aspects of Native American cultures of oral performance in which words and signs accompany and inflect one another, including public oratory, storytelling practices (for which it may serve a unique mnemonic function), and religious ritual.[33]

As Laura Murray has argued, completed Indian vocabularies and linguistic questionnaires represent a significant though underexplored literature of contact, enacting conventions of epistemology and representation according to a unique "I-Thou" relationship that deserve consideration as a distinctive literary genre.[34] Murray's focus is oral language vocabularies, but her cogent claims deserve special consideration in the context of signed language vocabularies as well. Close attention to the formal properties of the latter reveal them to be distinct literary artifacts that require different interpretive strategies for literary scholars and cultural historians. The production of an oral language vocabulary is an act of alphabetic and diacritical mimesis in which words of the source language are transformed into a written phonetic code that must index a host of linguistic attributes: syllable, cadence, vowel sounds, and other aspects of prosody such as intonation and vocal stress (a dauntingly complex task that, as I discussed in chapter 1, was prone to disabling ambiguities for collectors untrained in techniques of orthography). In addition, in order to provide usable linguistic data, lexical collectors must also strive for internal regularity across words so that morphemes and word stems are consistently rendered. One might think of these aspects of the documentary process as a kind of deferred ventriloquism, in which the recorder must actively imagine a distant reader and fashion the means for the successful reproduction of an unfamiliar phonetic event at a future time.

By contrast, a manual sign is an embodied physical gesture that unfolds in a temporal sequence. Consequently, sign language vocabularies are compendia of short descriptive narratives that require a different set of representational choices on the part of the language collector. When does a manual sign begin, and when does it end? How is one to distinguish between the intrinsic components of a linguistic sign and other forms of casual or unconscious gesture (simple pointing, head nodding, and so on) that may accompany it?[35] How, and on what logic, are phonemes and manual stems to be identified, designated, and accorded proper emphasis in compound signs? Finally, because manual signs often express remarkable semiotic and semantic complexity, how should those complexities be labeled and evoked in literary discourse? Consider, for example, the Long Expedition's entry under the label *"Combat"* in the "Indian Language of Signs": "The clenched hands are held about as high as the neck, and five or six inches asunder, then waved two or three times laterally, to show the advances and retreats of the combatants; after which the fingers of each hand are suffered to spring from the thumb towards each other, as in the act of sprinkling water, to represent the flight of missiles."[36] This rendition of *"Combat"* expresses a clear narrative sequence and would appear to contain both pantomimic and conventional elements. The recorder (likely Thomas Say) suggests that the clenched hands, "waved two or three times laterally," figuratively depict, "the advances and retreats of the combatants." This inference may be correct (and may have been communicated explicitly at the time of transcription), but this iconic act is conventionalized rather than "naturally" pantomimic, a fact illustrated by a more common dialect variant for the concept that places partially closed hands in alternating perpendicular motion to and from the body (see figures 2.2 and 2.3).[37] The final manual component, in which "the fingers of each hand are suffered to spring from the thumb toward each other, as in the act of sprinkling water," is an iconic act of physical pantomime. It is also what linguists call a bound morpheme, a primary linguistic unit that requires combination with other morphemes to form a complete sign (in contrast to free morphemes, which do not require such attachments).[38] Specifically, the example above is the same gesture used as a component of two additional signs recorded in "Indian Language of Signs": *"Discharging the arrow"* (in which the release of the arrow "is indicated by springing the fingers from the thumbs, as in the act of sprinkling water"; and in the conclusion of *"Copulation"* (in which the right hand advances within the left, "until the last motion [in which] its fingers are so far advanced as to admit being sprung two or three times from the thumb, as in the act of sprinkling water," presumably to signify ejaculation).[39] These descriptions seem to express a pattern of morphological variance with respect to a common root stem; either one sign is the root for the other two, or they are perhaps all cognates of an unrecorded manual antecedent. In this light it is tempting to consider that the morpheme common to these signs expresses a semantic metonymy as well, that discussions of physical violence in PISL may evoke the erotics of human sexuality, and sex violence. Such possibilities are matters of poetics as well as linguistics and are therefore open-ended. But what is indisputable is the fact that the phrase "as in the act of

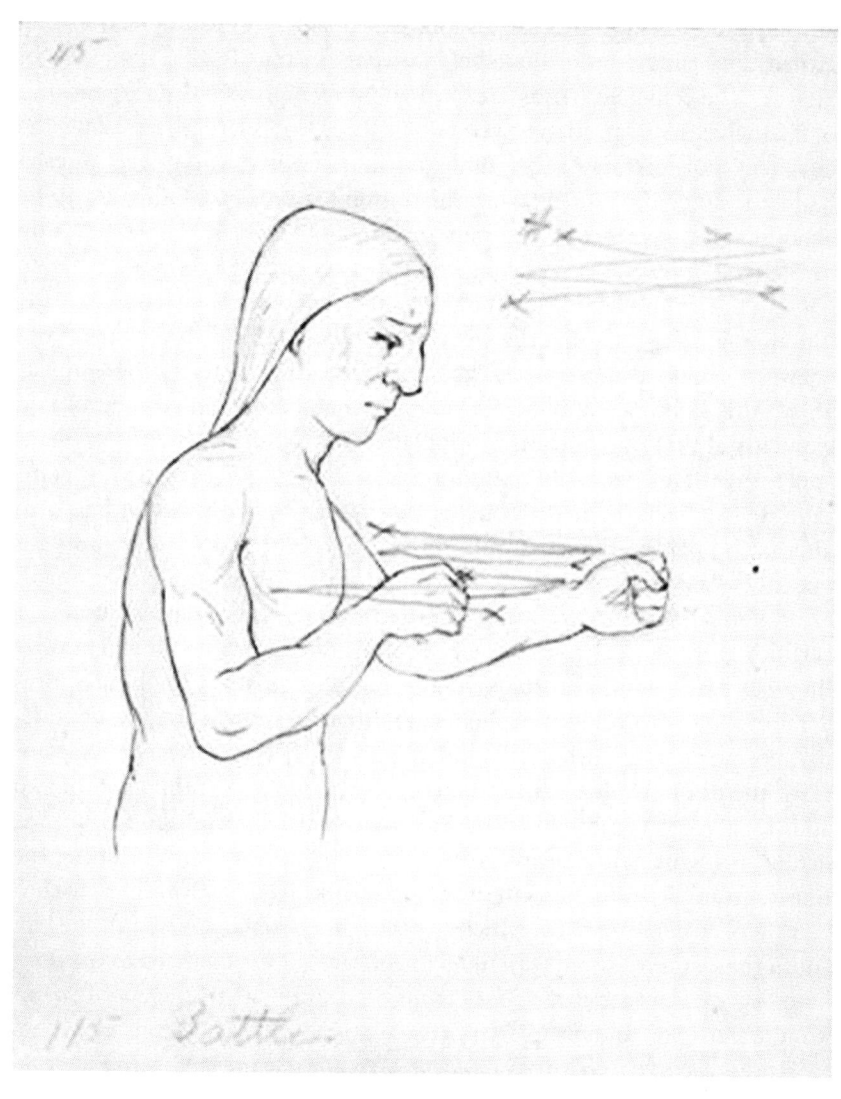

Figure 2.2. "Battle." Garrick Mallery Collection on Sign Language and Pictography, Numbered Manuscripts 1850s–1980s, NAA MS 2372, Smithsonian Institute, Washington, D.C.

Figure 2.3. "Speak." Garrick Mallery Collection on Sign Language and Pictography, Numbered Manuscripts 1850s–1980s, NAA MS 2372, Smithsonian Institute, Washington, D.C.

sprinkling water" is a simile provided by the recorder to evoke a familiar image in the readers' mental inventory and is not intrinsic to the signs themselves. Granting that the simile has clear illustrative value, the obvious location of its figurative content outside the linguistic system it purportedly describes underscores the difficulty of generating a stable data set about signed language properties within a nonmanual (i.e., a spoken, written) language. By way of further illustration, let me turn briefly to one final related example, the description for the indexical sign "*To Speak*": "The motion is like sprinkling water from the mouth by springing the fore finger from the thumb, the hand following a short distance from the mouth at each resilience, to show the direction of the word, or to whom it is addressed" (1:381).[40] Clearly, the action of springing a single forefinger from the thumb is physically distinct from springing all fingers from the thumb, but the repetition of the simile "like sprinkling water" figuratively implies a semantic homology that is an artifact of the printed vocabulary, rather than manual discourse itself.

Such technical challenges inherent to the act of transcription hinge on questions of literary representation that underscore the epistemological ambiguities of a linguistic system that lacked explicit classification within existing philological discourse. Reflecting on the slippage between words and signs at a later period, the pioneering theorist of PISL, Garrick Mallery, would suggest that PISL is best understood as a kind of writing, "though dissolving and sympathetic, and neither alphabetic nor phonetic." Positing an analogy with Egyptian hieroglyphics, Mallery theorized that reading this "writing" depends on a cognitive apprehension of the "luminous track impressible on the eye separate from the members producing it." For Mallery, what begs to be read is not the body but rather its traces in the air: "an immateriate graphic representation of visible objects and qualities which, invested with substance, has become familiar to us as the *rebus*."[41] Although members of the APS had speculated about the relationship of PISL to the supposedly iconographic character of Chinese written script, Mallery's theory of rebus-like "immateriate graphic representation" and its implications for producing a written sign vocabulary were not imagined by members of the Long Expedition. Indeed, the written instructions provided by the APS Historical and Literary Committee inquire only in general "whether any particular set of signs be employed in the communications of the tribes unacquainted with the language of each other" (a phenomenon sought in conjunction with "any species of dramatic representation"), but in a separate section from the more specific instructions labeled together under "Languages."[42] This demarcation of sign languages from linguistic matters proper is reflected in the "Indian Language of Signs" themselves. The Long Expedition observed the practice of sign language by ten different Native American groups—the Omaha, Osage, Caddo, Pawnee, Cherokee, Kiowa, Kaskia, Cheyenne, Arapahoe, and Ietan Comanche—across a vast extent of geography that spanned from Council Bluffs on the Missouri west to the Rocky Mountains, and thence east along the Arkansas, Red, and Canadian Rivers as far as present-day Louisiana. Yet the tribal source of the linguistic data collected in the "Indian Language of Signs"—the primary organizing category of comparative Indian linguistics in the nineteenth century—is never specified. Moreover, of the 110 manual signs recorded in the "Indian Language of Signs," only 29 correspond to those included in the "Vocabulary of Indian Languages" appended to the second volume, suggesting that systematic comparison between oral and signed languages was not intended.

Absent a clear analytical objective, the "Indian Language of Signs" sits uneasily alongside the "Vocabulary of Indian Languages" as an unincorporated data set that implicitly questions the cultural and epistemological assumptions embedded in standardized acts of oral vocabulary collection. If the instrumentality of PISL as a lingua franca was observed across intertribal boundaries, what social and cultural rules governed practices of code-switching within common linguistic groups? What metaphysical or epistemological bearing might communication via manual sign have for those religious practices, dances, and storytelling rituals in which PISL was commonly employed? In addition to these social and cultural questions are more fundamental questions of body and mind. What cognitive paradigm is manifested by sign language, and what are its salient organizing properties? Do manually expressed concepts differ semantically from those organized through speech? If so, how? Does the grammar of sign language express linguistic analogy to the principle of polysynthesis observed in oral Indian languages? Or might its rule-based syntax be contingent upon the physical mechanics of human anatomy? Are manually expressed concepts, perceived by the brain through the eye, different in kind (cognitively, semantically) from those transmitted to the ear through the medium of the voice? Finally, what implications might an embodied language of sign, with its uniquely developed coordination of mental and physical articulation, have for a developing linguistic discourse of human difference, what I described in chapter 1 as the philology of race?

Lacking a stable model of linguistic classification for PISL, the narrative portion of James's *Account* of the Long Expedition ignores some of these questions but answers others by mapping the practice of sign language onto an existing discourse of affective Indian embodiment.[43] Throughout the two-volume narrative, imagined interiorities provide a reflexive means by which to organize and interpret a linguistic system for which existing taxonomies failed to account. This shorthand—in which signs are used to index emotion, and emotion to index embodied expression—draws heavily on existing discourses on Indian eloquence and Indian emotionality. A subtle descriptive cue here is the distinction maintained between "gesture" and "gesticulation." As Pauline Moffitt Watts has pointed out in a discussion of Franciscan missionary activity in sixteenth-century Mexico, Anglo encounters with Indian groups were informed by classical understandings of rhetoric in which "gesture" was a recognized and refined element of civilized oratory. By contrast, "gesticulation" was regarded as "exaggerated, uncontrolled, and inappropriate gesture ... [and was] morally, socially, politically subversive, redolent of bestial, uncultivated human origins."[44] This division prevails across the Long *Account* as well, but with key differences. Whereas classical oratory extols the formality of conventionalized gesture, James's representations of formalized Indian oratory are characterized preponderantly by the more offensive term "gesticulation." The difference may be explained, in part, by what Jay Fliegelman identified as the American "elocutionary revolution" of the late eighteenth century, a movement to recalibrate the modes of classical rhetoric to promote the republican practice of American democracy and that "made the credibility of arguments contingent on the emotional credibility of the speaker."[45] For Fliegelman, the republican promotion of an embodied basis for the public expression and confirmation of sincerity was the rhetorical countermeasure to a world increasingly influenced by a play of texts that could not be trusted, but were potentially mere disguises of hidden thought:[46] "By insisting that the universality of language lay less in the features of language than in the features of delivery and countenance, the body of the speaker and its attitudes, not the body and attitudes of the text, become the site and text of meaning."[47]

In the discourse of affective Indian embodiment "gesticulation" signified both untrustworthiness and barbarity, providing a shortcut to a volatile Indian interiority that could not be masked by oral eloquence. Following the theft of a number of articles from the expedition in the vicinity of a Konza village near Council Bluffs (and a separate violent incident involving Anglo beaver trappers), a council was convened by the local Indian agent, Major Benjamin O'Fallon (who had joined the expedition temporarily), with representatives of the Grand Pawnee, Pawnee Loups, and Pawnee Republicans in October 1819. Although the Pawnee Republicans were felt confidently to have been responsible for these incidents, all three groups were called upon for accountability. Rising first to speak was Tarrarecawao (also known as Long Hair), a respected chief of the Grand Pawnee, who "stood for a short time immoveable, then slowly advanced nearer to the agent, and with a very loud, powerful voice, fierce countenance, and vehement gesticulation . . . addressed him."[48] Like Laceechnesharu, the Pawnee Loup chief who followed him, Tarrarecawao expressed his peaceful intentions and ignorance of the crimes committed; both chiefs solemnized their words by indicating the peace medallions they wore around their necks, which had been presented to them by William Clark. O'Fallon's reply indicates that their eloquent speech was not to be trusted: "I am not satisfied with what you have said," is his recorded reply. "What you have said is good, but it is not enough. Until you drive those dogs from among you, I will not consider you in any other light than as dogs."[49] In another episode near the Great Bend of the Arkansas River in August 1820, a retreating war party of wounded and impoverished Ietan Comanche encounters the expedition. Their conduct immediately places the expedition on its guard: one Ietan attempts to steal a gun; another, a horse. These incidents are contained quickly, however; the peace pipe is exchanged, gifts offered, and an attempt is made to record a vocabulary. But here an intriguing disjunction emerges within the narrative. As Thomas Say writes, their oral language presents a pleasing image: "Their words seem less harsh, more harmonious, and easier of acquisition, than those of their neighbours."[50] But this contrasts with their more revealing employment of sign language, which is characterized by "a violent shivering gesticulation" that accompanies their voices and seems bodily to insinuate their "importunateness" and the "incipient symptoms of disorder among them."[51] The expedition soon retreats. By contrast, when the more refined term "gesture" is used in the narrative to describe sign language practice, it signifies peacefulness, trustworthiness, and loyalty to the United States. Shortly prior to this episode, an assembled group of Kiowas, Kaskias, Cheyennes, and Arapahoes swiftly approach the expeditionary party: "A minute afterwards we were surrounded by them and were happy to observe, in their features and gestures, a manifestation of the most pacific disposition; they shook us by the hand, assured us by signs that they rejoiced to see us, and invited us to partake of their hospitality." Gifts of jerked bison, tobacco, knives, horses, and other items are exchanged (Say reflects that their gifts out-valued those of the expedition), which forms a prelude to satisfactory trade of equipment, heralded by both parties as a token of more formalized and extensive trade to come. Say is gratified to observe that they "hold in exalted estimation, the martial prowess of the Americans" and have a low opinion of the Spanish. Further time in the camp results in the acquisition of new vocabularies, and additional linguistic observations that contrast their oral and signed languages. Where the Ietan Comanche's spoken language was "less harsh, more harmonious, and easier of acquisition" than others of the region, Say writes that "these languages abound with sounds strange to our ears, and in the noisy loquacity of some squaws . . . we distinguished preeminently, sounds which may be expressed by the letters koo, koo, koo." Where the Ietan use of sign language is characterized by "violent shivering gesticulation," Say writes: "It was no uncommon occurrence, to see two individuals of different nations, sitting upon the ground, and conversing freely with each other, by means of the language of signs. In the art of thus conveying their ideas, they were thorough adepts, and their manual display was only interrupted at remote intervals by a smile, or by the auxiliary of an articulated word of the language of the Crow Indians, which to a very limited extent, passes current amongst them."[52] The juxtapositions are striking: in one group, perceptions of hostility and mistrust correspond to an accessible and aesthetically pleasing oral language that is the inverse image of a discordant sign language practice; in the other, an experience of trust and hospitality corresponds to an inaccessible and phonetically strange speech that is the inverse image of a sign language practiced by "adepts" whose fluency is interrupted only by a smile, another physical cue that speaks to a pacific emotional interior. It is a remarkable equation, an implicit taxonomical chiasmus most striking in that, for each, the language of embodiment rather than voice emerges as the more reliable index of emotional posture and political intention. Language may present a deceiving image, and speech may mislead, but the body does not lie.

Eloquent Bodies: Race, Language, Disability

Thomas Say's implicit yet specific organization of manual expression contra oral speech to divine the secrets of Indian interiority participates in a wider cultural discourse that encoded Indian bodies, gestures, and speech in terms of the developing politics of Indian land and forced removal. A key document in this vein is the archaeologist and Indian commissioner Caleb Atwater's *Remarks Made on a Tour to Prairie du Chien; thence to Washington City, in 1829*, which records his work as a commissioner appointed by President Jackson to negotiate with the Winnebago a cession of mineral-rich territory in the vicinity of Green Bay, Wisconsin, claimed by the Winnebago, Potawatomi, Ojibwe, and Ottawa peoples. Asserting that the "violent gestures" of Native Americans are a result of "the poverty of their languages [which] tends strongly to excite exertions to express ideas by figures, which their language is not copious enough, to enable them, by words, to convey," Atwater offers his general impressions of the tenor of Indian oratory during treaty deliberations according to the following prototype:

> He thanks the Great Spirit, that he has granted them a day for holding their council, without or with a few clouds, as the case may be—that their several paths between their homes and the council fire, have been opened and unattended with danger—that the storm is passed away and gone—and he hopes that during the time, he may be detained from home, [his] beasts may not destroy his corn, nor any bad birds be suffered to fly about the council with false stories. All this is uttered without much gesticulation, and without enthusiasm; but should he touch upon the subject of a sale of his country, his whole soul is in every word, in every look, in every gesture. His eye flashes fire, he raises himself upon his feet, his body is thrown in every variety of attitude—every muscle is strained—every nerve its exerted to its utmost power, and his voice is loud, clear, distinct and commanding. He becomes, to use his own expressive phrase—A MAN.[53]

By such indications, Atwater suggests that Indian eloquence "is easily conceived," but eloquence, however forceful in its expression, is not evidence of the emotional fullness of personhood. In this sense, Atwater's final qualification, that the Native American thus becomes "A MAN," but only in "his own expressive phrase," cuts precisely to the point. Indian manhood thusly conceived is a form of self-fashioning on a closed emotional circuit, circumscribed by culture and race, rising into itself from a stasis without the "enthusiasm" of meaningful affect into an intensity of bodily outrage. Eruptive gesticulation is for Atwater a telltale signifier of interiority, an index of what Ezra Tawil has termed "racial sentiment," the belief that "different races were thought to feel different things, and to feel things differently."[54] Atwater repeats this equation in his discussion of the Winnebago Chief Hoowaneka (Little Elk): "His gestures were very graceful, but, in those parts of his speech, where he felt deeply, what he said, his gesticulation was violent, and his whole soul appeared to be agitated in the highest degree."[55] "Gesticulation" functions here as a figure of weakness, a signature lapse from recognized oratorical standards into ungovernable emotionality: "Thus, we see, that our red men are not sufficiently advanced in the arts" to achieve the heights of true oratory, an assessment he grants to be remediable if the Indian could repudiate "aristocracy, his love of war, [and] his indolence.... Until then, he will rise no higher than he now is: his speeches will be vehement, his gesticulation violent, and repetitions, and darkness, and obscurity, mixed with some beautiful allusions to nature, and vague traditions, handed down, from ages gone by, will be found in all his harangues."[56] The loss of land and cultural defeat are the topics at hand in this pair of examples, but for Atwater those topics are largely incidental to the phenomenon of Indian oratory more generally. In this, violent bodily agitation in the act of speechmaking is the intensified expression of an essential emotional insipidity, the amplification and semantic fulfillment of the "darkness" and "obscurity" of a dead and primitive civilization.

Atwater's own fashioning of Indian eloquence conforms to a prototype as well, specifically that of Chief Logan's famous speech for Lord Dunmore, which Atwater praises as "simplicity itself" and whose effectiveness he attributes to Logan's close connection to whites, "whom he more resembled in all his ideas, than his own people."[57] Logan's speech had been publicized and celebrated by Jefferson as an oration unsurpassed by Demosthenes or Cicero, or "of any more eminent orator, if Europe has furnished more eminent"; in juxtaposition with Hoowaneka's speech here, what is most striking is the flattened emotional profile Logan's speech projects—traveling on a narrow continuum that includes pride, lamentation, and spent vengefulness but that (unlike Hoowaneka's) is devoid of any vehemence, observable agitation, or implied threat of future violence.[58] There is a certain irony that Atwater should cite Logan's speech as the moderated counterpoint to the savage exemplarity of Hoowaneka's emotional style of oration. Jefferson had offered Logan's speech as counterevidence to Buffon's degeneracy theory as it applied to Native Americans, and the latter's claim that "he lacks vivacity, and is lifeless in his soul; the activity of his body is less an exercise or voluntary movement than an automatic reaction to his needs; take from him hunger and thirst, and you will destroy at the same time the active cause of all his movements; he will remain either standing there stupidly or recumbent for days at a time."⁵⁹ Subtracting the leavening influence of whiteness Atwater finds to mark the difference between Logan and Native Americans like Hoowaneka, Atwater effectively returns the prototype of Indianness as one given to spontaneous eruptions into violent gesticulation to Buffon's image of a being for whom "the activity of his body" is "automatic" but whose natural state is "recumbent" inactivity. As Atwater sums up the matter: "A savage has but few words by which, to convey his ideas, yet, he does not often use one half of these in his conversation. Generally grave and sedate, and too indolent to use many words, he converses by signs."⁶⁰

Language, oratory, and a semiotics of embodiment combine here in an evolving racial politics yet rooted in an eighteenth-century discourse of primitivism that figures differences of human endowment on a developmental (rather than essential) scale conditioned primarily by environment. In this light, perhaps the most intriguing reaction to the sign language documented by the Long Expedition was that of Samuel Akerly, an M.D. and professor at the New-York Mechanic and Scientific Institution, who delivered a lecture on the topic before the New-York Lyceum of Natural History in June 1823. Akerly was also the cofounder, with Samuel Latham Mitchill, of the New-York Institution for the Deaf and Dumb—a school that, under Akerly as director, experienced friction with Gallaudet's more celebrated institution in Connecticut but that likewise applied the methods of Abbé Sicard for the education of the deaf in manual sign language. Akerly declared that the American Indians documented by the Long Expedition were unique among the known peoples of the world in that, being possessed of the faculty of speech, they had also developed "a system of signs, by which they could freely express their ideas." In doing so, they expressed a universal principle of language formation: "Philosophers have discussed the subject of a universal language, but have failed to invent one, while the savages of America have adopted the only one which can possibly become universal. The language of signs is so true to nature, that the deaf and dumb, from different parts of the globe, will immediately on meeting, understand each other."⁶¹ The universality of gesture was a common refrain of early American deaf education, drawing philosophical currency from a transatlantic discourse inquiring into the nature of language itself. For the Scottish Common Sense philosopher Thomas Reid, language was composed of two sign types: the "natural" (which originated human expression in a state of nature prior to all social covenants); and the "artificial" (which are essentially arbitrary and become meaningful only "by compact or agreement among those who use them").[62] Despite their archaic origins, "natural" signs are not dead but "have a meaning which every man understands by the principles of his nature" and are conveyed through modulations of voice, gesture, and expression as the chief means by which "we give force and energy to language."[63] By contrast, "artificial signs" compose a system that has been grafted onto natural language, and have proliferated to such a degree that they have occluded the primary qualities of human nature itself: "Is it not a pity that the refinements of a civilized life, instead of supplying the defects of natural language, should root it out, and plant in its stead dull and lifeless articulations of unmeaning sounds, or the scrawling of insignificant characters?"[64] Rather than perfecting the expression of thoughts and sentiments, the skillful use of artificial language "is surely the corruption of the natural."[65] For Reid, the signposts that might lead us back to nature were offered by the deaf and by "savage" peoples, both of whom retained a greater share of natural language by conditions of necessity.

Reid's theories offer a valuable context for explaining that, although the thrust of Akerly's claim above is complimentary to the inventive powers of American Indian peoples, his primary motivation was not to herald the cultural accomplishments of Native Americans but, in a sense, to assert the primitivism of his own deaf students. After all, despite the dramatic developments in deaf education in France in the latter half of the eighteenth century, the commonplace view was that the deaf were ineducable—Kant, for example, declaring them capable only of an *analogue* of reason but not reason itself.[66] From Akerly's point of view, if Indians and the deaf expressed manually a human capacity for iconic expression that was truly universal among the hearing and nonhearing alike along the lines imagined by Reid, the physical limitation of deafness did not enforce an impassible upper limit of cognition but merely froze linguistic development at a primitive state—a condition that could be mitigated and elevated by rigorous instruction in language that contained both iconic and symbolic elements.[67] Thomas Gallaudet, who also took instructive note of the Long Expedition, agreed with this sentiment but went further, championing the "natural language of signs" not only as a vehicle of deaf instruction but as a language whose "genius" was demonstrably superior to oral language for moral instruction because of its "peculiar adaptation to the mind of childhood and early youth, when objects addressed to the senses, and especially the sight, have such a sway over the mind."[68] In this, Gallaudet's recommendations track closely with Reid's, who predicted, "Where speech is natural, it will be an exercise, not of the voice and lungs only, but of all the muscles of the body; like that of dumb people and savages, whose language, as it has more of nature, is more expressive, and is more easily learned."[69]

Joining threads from a diverse array of cultural discourses and human geographies, the philosophical dream to restore the perfection of the natural through language connects a transatlantic vogue of the primitive to an emergent discourse of disability. What unites them is a romantic nostalgia, and a common sense that non-normative experiences of embodiment (marked by deafness, or racial difference) correlated to a desirable state of expressive freedom—a sort of negative capability, rooted in the body, that was untainted by the artifice of reason. Overburdened by artificial language, nondisabled white bodies were, in a sense, physically and emotionally impaired because the naturally expressive impulses of the body were disconnected from the governing systems of an acquired order of thought.

A similar vision of natural language was cherished also by Peter Du Ponceau at the American Philosophical Society. Writing in his private notebook on philology, Du Ponceau projects an uncharacteristically romantic fantasy of linguistic emancipation:

> There is an intuitive language which man speaks only to himself. What crowds of ideas rush at once upon the mind in case of a sudden disappointment or good fortune. There is no time to clothe them in words, the past, the present, & the future pass at once in review before us, accompanied with fancies of what might & did not happen. Such probably will be the mode of communication of immortal minds when freed from the shackles of our earthly bodies—The nearest a language comes to this mode of communication, the more perfect I would conceive it to be.[70]

In this, Du Ponceau posits ideas as cognitively prior to their representation in language; languages give the form to ideas that makes possible their social expression, yet the external relays of thought through language distort and temporally delimit an underlying essence of mental activity that is unalloyed by linguistic structure. Unlike Gallaudet, Akerly, or Reid, Du Ponceau does not figure expressive liberation explicitly in a return to the uncivilized body but rather in the emancipation of immortal minds "from the shackles of our earthly bodies." But "bodies," in this sense, are less literal than existential—a generalized figure of post-Babel linguistic embodiment that measures the distance from which we are separated from the primacy of intuition through the impassable cognitive limit of death. And yet there is a sense that not all languages have fallen equally into fragmentation, and a hope—suspended on the dash that follows that sentence, and resurrected in the subjunctive mood of the one that follows—that a language approaching the purity of primary intuition may yet be a living reality on earth. In these private notebooks, crucibles for his researches into Native American linguistics and his evolving ideas about language, Du Ponceau projects a careful and studious method that meticulously synthesized vocabularies, grammars, and travel dispatches from a range of printed and epistolary sources. But in passages like that above, he indulges also his visionary cast of mind and ruminates on the metaphysical wish that animated his investigations. That wish joins science to a form of romanticism that is proto-Emersonian in its desire for transcendence. In Emerson's circular scheme, nature is "the vehicle of thought": words are the signs of natural facts, which in their particularity are signs of spiritual facts; nature is both "the symbol of the spirit" and "a metaphor of the human mind." To return to nature is to return language to the primary intuitions of mind in consonance with the elemental order of the world, a process that correlates the expressive component of individual self-fashioning with spiritual enlargement. This process has a primary moral dimension for Emerson that, like Gallaudet before him, he identifies prototypically with "children and savages."[71] Like Emerson, who also grapples with the earthly limitations of our means to know in "Experience" and declares that he would "die out of nature, and be born again into this new yet unapproachable America I have found in the West," Du Ponceau imagines a state of rebirth from earthly shackles.[72] But even though he shares with Emerson a transcendent ideal, for Du Ponceau this ideal is joined to a living research agenda that sought material verification in the Indian languages of the American West—not, in other words, in that "new yet unapproachable America" that was an ever-retreating figure for a national and individualistic imagination but in a proximate, undiscovered linguistic territory that might be documented as living fact through the coordinated actions of the APS and the War Department. Proper description and classification of new languages was the focus, the object of investigation, but this object was also the means of discovery of the "more perfect" language, which, though, conceived in the ideal, was anticipated as a living achievement on earth. Did sign language answer to this "more perfect" conception, the fulfillment of a long-anticipated wish? In notebooks from later years, Du Ponceau includes entries on Plains Indian Sign Language, suggesting that it eventually formed a serious object of his linguistic contemplations and that it had been upgraded, in a sense, from the instructions he had coauthored for the Long Expedition, which classified them in passing only as a kind of dramatic performance.[73] But the evidence suggests that Du Ponceau had not arrived at anything approaching a final determination on the question when the notebooks break off gradually after 1829—the open-ended entries on sign language persist alongside other unresolved questions and mental impressions. An offset remark in his notebook from 1826 speaks suggestively to those questions that remained unanswered and were perhaps for him unanswerable: "Ideas rush in masses upon the mind."[74]

* * *

In one sense, the literary and linguistic assemblage constructed across this chapter comes full circle here—from the material apparatus of empire; to the misrecognized prevalence of Plains Indian Sign Language across a vast extent of borderlands territory; to Euro-American meditations on the expressiveness of the racialized Indian body; in an emergent discourse on deafness, disability, and universal language; and once again to a philosophical vantage point that gazed west in anticipation of theoretical fulfillment and relied on the material apparatus of empire to fulfill that purpose. If this itinerary is perhaps a circuitous one, that circuitousness is also one part of the point I am making. To return to one of the theoretical vantage points with which this book began, what Deleuze and Guattari's figure of the rhizome offers in this context is a means to imagine more fully the often indirect relays that accomplish the theoretical and material work of westward expansionism. Undertaken as a surveying enterprise to demarcate a new international boundary, the Long Expedition was, from one point of view, a series of physical and documentary actions across an ill-charted physical territory that took its bearing from a coordinated network of political and scientific agendas. But the Long Expedition assumed a second material form in the guise of documents, a literary record—or, as the *New York Globe* put it, an earlier imperial "scheme to be filled up"— that triggered various forms of ideological and philosophical consolidation in a politicized climate of literary reception. The Long Expedition is, in other words, both a set of imperial actions and a set of representations about the nature of those actions; and it is the second life of the expedition, in its multiple circulating representations, that offers a broader rhizome of social, philosophical, and print relations, one that maps retroactively a supplementary set of meanings onto the original imperial undertaking. What this suggests is that a full view of U.S. expeditionary actions in the western borderlands must include a discussion of, for example, disability; and that to understand an emergent discourse on deafness and universal language theory, one must compass also the extents of western U.S. empire. Constituted in these terms, such an archive privileges an elastic understanding of common historiographical binaries: center and periphery; national and international; social linguistic exchange and documented vocabulary; "savage" and civilized; bodies and print. But in charting the path of linguistic misrecognition through an imperial lens, such an archive risks passively reproducing the very documentary procedures that consigned Native peoples to historical oblivion—the point at which, as Larzer Ziff put it in a passage quoted above, "sign language gave way to interpreted speech . . . and cultural equality gave way to dominance and the process of literary annihilation."

By way of transition into the next chapter, then, let me reference an important alternative for thinking about networks that offers an indigenous counterforce to the imperial rhizome. Contra the hegemony of Euro-American ideas that effaced Native claims of sovereignty and self-representation, Robert Allen Warrior has championed the figure of "intellectual trade routes" as a means of recuperating and reimagining indigenous networks of knowledge and cultural exchange. Whereas conventional histories of the movement of ideas in the Euro-American/Native encounter "has most often been considered a one-way process, with Western ideas and the Western classical tradition making their way to the Indian world from metropolitan centers to colonial indigenous margins," Warrior writes that trade routes are "pathways [that] became trails and then networks of trails that criss-crossed the single landmass that is the Americas".[75]

> The many hundreds of cultures and civilizations that dot the American landscape are connected by those crisscrossing trails, and the supposed European discovery of the continent took place along those trails. Different indigenous groups have made more or less extensive use of these routes, but certainly all of them have had some knowledge of the world beyond their homelands. Even among a highly insulated group of people who exhibit next to no interest in such a world, it is hard to imagine that a generation

could pass without at least a few people developing a strong curiosity about the world over the next hill, through the next stand of trees, a little further downriver, or over a looming range of mountains.[76]

The totality of Native sign language practice epitomizes one network of the intellectual trade routes Warrior describes. Circulating on Warrior's criss-crossing networks of trails that pre-dated Columbus, PISL and other forms of sign constituted a key embodied medium for the circulation of indigenous knowledge from homeland to homeland that developed new forms of political and cross-cultural significance in the context of Euro-American colonization of the North American continent that also "took place along those trails." Recuperating indigenous networks that have been forgotten or lost, the figure of intellectual trade routes—such that can arise in "a serendipitous moment in an archive or the sudden realization of a connection between things that had seemed disparate"—also accounts for the transformation of indigenous networks in light of Euro-American contact and the forms of intellectual and human traffic to which the circumstances of encounter gave rise.[77]

In this light, consider one final example in which the diverse elements of the imperial rhizome and the intellectual trade routes of indigenous America converge in a powerful romantic embodiment: a man named John Dunn Hunter, who walked into Samuel Akerly's New-York Institution of the Deaf and Dumb one day in the fall of 1822. As Akerly observes, Hunter was "the white Indian who had been restored to civilized society," noting that "a sign language was used as a medium of communication between the tribes west of the Mississippi, among whom he had resided from his infancy." According to Akerly, Hunter "observed every thing with that apparent indifference peculiar to the Indians of this country and yet his repeated calls at the school were the indications of a more than common interest, excited by seeing instruction imparted through the medium of signs, to those who could not hear."[78] The author of a fascinating Indian captivity narrative that was published in 1823, Hunter was celebrated on both sides of the Atlantic and then widely condemned as an imposter, his autobiography "exposed" to be a fraud. Literary critics and historians today are less sure. Although credible evidence suggests that his account was truthful, that evidence is not conclusive; he persists as a figure resistant to literary or historical classification. Hunter died in 1827 in Texas, following an unsuccessful bid to found the Red and White Republic of Fredonia, a multiracial utopia that sought to unite twenty-three local and displaced Native American tribes with members of the Edwards *empresario* grant near Nacogdoches under a republican constitution. According to Hunter, that effort was inspired by his experience of a powerful speech delivered by Tecumseh, the Shawnee icon of the Pan-Indian Confederacy, imploring the cause of collective Indian resistance to white depredations—a message that, for Hunter, was conveyed substantively through Tecumseh's extraordinarily expressive powers of manual gesture. I have not found any other historical or secondary source discussing Hunter that notes his visits to the New-York Institution of the Deaf and Dumb or that comments on his knowledge of sign language. And yet his knowledge of PISL, corroborated in several instances by his *Memoirs*, suggests intriguing possibilities for cultural historians. In chapter 3, I explore the conjunction of oral and embodied speech within the literary domain of Hunter's *Memoirs* as a means of opening up broader questions about the linguistic complexities of Indian political identity for Tecumseh's Pan-Indian Confederacy in the borderlands region of the Northwest Territory and Canada. When traced schematically, if fragmentarily, across a broad array of textual topographies, social spaces, and historical silences, what emerge are extensive multilingual networks that may prompt us to reimagine patterns of exchange, political and social relations, and contested identity formations across the multiple commons of Native America.

3

John Dunn Hunter, Tecumseh, and the Linguistic Politics of Pan-Indianism

The Troubling Case of John Dunn Hunter

By the time Samuel Akerly met him at the New-York Institution for the Deaf and Dumb in the fall of 1822, John Dunn Hunter had studied English for at least three years, traveled east over the Alleghenies to gain an audience with Jefferson at Monticello, and traveled from Philadelphia to New York.[1] He is an enduring cipher of American literary and political history. The author of an internationally famous captivity narrative, Hunter was celebrated first as a gifted "white Indian" on both sides of the Atlantic, only to be maligned as an imposter in a campaign orchestrated by Lewis Cass and supported by such prominent figures as William Clark, Henry Rowe Schoolcraft, Jared Sparks, Peter Stephen Du Ponceau, and John Neal.[2] Hunter was assassinated, unaware that Cass's campaign had shifted public opinion decisively against him, in obscure circumstances in Texas, in 1827, following his unsuccessful efforts to found an independent multiracial utopia called the Red and White Republic of Fredonia. By the end of the nineteenth century, the prevailing view remained that Hunter had been a literary and personal fraud. Contemporary scholarly discussion of Hunter, however, largely has followed the lead of Richard Drinnon's 1972 reappraisal of Hunter's claims of authenticity, in which Drinnon finds all of the major charges levied against Hunter to be politically motivated and either unprovable or demonstrably false.[3] Amid ongoing speculations about the reliability of Hunter's life story and its significance for cultural and political history, his knowledge of Plains Indian Sign Language has been unexplored.[4] Yet much of the controversy originally surrounding Hunter involved questions of language. Revisiting his case in the present context reveals the degree to which the ideological struggle to shape an emergent national narrative concerning Indian Removal in the 1820s was impacted by nineteenth-century Indian linguistics (and, more to the point, impacted by the limitations of that discourse), even as it underscores the challenges of working with oral and manual sources of evidence that are often ambiguous and not always resolvable within traditional methods of historical verification.

Excavating the full horizon of Native expressive practices and communication systems along what Matt Cohen has described as "a spectrum of media modes" is an essential task for an American studies project that is committed to transcending the conceptual binary of orality and print and bridging the disciplinary divide between indigenous studies and the history of the book. "To do so means engaging the implications of dissolving orality and literacy into a continuous topography or spectrum," Cohen writes, "rather than thinking of them as a series of overlapping but always distinct cognitive categories or habits."[5] Favoring the open-ended dimensionality of the word "communication" to characterize that spectrum, Cohen's work invites us to dismantle constructed hierarchies of expressive practice in order to assemble a comprehensive view of the "networked wilderness." A critical investigation of manual linguistic discourse is a necessary step in the goal of disrupting a binaristic historiography rooted in orality and literacy, a step that foregrounds questions of embodiment as a semiotic and social generator in combination with other Native modalities of communication, performance, and resistance. At the same time, there are compelling reasons to retain critical approaches to nonoral linguistic systems that recognize them as "distinctive cognitive categories or habits." As Diana Taylor has argued, "part of the colonizing project throughout the Americas consisted in discrediting autochthonous ways of preserving and communicating historical understanding."[6] Historical misrecognitions of sign language effectively consigned it (and other Native nonoral, nonprinted expressive practices) to the margins of Euro-American understanding, even as embodied forms of speech quilted social geographies, enacted and reproduced tribal memories, and brokered significant forms of colonial and imperial resistance for Native actors.

Approached from this perspective, the widespread practice of Indian sign language offers a compelling opportunity to reimagine Native political alignments along a shifting international borderland that remained largely opaque to Euro-American eyes in the 1820s. As Eric J. Sundquist and Stephanie LeMenager have argued persuasively, James's *Account* of the Long Expedition was a key document popularizing the idea that the southern prairies were impenetrable and uninhabitable by whites, provoking, in LeMenager's words, "crises of imagination" within the dream of westward expansion on an agrarian model.[7] While the desolate image of the "inland deserts" evoked a climate of denial to U.S. national and territorial fulfillment, it also occluded complex intertribal economies of the southern plains that were rapidly transforming under pressures of forced emigration and complicating the political status of the border between the United States and post-Revolutionary Mexico. In this context, perhaps the most important unasked question concerning the sign language documented by the Long Expedition was a political one: To what degree did broad fluency in American Indian sign languages enable the forging of intertribal political alliances, and the organization of resistance to U.S. and Spanish (after 1821, Mexican) encroachment, on Indian lands across a long geographical frontier? In pursuing this question, the following two chapters treat in depth the case of John Dunn Hunter as a writer, political activist along the U.S./Mexico border, and troubling case study for a bevy of influential figures striving to control the ideological and narrative shape of western expansionism. Using Hunter as fulcrum to open up discussion of the linguistic politics of Pan-Indianism, in this chapter I treat in depth the role of sign language in the development of Tecumseh's Pan-Indian confederation in the Northwest Territory and, in chapter 4, connect that history to the remarkable story of the Fredonian Rebellion in Texas, and the efforts of the Mexican Comisión de Límites to reckon with the complex racial and national implications of that event at the end of the 1820s.

Some background on Hunter's life is warranted here. John Dunn Hunter was a phenotypically white man, who, by his own account, was captured by the Kickapoo during early childhood. Following a Pawnee raid, he was conveyed to the custody of an itinerant band of Kansas Indians, with whom he lived for several years before being transferred subsequently to the protection of the Little Osage near the Vermillion branch of the Arkansas River. At the time of this final transfer, Hunter was, by his estimate, ten to twelve years of age; he then spent the remainder of his youth with the Osage, under the adoptive and solicitous care of the warrior Shen-thweeh and his wife, Hunk-hah, who had recently lost a son. During this period, he was bestowed the name "Hunter," for the speed with which he acquired proficiency with a rifle. Following his adoption as a full member of the Osage, Hunter's account of his individual life story blends into a story of his people; in his *Memoirs* he is both witness to and fully invested as a participant in a Native American history dominated by complex political frictions and shifting alliances between the Grand and Little Osage, the Kansas, Pawnee, Maha, Otoe, and Potawatomi, and white traders across a contested geography in the lower Arkansas River basin. Hunting expeditions, dramatic episodes of armed conflict, and tense intertribal negotiation characterize this part of his account of his life story and are highlighted in a series of extraordinary narrative sequences, including the record of a remarkable sixteen-month journey with a small group across the Rockies to the Pacific Ocean, and Hunter's account of Tecumseh's impassioned speech before the Osage in 1811 (which I discuss in detail below). In 1816, rejecting on moral grounds an alcohol-fueled plan to rob and kill a white trader named George P. Watkins (who had previously displayed kindness to Hunter and had urged him to return to white civilization), Hunter abruptly left the Osage and warned Watkins of the plan against him. In response, Watkins declared that it was Hunter's duty as a white man to join forces with him and fight the Osage—voicing a politics of racial essentialism Hunter was unprepared to accept. Disillusioned, and feeling acute misgivings at having "betrayed my countrymen," Hunter then wandered alone for several months in the wilderness. Within the storytelling progression of the *Memoirs*, Hunter's rejection of Watkins's demand of loyalty to white civilization is less personal than it stands as a rejection of the culture for which Watkins and his crew serve as a disturbing synecdoche. Conversely, his abrupt repudiation of the Osage is directed less at the broader culture of "his countrymen" than it is a rejection of the moral degradation of his people that contact with white culture had produced (exemplified specifically by the introduction of alcohol), and that threatened to transform Osage society overall.

Hunter's account of his subsequent period of solitude marks a final transition in the development of his hybrid subjectivity and authorial identity. Remarkably, the figure that emerges from this crisis is a natural historian, ethnographer, and political visionary. Following his acquisition of English (Hunter enrolled in several schools in the vicinity of Cape Girardeau and points south along the Mississippi and studied English for three years), Hunter characterized his new resolve in Humboldtian grandeur: "From the ready proficiency I had made, I thought of nothing less than the subjugation of the empires of science and literature, and when this had been accomplished, to have penetrated into unexplored regions in search of new truths" (79). The book to which this ambition gave rise has the unusual distinction in first-person accounts of Indian captivity to be accompanied by a lengthy ethnological treatise documenting the social and political practices, *materia medica*, and religious and cultural systems of the Native American peoples among whom he had lived. Indeed, the title of the first edition of his book emphasizes this contribution to knowledge of Indian peoples ahead of the significance of his own remarkable life story and experience of captivity: *Manners and Customs of Several Indian Tribes Located West of the Mississippi; Including Some Account of the Soil, Climate, and Vegetable Productions, and the Indian Materia Medica: To Which Is Prefixed the History of the Author's Life during a Residence of Several Years among Them* (Philadelphia: J. Maxwell, 1823). Prioritizing objective knowledge over subjective experience, the book's title stands as its own kind of narrative outcome to the experience of captivity. Prototypically, captivity narratives enact cycles of loss and return, community disincorporation and restoration, trial and salvation. Both Hunter's title and book depart from this paradigm. Fashioning its author as an objective authority detached from the people the book describes, the title to the first edition does not figure Hunter as a captive redeemed by providence (as Rowlandson's does) or restored to the social body of the United States in which the identities of captive and community are reestablished (as James Smith's does). Instead, it figures a displacement of identity from experience to disembodied objectivity; the life is literally a prefix, implicitly devalued further by virtue of its placement at the end of the title sequence.

The transformation of a preliterate experience of Indian captivity into an authorial persona capable of detached objectivity about the nature and ethnographic meanings of that experience forms the primary narrative arc of Hunter's autobiography and stands as a significant innovation on the captivity genre. Written following his acquisition of English, the autobiography stages a literary reconciliation of these two postures as an ongoing meditative theme that highlights the linguistic constitution of experience, memory, and scientific discourse. For example, during his transformative episode of solitary wandering, in which he writes, "I looked back with the most painful reflections on what I had been, and on the irreparable sacrifices I had made, merely to become an outcast," Hunter did not yet know English, nor had he dreamed of "the subjugation of the empires of science and literature" that a "ready proficiency" with books would later inspire (66, 79). What he had instead was time and the power of patient observation. Hunter relates that experience in the following manner:

> The conflicts of the male buffaloes and deer, the attack of the latter on the rattlesnake, the industry and ingenuity of the beaver in constructing its dam, &c., and the attacks of the panther on its prey, afforded much interest, and engrossed much time. Indeed, I have lain for half a day at a time in the shade to witness the management and policy observed by the ants in storing up their food, the maneuvers of the spider in taking its prey, the artifice of the mason-fly (*Sphex*) in constructing and storing its clayey cells, and the voraciousness and industry of the dragon-fly (*Libellula*) to satisfy its appetite. (66)

This passage enacts an intensive moment of temporal, linguistic, and epistemological compression, what in Freudian parlance might be termed condensation. Rendering in English a moment of engrossed attention and knowledge formation governed originally by an Osage linguistic reality, Hunter exalts a Native modality of natural observation even as he rewrites that modality according to Euro-American conventions of taxonomy (marked pointedly by his incorporation of the Latinate terms, *Sphex* and *Libellula*). Linnaean classification is seemingly ascendant here, the organizing system that encompasses and signposts for his readers a prior order of understanding ultimately consonant with a Euro-American scientific worldview. But even as this particular literary consolidation of a preliterate experience of mind culminates in taxonomic clarity, Hunter's *Memoirs* expresses throughout an ongoing struggle to reconcile incommensurable orders of linguistic understanding. Upon entering school at Cape Girardeau, Hunter reports initially having "great difficulty in learning the pronunciation and meaning of words," which, when "partially surmounted," leads to his becoming "literally infatuated with reading"—a description that suggests a relationship to the written word that was equally ardent and stupefying (77). "My judgment was so confused by the multiplicity of new ideas that crowded upon my undisciplined mind, that I hardly knew how to discriminate between truth and fable" (77). Dedicated study improves his confidence; but, even at the moment of the book's writing, some six years following his departure from the Osage, Hunter voices in his opening pages acute ambivalence about the reconciliation of his preliterate self with his literary consciousness. Hunter opens his preface with an expression of reluctance that was an established convention of nineteenth-century autobiography, that "in presenting myself to the world as an author, I have complied more with the wishes of friends than my own inclinations," even as he specifies that reluctance in a manner that announces his own authorial unconventionality: "This conviction arises from an imperfect acquaintance with the English language, and total ignorance of the art of book-making." Moreover, Hunter emphasizes that the subject of his book is drawn entirely from memory "of events, persons, and things, which are many years separated from the present, and some of them so remotely, as barely to come within my recollection" (1). In light of these limitations, what enables the production of the manuscript is the successful interface of Hunter's memory of experience with Euro-American epistemological and literary techniques. On one hand are the "interrogations respecting some of the subject matter" by his editor and associate Edward Clark, a process of inquiry that precipitated the organization and presentation of "events, persons, and things." On the other is the retrospective bifurcation of his memory according to distinct literary frameworks and narrative postures: "the story of my captivity," written in the first person according to the conventions of the captivity narrative; and in "a detached form, under appropriate heads, my observations on the Manners and Customs of the Indian tribes dwelling westward of the Mississippi, and my notices on the climate, soil, and vegetable productions of the territory occupied by them," written primarily in a detached third-person voice (1–2).

Language, and its fraught relation to lived experience, is thus both the inaugurating and overarching theme of Hunter's *Memoirs*, even as it stages an ongoing difficulty of narrative presentation and literary self-fashioning in the text itself. At stake in the act of authorship is not only the publication of his life story and knowledge of the lifeways and culture of southern Plains Indians, but the production of a white personhood premised on an identification with the English language and organized subjectively through the literary conventions of both the captivity narrative and the ethnological treatise. For Hunter, this project entailed a bold claim to exceptionality. "It is a remarkable fact," he writes, "that white people generally, when brought up among the Indians, become unalterably attached to their customs, and seldom afterwards abandon them.... Thus far I am an exception, and it is highly probable I shall ever remain such" (11). In language that anticipates the Whorf-Sapir hypothesis of linguistic relativity—the twentieth-century linguistic theory inaugurated by Edward Sapir and developed by his student Benjamin Whorf that language determines the structure of thought and that different languages constitute cognitively distinct worldviews—Hunter goes on to remark that his mind often still returned to "the innocent scenes of my childhood, with a mixture of pleasurable and painful emotions that is altogether indescribable." Yet he also avows that his "intercourse with refined society, acquaintance with books, and a glimpse at the wonderful structure into which the mind is capable of being molded, have . . . unalterably attached me to a social intercourse with civilized man, composed as he is of crudities and contradictions" (11).[8] Although he finds the recollection of childhood to be characterized by feelings that are "indescribable," this is an expression of emotional rather than linguistic ambivalence and reflects a common romantic conceit that language corrupts the experience of natural innocence. But his affirmation of the benefits of civilized society, particularly "the wonderful structure into which the mind is capable of being molded," expresses something else: a perception that literate and Euro-American world and self-understandings represent a cognitive space apart, a form and composition of mental experience that carries distinct and alternative advantages to the Osage linguistic reality of his youth.

For Hunter's early readers, the nature of this linguistic and cognitive traversal was a point of guarded meditation. One anonymous early reviewer for the *Monthly Review* granted the authenticity of Hunter's self-representations but still wondered "that a person kidnapped in his infancy; torn away from all civilized society before he could lisp his mother's tongue . . . should, in the short space of a few years from his escape, have been able to compose a volume in the English language, in which terms of art and science are frequently and appropriately used."[9] Marveling outwardly at Hunter's quickly acquired literary competence, this assessment expresses also a peculiar unease—not, perhaps, that such an acquisition was impossible (and that the text was fraudulent) but rather that its evident achievement presented something troubling, even uncanny. Seeking out but failing to discover points of slippage between Hunter's literary performance and the contours of his life story only underscores the ambivalence of what Homi Bhabha has characterized as the discourse of mimicry. For Bhabha, "the desire of mimicry" is to elicit perceptions of reformed, but recognizable, difference, representations that reveal the colonial subject as *"almost the same but not quite"*—or, in Bhabha's revision of Freud's phrase, *"almost the same but not white."*[10] From the perspective of this reviewer, Hunter was, it would seem, a white man who was nevertheless mimicking whiteness, a scenario particularly unsettling because the acquisition of a racially coded form of objectivity was all too attainable.

What did it mean to embody, or inhabit, a white, as opposed to Native, authorial voice? In Hunter's case, phenotypical embodiment did not correlate seamlessly with the inhabitation of a style of literary objectivity identified prototypically with whiteness. The racial nexus here is language itself, or more specifically the capacity of acquired English literacy to transcend and document reliably what was assumed to have been a bounded Native worldview. With Hunter, the "terms of arts and science are frequently and appropriately used"; but, premised on the fact that Hunter was "torn away from all civilized society before he could lisp his mother's tongue," the epistemological mastery coded as a white possession is assigned to a linguistic realm he did not acquire in childhood and only belatedly came to command as something external to himself. This view was not limited to a skeptical reading public; indeed, within the *Memoirs*, Hunter had already anticipated something close to this outlook on the relationship of language to identity. Not long after his lone sojourn in the wilderness, he describes his first acquisition of English words in a remarkable passage that figures English as a kind of racial costume: "While in this place, I acquitted a knowledge of many words in the English language, and, at the repeated and not to be denied instance [*sic*] of the American women, for the first time in my life arrayed myself in the costume of the whites; but it was a long time before I became reconciled to these peculiarly novel fetters" (69). It is a remarkable sentence. In the first compound independent clause, Hunter speaks of his acquisition of what appear to be two separate articles: English words and "the costume of the whites," presumably Euro-American clothing provided at the insistence of the American women at Flees' Settlement. Yet the ambiguity of that clause suggests that it may not, in fact, have been articles of dress with which he was urged to "array" himself but rather the English language itself—an ambiguity whose deliberateness is reinforced in the second independent clause, in which he again links the two in the artful phrase "novel fetters." In this evocative moment of retelling, Hunter speaks ironically of his discomfort with both English-style clothing and the English language in a passage that advertises the eventual sophistication of his literary command at the moment of composition, even as it figures language itself to be akin to a racially coded costume that may attire, but perhaps not transform, the identity of speaker beneath. For contemporaneous readers like John Neal who suspected Hunter of a bold literary forgery (and, perhaps, for skeptical modern readers as well), the passage might have provided something else: a wry hint of the author's gambit, a signal that "the costume" in play is the writer's own literary persona, and that the *Memoirs* themselves have the fictional trappings of a "novel."[11]

Within the *Memoirs*, Hunter frequently renders linguistic variety in comparative terms and emphasizes the experience of speaking, listening, and thinking in Indian languages in episodes of cross-cultural encounter. Communication via Plains Indian Sign Language is depicted as an integral element of these experiences, serving variously as an auxiliary to oral speech, a substitute for it when oral communication is impossible, and as the transcendent communicative component of formal oratory that completes an exemplary scenario of public participation.[12] The sum of evidence presented by Hunter's book strongly suggests that, whatever questions remain about the veracity of his overall account, his knowledge of Plains Indian Sign Language was real. In the first chapter of the *Manners and Customs* counterpart to his personal captivity narrative, "Considerations on the Physical and Moral Conditions of the Indians," Hunter writes that in southern Plains cultures, "they use many signs, which convey ideas of entire sentences: such, for instance, as a circular motion of the extended arm in the direction of the sun's course, to represent a day or half day; the rapid sweep of the hand represents a violent wind; the uplifted hands and eyes, an invocation to the Great Spirit, &c" (87). Albeit referenced here only in passing by way of general illustration, the descriptions of these three manual signs (the passage of a day; violent wind; an invocation to God or the Great Spirit) are accurate.[13] In this light, it deserves pointing out that the most common charge levied against Hunter by his detractors was that he plagiarized his account of the peoples and territories referenced in his book from existing sources (Nuttall and the Biddle edition of Lewis and Clark's journals are cited most frequently as his likely sources). However, not one of these three signs had been published in any source prior to his initial application for copyright in Philadelphia, in February 1823. In other words, Hunter's knowledge of PISL could not have come from a printed source (including the James account of the Long expedition, published later that year). Whether or not his acquisition of PISL reflects the life story he reports in all of its specificity, that acquisition transpired in a social scenario governed multiply by PISL, oral speech, and potentially other signifying practices as well.

This may seem like a labored point to establish, but it is worth demonstrating that Hunter's ethnographic claims bear some close scrutiny—an exercise particularly worthwhile given Hunter's own insistence on the extraordinary complexity of the totality of Osage social and cultural practices. Affirming that PISL functions at times as an independent linguistic system while demonstrating his knowledge of it,

Hunter also insists that the full significance of manual sign language practice is knowable only by experience and a situated understanding of Native "idioms and habits": "In regard to the signs used by the Indians to connect their words, and render their languages intelligible, very little of a satisfactory nature can be said; because they are so variously adapted to their different subjects of conversation, as in general to baffle description" (86). In this subsection, titled simply "Signs," Hunter contextualizes manual linguistic signs within a broader cultural and bodily discourse that includes significant aspects of posture and bearing, and acts of pantomime referencing animals, plants, and action. Added to this catalogue of bodily actions are what he calls "significant emblems," such as wampum, war clubs, and the wings of birds (some of which are, when appropriate, painted red or black to indicate climates of hostility or war), which Hunter characterizes as inflectional objects that organize the grammar of social and political practices and structure the semantics of cross-cultural exchange.

Ironically, Hunter fulfills his insistence of the legibility of Indian difference by confessing his inability to represent that difference adequately within the Euro-American literary discourse he has come to embrace. But even though the challenges of ethnographic and self-representation are framed in the *Memoirs* largely as an issue of language, linguistic translation is not the ultimate barrier to literary transparency. Rather, it is the (literally) embodied nature of the social in its relations to various signifying practices that "baffle[s] description"—an issue that in this instance may have less to do with the multiform adaptations of sign language (complex though they are) than it does with the ungraspable totality for which embodied forms of speech are an unconsciously integrated component. Approached from such a vantage point, this representational difficulty reflects an epistemological horizon of firsthand social experience. As the influential French sociologist Pierre Bourdieu writes in *Outline of a Theory of Practice*, what is at stake here are the social and cultural processes whereby individual actors experience social reality as commonsensical and natural rather than as constructed or artificial. Consider, in this light, Bourdieu's major innovation in sociological theory in his famous elaboration on the concept of *habitus*, by which he means not the experience of a socially sanctioned reality (or that reality itself in its objective qualities) but rather a regenerative principle of unconscious "dispositions" held by individual agents that orchestrates social and cultural practices into a coherent, embodied, and collective worldview:

> One of the fundamental effects of the orchestration of habitus is the production of a commonsense world endowed with the *objectivity* secured by consensus on the meaning (*sens*) of practices and the world, in other words the harmonization of agents' experiences and the continuous reinforcement that each of them receives from the expression, individual or collective (in festivals, for example), improvised or programmed (commonplaces, sayings) of similar or identical experiences. The homogeneity of habitus is what—within the limits of the group of agents possessing the schemes (of production and interpretation) implied in their production—causes practices and works to be immediately intelligible and foreseeable, and hence taken for granted. (emphasis in original)[14]

According to Bourdieu, the objective cast of a commonsensical worldview is reproduced through a noncoordinated aggregate of social action, but the ultimate structure of that worldview is always opaque to the individuals who identify with it at any given moment. In other words, what makes complex social and cultural practices intelligible to their actors does not necessarily make them explicable by them. For Bourdieu, the unconsciously internalized aspects of social competence mean that subjects are forever hidden from understanding precisely why or how they act and express themselves as they do: "It is because subjects do not, strictly speaking, know what they are doing that what they do has more meaning than they know."[15] In Hunter's case, what this suggests is that even the most careful literary dissection of, for example, the various adaptations of embodied gesture and sign language in Plains Indian culture may "baffle description" because that dissection will always fall short of articulating the global *sens* of cultural practices in their constitution of a shared social world. "Communication of consciousnesses," Bourdieu suggests, entails an a priori sharing of unconscious dispositions also (80). This, of course, Hunter's readers lack—even as the reviewer for the *Monthly Review* discussed above senses that Hunter lacks his own Euro-American social and cultural dispositions as well.

This is one way of describing how the body may encode speech that cannot be written, but that is not to say that the unconscious "dispositions" constitutive of a *habitus* do not signify in cross-cultural scenarios or that the body itself is unreadable in the absence of a shared social context that might make the semiotics of embodiment (and its underlying unconscious dispositions) fully intelligible. In the reminiscence of the London newspaper editor Cyrus Redding, for example, one of Hunter's most striking physical traits centered on "certain habitual movements of his limbs ... and again and again the lifting of the hand on particular occasions towards the ear when he was speaking." These actions, according to an American acquaintance who also took note of Hunter's unusual physical mannerisms, appeared to be "most likely unconscious"; he reported to Redding that they were characteristic of Native American tribes of the South he had encountered and that "he had seen no white but Hunter having it."[16] Another of Hunter's posthumous defenders, H. B. Mayo, who had joined Hunter in the Fredonian Rebellion and was a cosignatory of the Fredonian Declaration of Independence, remembered him in this way: "His manners were, in general, quiet, grave and gentlemanly; but they would burst out into singular vivacity, when his feelings were raised, and then, at times, his high excitement would render him masterless of himself, and while it made him eloquent in gesticulation, frequently deprived him of all command over words. Any discussion relative to the situation and character of the Indians would rouse the level of calm in his ordinary manner into a storm that agitated his entire soul."[17] Whether the physical traits observed by Redding echoed manual linguistic signs, were merely gestural, or were the ingrained habits of a studied racial masquerade is unknowable; by contrast, Mayo's claim that Hunter was "eloquent in gesticulation" in the absence of oral speech strongly suggests the use of sign language. Neither is conclusive, but whatever the case, where these two accounts coincide is their assignment of embodied elements of Hunter's speech to a realm of unconscious dispositions that was racially valenced. Bodies carry echoes, visible traces of former selves. When Hunter's body spoke, "masterless of himself," it was, for these white observers, the Indian talking.

Hunter, Tecumseh, and the Social Character of Manual Discourse

Embodied speech, social practice, and the limits of literary representation converge on what is surely the most powerful (and, following its publication the most pointedly contested) episode of the *Memoirs*, in which Hunter offers his account of Tecumseh's speech before the Osage during the latter's return voyage of his long southeastern tour following the New Madrid earthquakes in 1811 and 1812. As John Sugden has documented, Tecumseh informed William Henry Harrison on August 6, 1811, that he had already visited the Creeks and Choctaws and intended to visit the Osages; as Sugden speculates, it is quite possible that Tecumseh's Pan-Indianist mission canvassed other tribes as well, as his journey led him through the country of the Chickasaws, western Shawnees and Delawares, Iowas, Sacs, Meskwakis, Sioux, Kickapoos, and Potawatomis.[18] In his account of the speech, Hunter expresses awe at Tecumseh's oratorical prowess and testifies to the unprecedented effect Tecumseh's forceful eloquence had on his audience, for whom "the occasion and subject were peculiarly adapted to call into action all the powers of genuine patriotism," who felt keenly Tecumseh's "vehement narration of the wrongs imposed by the white people on the Indians," and who, "on this occasion, felt the portraiture of Te-cum-seh but too strikingly identified with their own condition, wrongs, and sufferings." Avowing that "to do justice to the eloquence of this distinguished man . . . is utterly impossible," Hunter twice indicates that Tecumseh's use of embodied speech was essential to the public transaction of his address and that a mere transcription of his orally spoken words must fail to convey the power of his oratory:[19] "This discourse made an impression on my mind, which, I think, will last as long as I live. I cannot repeat it *verbatim*, though if I could, it would be a mere skeleton, without the rounding finish of its integuments: it would only be the shadow of a substance; because the gestures, and the interest and feelings excited by the occasion, and which constitute the essentials of its character, would be altogether wanting" (28). Shadow and substance. In introducing Tecumseh's speech with the above qualifications, Hunter fashions an ideal of Indian oratory as socially transactional on multiple linguistic and affective registers. What stands out is the superior linguistic weight he grants to physical gesture relative to oral speech on an expressive spectrum for which even a *"verbatim"* transcription of the latter would be inadequate to convey that spectrum's full semantic and emotional richness. In chapter 1, I explored the commonplace reliance of nineteenth-century philologists on biological metaphors to organize research into the world's languages. For pioneers of comparative grammar such as Friedrich Schlegel and Peter Du Ponceau, grammar was akin to the enduring skeleton and words to the impermanent flesh; by devoting the weight of inquiry to comparative grammar (rather than etymology), they hoped to sidestep the evanescence of cultural change and arrive at a more stable image of the historical relatedness of languages. For this generation of philologists, physical gesture and Indian sign language were, at best, negligible points of reference. By contrast, Hunter employs a skeletal metaphor here to emphasize the inadequacy of spoken words to convey the linguistic reality of a momentous cultural event among the Osage, one given semiotic depth by manual components. The skeleton of words may have permanence on the page, but a skeleton "without the rounding finish of its integuments" lacks the fullness of life in all of its emotional, social, and political complexity for the Osage at a particularly urgent historical moment. Hunter's shift of emphasis in his choice of metaphors only enhances this impression. Spoken words are described first as a "skeleton" and upon their second iteration reduced to "the shadow of a substance," a diminishment of linguistic presence for spoken words in favor of the unrecorded "gestures, and the interest and feelings excited by the occasion," which he finds to constitute "the essentials" of the speech's social "character."

What follows in the text is Hunter's oral transcription of Tecumseh's speech from memory; it stands as the only historical record of his speech before the Osage.[20] The speech begins by positing commonality between all Native peoples, grounded in shared origins and shared loss, and with a plea for solidarity:

> *Brothers*—We all belong to one family; we are all children of the Great Spirit; we walk in the same path; slake our thirst at the same spring; and now affairs of the greatest concern lead us to smoke the pipe around the same council fire!
>
> *Brothers*—We are friends; we must assist each other to bear our burdens. The blood of many of our fathers and brothers has run like water on the ground, to satisfy the avarice of the white men. We, ourselves, are threatened with a great evil; nothing will pacify them but the destruction of all the red men. (29–30)

Tecumseh continues by invoking the charity of their common ancestors in providing for the "feeble" whites who "could do nothing for themselves"; shifting to the present, he then declares the whites are no longer friends to the Indians, that first they wanted Native lands but now will not be satisfied but with the extermination of all Native peoples. Moving to the purpose of his political mission, Tecumseh then makes a dramatic appeal:

> *Brothers*—The red men have borne many and great injuries; they ought to suffer them no longer. My people will not; they are determined on vengeance; they have taken up the tomahawk; they will make it fat with blood; they will drink the blood of the white people.
>
> *Brothers*—My people are brave and numerous; but the white people are too strong for them alone. I wish you to take up the tomahawk with them. If we all unite, we will cause the rivers to stain the great waters with their blood.

> *Brothers*—If you do not unite with us, they will first destroy us, and then you will fall an easy prey to them. They have destroyed many nations of red men because they were not united, because they were not friends to each other. (30–31)

Invoking the Shawnee alliance with the British on the Canadian border, Tecumseh promises that "Our Great Father, over the great waters" may be counted on for soldiers, rifles, and other material assistance. He then ends with an appeal to the Great Spirit, an explicit reference to the New Madrid earthquakes, and a prophetic vision of divine retribution against the whites in language that anticipates the Ghost Dance Religion nearly eighty years later:

> *Brothers*—The Great Spirit is angry with our enemies; he speaks in thunder, and the earth swallows up villages, and drinks up the Mississippi. The great waters will cover their lowlands; their corn cannot grow; and the Great Spirit will sweep those who escape to the hills from the earth with his terrible breath.
> *Brothers*—We must be united; we must smoke the same pipe; we must fight each other's battles; and more than all, we must love the Great Spirit: he is for us; he will destroy our enemies, and make all his red children happy. (31)

It is a powerful oration in Hunter's retelling. Tecumseh's message led Hunter to view war as imminent, and its consequences in restoring the rights and lands of Indians as inevitable. But according to Hunter, the Osage refused Tecumseh's overtures and request for armed confederation. Despite this political failure, and despite the unrecoverability of the "gestures" and the "interest and feelings" of an affective social reality Hunter exalts as forming "the essentials of its character," Tecumseh's speech crystallizes the nature of the cryptolinguistic archive. By Hunter's own reckoning, the oral documentation of Tecumseh's speech elides more semantic content than it discloses. Yet what remains offers to literary and historical interpretation an opportunity for a strategic rethinking of the extant Native American linguistic archive that is informed by its elisions and misrecognitions. In the first place, if the expressive and semantic subtleties of embodied speech are lost within the fine textures of an ephemeral social world in which it was a naturally recognized core component, what remains is a testimony that vouches not only for its presence but also for its power as a social and cultural bridge between mutually unintelligible oral languages.[21]

In this context what matters is not that Hunter was unable to manifest in literary discourse the unconscious social dispositions necessary to convey the full "character" of his experience in print (or that Hunter's readers likely lacked the complementary dispositions to grasp it). What matters is that Tecumseh did share those dispositions in the "network of relations" Lisa Brooks has characterized with the figure of "the common pot" and that the intertribal social compatibility brokered by manual gesture, documented here in a popular printed text, illustrated its wide currency as a potent political medium from the Great Lakes to the Great Plains and beyond.[22]

Tecumseh, Sign Language, and the Linguistic Politics of Pan-Indianism

Questions about language, land, and Indian political identity were crucially linked for both Native peoples and the United States government. Even as the cause of Tecumseh's Pan-Indian movement reflected the regional political aims of Native peoples who began forming tribal confederations to combat land dispossession in the Old Northwest at the end of the eighteenth century, emerging philological theories about the fragmentation of Native languages in the early nineteenth century grew more central to the rationale of U.S. federal policy concerning tribal land cessions.[23] To understand the roles of sign languages and embodied speech in Tecumseh's Pan-Tribal Confederation in the Northwest requires looking more closely at the political significance of Native multilingualism in the Great Lakes region in the context of the treaty system that governed U.S.-Indian relations through the nineteenth century (and that has lasting influence today). As Maureen Konkle has argued, treaties were paradoxical: designed as instruments to dispossess peoples deemed culturally and racial inferior, treaties also legally codified Native populations as quasi-sovereign political entities known as "Indian nations" and in so doing affirmed their right and political capacity to enter into lawful contract.[24] Routinely violated, circumvented, and divested, the political legitimacy recognized by the establishment of Indian nations as negotiating entities nevertheless carried (and carries) real power and cultural significance for Indian identity that should not be questioned. Yet from the historical standpoint of the Pan-Indian movements and confederacies led by such figures as Blue Jacket (Shawnee), Joseph Brant (Mohawk), Little Turtle (Miami), Tecumseh and his brother Tenskwatawa (often referred to as the Prophet [Shawnee]) across the Northwest Territory, treaties also carried an additional irony: the political autonomy recognized by the United States in the figure of separate "Indian nations" also entailed the divisibility of Native peoples.[25] Inscribing territorial boundaries of national difference largely on the basis of oral linguistic difference, the treaty system reflected a basic political and philosophical assumption that, as Walter Mignolo has put it, "languages were attached to territories, and nations were characterized by the "natural' links between them."[26] But if this assumption reflected philological theories about the "natural" evolution and dispersion of oral languages, that assumption was also mobilized as a political tactic for eclipsing Native forms of political collectivity that crossed shifting territorial locations in a multilingual and highly interactive world.

In making this observation, I don't mean to devalue the eighteenth-century emergence of the concept of "Indian nations" as a colonial construct or to exaggerate falsely confederated forms of Native political identity in favor of more permanent bonds of cultural and social cohesion realized at the level of tribe, village, or clan. What interests me instead here is the linguistic interface of a federal system of administration aimed at Indian land dispossession, and acknowledging the performative contexts in which political recognition of Native multilingualism (and specifically embodied language) was sought and rejected.[27] In exploring this issue, I take further insight from Mignolo and his concept of the "locus of enunciation" from which to imagine the embodied syntax of indigenous forms of knowledge and self-understandings in a larger political agenda of decolonization. A "locus of enunciation" is a site of speech, a borderland space of articulation—"border gnosis," in Mignolo's phraseology—that names the work of "subaltern reason striving to bring to the foreground the force and creativity of knowledges subalternized during a long process of colonization" and as such has the potential to remap our understandings of social and political geographies.[28] Mignolo's development of that figure aims preponderantly at sites of postcolonial emergence in contemporary settings; in my use of it here, I aim at a kind of historical and colonial reconstruction—fashioning, as Diana Taylor's work suggests, both archives (textual histories, bodies) and repertoires of performance (in oral and embodied speech) in contest and conjunction with colonial processes that conspired in their very erasure.

In the highly interactive cultural and social environment of a region the French called the *pays d'en haut* and that Richard White influentially characterized as an exemplary "middle ground," Algonquian peoples traded and intermarried among each other and with other Algonquians to the east and south, Iroquoian peoples to the east, Catawban-Siouan people to the west, and French, German, Scotch-Irish, and Anglo-American traders and backcountry settlers.[29] This was a world rich with linguistic diversity, and lexica from PISL users in the Trans-Mississippi region to the west would have blended with other variants of American Indian Sign Language (AISL), the Illinois trade language, trade jargon, and other media of cross-cultural exchange.[30] Writing of the Sauk and Meskwaki (Fox) peoples in Illinois, for example, Isaac Galland noted that

> the visible or written language of these people, consists principally of significant signs and gestures, by which they communicate their ideas to strangers, and a limited method of picture writing, which they have in use among themselves; such as are often seen engraved on their war clubs, gun stocks, or the wooden cases of their looking-glasses, and also such as are painted on trees, grave posts, and on the walls of their dwellings. They likewise have their simple hieroglyphics, wherein the delineation of part of the object or action, represents the whole; as the painting of a man's hand, denotes the act of having *struck* an enemy.[31]

In their range of travel and patterns of intertribal affiliation, the Shawnee exemplify the cosmopolitan scope and linguistic diversity of this borderlands region. In addition to their native language, varieties of Central Algonquian, Muskogean, and Northern Iroquoian languages formed elements of a common linguistic inventory for the Shawnee.[32] Tecumseh was a powerful embodiment of Shawnee multilingualism. Renowned for his gifts of language and powerfully eloquent oratory, Tecumseh is known to have been fluent in Shawnee, Muskogee (his mother was Creek), and English, and in the broad range of his diplomatic travels—from Ohio, Indiana, and Illinois to west of the Mississippi, across the south as far as Alabama and Florida, and possibly as far east as New York—he was unusually well-versed in practicing communication in diverse linguistic environments.

Although it has not been acknowledged previously to my knowledge, the weight of evidence very strongly suggests that Tecumseh knew sign language and employed elements of it in his oratory.[33] This probability has far-reaching, if to this point unexplored, significance for the linguistic politics of Tecumseh's Confederacy and as a case study of Pan-Indianism more broadly, and more work needs to be done to realize its full implications. But the circumstances of his exposure to various forms of sign language are easy to track. Although Plains Indian Sign Language was practiced far more extensively among Native peoples west of the Mississippi, it has been documented among the Shawnee and other Great Lakes tribes on the territorial borders of the Trans-Mississippi region in the nineteenth century as well.[34] In his extended contact with Sauks, Meskwakis, Kickapoos, and Ojibwes (and in less extensive but still substantive diplomatic relations with Iowas, Otoes, Missourias, and Osages), Tecumseh communicated with peoples who were also documented practitioners of PISL. In addition, other variants of American Indian Sign Language were present in the wider Great Lakes region the Shawnee called home. Among the Winnebago (who have not been classified as practitioners of the PISL variant), for example, Tecumseh exchanged speeches with people in present-day Wisconsin for whom (according to Caleb Atwater, as I discussed in chapter 2) sign language was a signature element of formal oratory.[35]

Among surviving accounts of those who witnessed Tecumseh's speeches firsthand, there is a striking level of consensus about the eloquence and semantic significance of his use of manual gesture as a central and routine element of his oratory in cross-cultural settings. Moreover, several of these testimonies suggest that he was both deliberate and selective in his employment of it. The most authoritative of these is offered by the former Shawnee captive and adoptee, interpreter, and Baptist preacher Stephen Ruddell. The same age as Tecumseh (twelve) at the time of his capture, Ruddell was a close companion of Tecumseh during the fifteen years he spent with the Shawnee and regarded Tecumseh as a brother. His relationship with Tecumseh continued following his return to white society, and he served as his interpreter on a number of important occasions including the 1807 Council of Greenville. In Ruddell's words, Tecumseh was "naturally eloquent—very fluent—graceful in his gesticulation but not in the habit of using many gestures—There was no violence, no vehemence in his mode of delivering his speeches—He always made a great impression on his audience."[36] Other sources affirm this view. As a witness quoted by Henry Rowe Schoolcraft put it, "all he used [i.e., of "gesticulation"] was necessary and properly placed—every motion of his hand appeared to correspond with his feelings and added weight to the sentiments he wished to enforce."[37] Others witnesses found him forceful and animated in his use of gesture, though no less eloquent. In attendance at the 1807 Council of Greenville, John A. Fulton, later mayor of Chillicothe, described Tecumseh's speech as "rapid and vehement; his manner bold and commanding; his gesture impassioned, quick and violent, and his countenance indicating that there was something more in his mind, struggling for utterance, than he deemed it prudent to express."[38] During Tecumseh's famous speech reproaching General Henry Procter at the September 1813 British retreat from Fort Malden—a speech that, according to John Heckewelder, "was in every body's hands"—a contemporary British witness recorded that Tecumseh, "accompanied by powerful energy and gesticulation, protested against the infamy of abandoning the position."[39]

To be sure, "gesture" and "gesticulation" are common elements of public oratory (and private conversation) for people unacquainted with any form of sign language, and none of the sources cited above specifically use the words "sign language" to describe the manual component of Tecumseh's style of address. As William Stokoe pointed out, if sign language is always gesture, gesture is not always sign language.[40] But if this recognition urges caution in classifying Tecumseh's use of gesture, the evidence suggests that Tecumseh's use of gesture contained signed linguistic components. In the first place, "sign language" was not a consensus label in the early nineteenth century. As I have discussed at length already, it was predominantly misclassified as sublinguistic in the antebellum period; given these limits to contemporary understanding, many Anglo observers simply did not perceive American Indian Sign Languages as anything other than racially specific modes of ordinary gesture. But even where it was recognized as a developed linguistic system, terms such as "language of gesticulation" and "gesture language" were used to denote what we now recognize as AISL interchangeably with, and perhaps even more frequently than, more modern-sounding labels such as the "Language of Signs" recorded during the Long Expedition. In this light, the testimonials above are highly congruent with other accounts in which the presence of sign language is not in question. Second, although sign language had functional utility as a lingua franca and spread on that basis, it was also a language of prestige (sometimes reserved only for men, but commonly among elders, chiefs, and keepers of medicine) that enhanced the authority of those who used it; in that context, given Tecumseh's experience with varieties of AISL, it would be far more unsound to assume that he did not incorporate sign into his oratory than to consider the possibility that he did.[41]

Analyzing the above accounts more closely lends further credence to this conjecture. Ruddell states: "He was naturally eloquent—very fluent—graceful in his gesticulation but not in the habit of using many gestures."

The ambiguity of the offset phrase "very fluent" might conceivably be thought to modify alternately the language on either side of it but in context seems to refer to Tecumseh's "graceful" use of "gesticulation": while it makes sense to be "very fluent" in knowledge and use of a language, "very fluent" is a nonsensical descriptor for a static condition or personal talent, such as natural eloquence. Moreover, to describe gesticulation as "graceful" runs counter to conventional understandings of the term, which typically is used to denote gesture that is *un*-graceful, exaggerated, and ill-modulated—a characterization that would appear to be incongruous on its face unless Ruddell (like many others who used the term in this way) intended "gesticulation" to designate sign language.[42] This likelihood gains additional weight in light of the closing clause, in which he suggests "gestures" were something he was "not in the habit of using." Spontaneous gesticulation in the act of oral utterance may be highly expressive, but it is also largely unconscious and not something consciously (or nonhabitually) put to "use." This sense accords with Schoolcraft's unnamed source, whose suggestion that Tecumseh's use of "gesticulation" was "necessary and properly placed" also strongly implies that it was deliberately coordinated with his oral speech.

To be clear: I am not arguing in this moment that Tecumseh should be assumed to have signed all of his major speeches in concert with their oral delivery in a parallel physical narrative (Ruddell's remarks alone seem to suggest this was not the case), or even that we can have any certainty about his likely degree of fluency in one or more varieties of AISL. But it does seem logical that Tecumseh certainly could have incorporated, and in fact almost certainly did incorporate some elements of the sign language that formed a commonplace component of his linguistic world into the communicative repertoire of his oratory in cross-cultural settings—even if those signed elements were largely perceived by his white audiences as ambiguous signifiers that denoted only his embodiment of racial eloquence. But if so, what does this mean? To credit sign language as a regular component of Tecumseh's oratorical practice across a range of cross-cultural settings is also to acknowledge a compelling linguistic performance of the fundamental cultural and social unity of Native peoples that formed the core message of Tecumseh's Pan-Indian argument. Despite his knowledge of English, Tecumseh made a point to speak in Shawnee in his orations before American and British officers, a practice that reflects Tecumseh's commitment to represent the Shawnee people and not allow that symbolic position be vitiated by linguistic compromise with whites.⁴³ Given that his white audiences on these occasions were, preponderantly, conversant neither in sign language nor Shawnee, Tecumseh's likely employment of both would have carried potent political symbolism: Tecumseh was not to be thought of only as a representative of the Shawnee but also as a figurehead who spoke for, and to, all Native peoples. Even so, wide misunderstanding of sign language as merely a physical embellishment of oral speech by Anglo audiences ensured that this message was either not received or marginalized in the literary record. John Richardson, the British witness to Tecumseh's speech before General Procter noted above, would later transform his memory of Tecumseh at the Battle of Detroit into the eponymous hero of an epic poem; but where Richardson's firsthand account of the battle recorded Tecumseh's "powerful energy and gesticulation," Tecumseh's employment of sign language is absent completely within the classical mode of Richardson's epic reconstruction of Tecumseh's oratory.⁴⁴

Tecumseh at Vincennes: Rereading the Archive

Reading Tecumseh's combination of Shawnee and sign language in transnational oratory works against such instances of literary erasure, while illustrating the fundamentally cosmopolitan character of the Pan-Indian argument he embodied for official British and American audiences—an oratorical staging of political identity that was both tribal and intertribal, particularistic and universal. In this light, I want to reconsider one of the most significant political episodes of Tecumseh's life: his famous meeting at Vincennes with William Henry Harrison, then governor of Indiana Territory, in August 1810. At that meeting, Tecumseh claimed that Native peoples owned their land in common, that the 1809 Fort Wayne Treaty ceding lands in the vicinity of the Wabash River (negotiated by Harrison with representatives of the Miami, Potawatomi, Lenape, and Eel Rivers tribes) was illegitimate, and accused Harrison of arbitrarily dividing Native peoples against one another in a strategy designed to effect their total ruin: "You want by your distinctions of Indian tribes in allotting to each a particular track of land to make them to war with each other. You never see an Indian come and endeavour to make the white people do so. You are continually driving the red people when at last you will drive them into the great lake where they can't either stand or work."⁴⁵ In response, Harrison flatly rejected Tecumseh's claims for Indian unity, positing (among other things) Native linguistic diversity as the primary and defining condition of nonaffiliation: "It was ridiculous to assert that all the Indians were one nation. If such had been the intention of the Great Spirit, he would not have put different tongues in their heads, but have taught them all to speak a language that all could understand."[46] As if to underscore the claim that linguistic diversity expressed ancient national divisions among Native peoples, Harrison's translator first conveyed Harrison's reply in Shawnee, and then again in Potawatomi. But before the interpreter could finish this second translation, Tecumseh rose to his feet and, in the words of Moses Dawson, "began to speak with great vehemence," declaring that "all the Governor had said was false" and accompanying his words with "violent gestures" that served as a kind of "signal" to his men: "The governor was surprised at his violent gestures, but, as he did not understand him he thought he was making some explanation."[47] As Harrison recounts the episode in a letter to William Eustis, Madison's secretary of war: "[Tecumseh] interrupted me before the interpreter could explain what I had said to the Potawatomies and Miamis and with the most violent jesticulations and indications of anger began to contradict what I had said in the most indecent manner."[48] Dawson appears to have relied on sources additional to Harrison's letter to Eustis for his narrative, but the consonance of both sources on Tecumseh's "violent" bodily expression at this moment (characterized alternately as "gestures," "signal," and "jesticulations") indicate that Tecumseh was almost certainly interjecting in sign language—a choice that ensured his objections could be known by all of those Native Americans present within and out of earshot.[49] Whatever semantic content Tecumseh's gesturing at Vincennes may have carried has not survived, but, whether or not Tecumseh's manual rejoinder responded specifically to Harrison's remarks about Native linguistic diversity, his signed expression at this important historical moment provides a powerful counterargument to Harrison's claim that the "Great Spirit" had not "taught them all to speak a language that all could understand." The weight of that counterargument is overwhelming. In degrees of mutual fluency in Algonquian languages, in the common employment of the wampum as a ritual tool of diplomatic exchange and technology of record keeping, in the "method of picture writing, which they have in use among themselves, such as are often seen engraved on their war clubs, gun stocks, or the wooden cases of their looking-glasses, and also such are painted on trees, grave posts, and on the walls of their dwellings," and in the common use of sign language, members of Tecumseh's Confederacy did indeed have at their disposal a richly developed common repertoire of linguistic and communicative practices that challenged the Jeffersonian view that asserted Native political disunity as a function of continental linguistic diversity.[50]

But the merits of this implicit counterargument, however cogent in theory, could not and did not prevail. The historical misrecognition of AISL was both epistemological and political; what became routine in the devaluation of sign languages by nineteenth-century linguists was staged in microcosm at Vincennes. As Charles Taylor argued in the modern context of the 1990s Québécois debate, claims of common identity turn in the first order on the politics of recognition.[51] Absent recognition as a developed form of human speech, sign language could not be acknowledged as the basis for a shared identity deserving of (or, in this case, forcefully demanding) political recognition. But if it was not translated, what message did Tecumseh's use of gesture at Vincennes convey? Harrison's words to Eustis betray suggestive ambiguities with respect to his perceptions of Tecumseh's manual interruption; ironically, he seems to have perceived Tecumseh's physical expression as an event that crossed supposedly fragmented linguistic and political boundaries. Noting "violent jesticulations and indications of anger" offered in "the most indecent manner," Harrison appears to be characterizing the use of sign language, rather than the content of Tecumseh's oral speech. Harrison reads this in the context of the spontaneous movements of other members of Tecumseh's party, who had "also sprung up, arm'd with war clubs, tomahawks, and spears and stood in a threatening attitude. Not understanding his language I did not know what he had said, until the Interpreter explained it to me, but the Secretary of the Territory General Gibson, who speaks the Shawonese language, and was sitting near me, apprehending some violence, requested Lieut. [Jesse] Jennings to make a guard of 12 men, who were at a little distance, to stand to their arms."[52] Although he did not understand it, Harrison is, after a fashion, interpreting Tecumseh's embodied expression here—not as speech, but as part of a broader semiotics of Indian hostility that betokened imminent violence. Tecumseh had arrived with a larger contingent of warriors than was expected; they were well-armed; their faces were painted vermilion; and as Tecumseh first spoke, Harrison observed the Potawatomi chief, Winamek (an ally to Harrison and enemy of Tecumseh's Confederacy), prime a pistol Harrison had presented to him a couple of days earlier. Even the earth was layered with portent. Refusing an invitation to convene the council on the portico of Grouseland, Harrison's home in Vincennes, Tecumseh is said to have declared "that the earth was the most proper place for the Indians, as they liked to repose upon the bosom of their mother" and accordingly seated his delegation on the grass—a piece of gamesmanship that was interpreted as "evidence that he either meditated or feared some fraud or treachery."[53] But it was only when Tecumseh began to sign that weapons were drawn. The Tecumseh biographer John Sugden has interpreted this pivotal linguistic shift as a failure of personal composure: "Tecumseh lost his temper," he writes, and thereafter, "for a few terrible moments it looked as if the council would disintegrate into bloodshed."[54] Certainly (and by all accounts) this was a tense interlude, but emphasizing the bloodshed that did not happen misses a larger point. Speech broke out; violence did not.

While the serial translation of Harrison's English into Shawnee, Miami, Potawatami, and Wyandot formally enacted the politics of national linguistic division at the level of negotiating procedure, Tecumseh's interjection in manual signs upended that divisive formal protocol and refashioned rhetorically the grounds of exchange—even if the bodily expression of that linguistic intervention was not recognized as language by his adversaries. But even though Harrison would not acknowledge Tecumseh's claims of Indian unity as politically legitimate, his actions and those of his men in response to Tecumseh's "violent jesticulations" do express an instantaneous and urgent recognition (if momentary) of the political power of signed Native speech. Tecumseh's ominous if inscrutable speech acts had changed the dynamics of exchange in a political arena, and he and his warriors were indeed united in opposition to the United States.

It is telling in this regard that Harrison's bid to regain control of the situation was linguistic and literary rather than physical: disbanding the council, Harrison declared he would no longer communicate with Tecumseh directly and would hereafter convey his answer to Tecumseh in a written message.[55] Ironically, during a subsequent meeting with Harrison arranged two days later, Tecumseh employed bodily expression once more—but this time in a manner and with a message that Harrison was prepared to accept. Following a second meeting, Harrison visited Tecumseh on August 14, when Tecumseh again affirmed his rejection of recent U.S. treaties and land purchases and vowed his reluctant intention to go to war with the United States in alliance with the British if these terms were not accepted and any further intention to negotiate treaties with Indians without their collective consent formally disavowed by President

Madison. In doing so, Tecumseh made clear his contempt for the British and recognition of their manipulation of Indian peoples for their own advantage, without regard for the interests of his own countrymen, "and here he clapped his hands, and imitated a person who halloos at a dog, to set him to fight with another, thereby insinuating that the British thus endeavored to set the Indians on the Americans."[56] Although it would be gratuitous to imply that Harrison was prepared to understand Tecumseh's embodied expression only in the form of pantomime that likened Indians to dogs, the episode carries a potent if unintentional symbolism: both the intertribal cultural basis and specific political content of embodied speech went largely unacknowledged on the assumption that signed expression could not be anything other than simple pantomime; regarded as a physical compensation for primitive oral languages, sign languages and embodied gesture only reinforced the ideological consignment of Native Americans to a lower developmental order of humankind.

The confrontation between Tecumseh and Harrison at Vincennes was depicted frequently in popular literary and visual representations throughout the nineteenth century and was a particular highlight in the developing lore of Harrison's military exploits in the run-up to his successful presidential campaign in 1840. Two of Harrison's campaign biographies from that year include illustrations depicting the tense moment of Tecumseh's manual interruption of Harrison's translated speech. In one, a lithograph by J. T. Bowen of Philadelphia titled *Council at Vincennes: Gen. Harrison and Tecumseh,* Harrison is seen at the head of his men to the left of the picture before the portico of Grouseland, in the act of drawing his saber after having risen from his chair; his soldiers, and Winamek among them, already have weapons drawn (figure 3.1).[57] Tecumseh and his retinue appear to be grouped on the lithograph's right. But here, there is a climate of confusion. Whereas Harrison and his men (including Winamek) are arrayed in a disciplined formation in collective recognition of Tecumseh's violent threat, Tecumseh's entourage is a cluster of disordered and contradictory intention. While one follower, in a kneeling position, is poised to strike with his war club, the remainder of Tecumseh's entourage is discomfited; fear and dismay play clearly across several faces, and one Native man, his back turned, appears to be in the act of abandoning Tecumseh in a hasty effort to flee. Only the figure that is presumably Tecumseh, his right hand uplifted with a knife, has the force of character to stand fast and the physical charisma to match and visually offset Harrison. The blocking of these

110 *John Dunn Hunter, Tecumseh, and the Linguistic Politics of Pan-Indianism*

Figure 3.1. J. T. Bowen, *Council at Vincennes: Gen. Harrison and Tecumseh*. Lithograph. Philadelphia. This image, in which Harrison's and Tecumseh's respective retinues flank and visually frame a signing translator and interpreter, was published in *The Life of Major-General William Henry Harrison: Comprising a Brief Account of His Important Civil and Military Services, and an Accurate Description of the Council at Vincennes with Tecumseh, as well as the Victories of Tippecanoe, Fort Meigs and the Thames* (Philadelphia: Grigg & Elliot, and T.K. & P.G. Collins, 1840). Courtesy of the American Antiquarian Society, Worchester, MA.

figures tells one kind of story about Vincennes and the conflict it represents, which would have been both flattering and familiar to Harrison and his advocates: U.S. military taciturnity, discipline, and competence, poised against savage anger, confusion, and cowardice. But what is most striking is not this rote ideological opposition, organized around the synecdochic bodies of Harrison and Tecumseh; it is that neither of them appears to be the focus of the picture at all. Instead, the focal point of the lithograph is devoted entirely to Harrison's interpreter—his position of visual emphasis enhanced by the space on either side of him (every other figure is part of one cluster or the other) and framed for the eye by two angled trees at the center rear of the scene. With his right index finger placed upon the open palm of his left hand, the interpreter clearly appears to be in the act of signing to Tecumseh and his host. And yet, visual details within the lithograph, coupled with the corresponding text in Harrison's biography, vex the particulars of the visual scenario. Notably, neither the primary source materials describing the episode nor the details of Harrison's biography in which the image is included suggest that that the interpreter was, in fact, gesturing at all. That action is attributed solely to Tecumseh: "As soon as [Harrison's speech] was interpreted in Shawanoese, Tecumseh interrupted the interpreter, and said it was 'all false;' and giving a signal to his warriors, they seized their knives, tomahawks and war-clubs and sprang upon their feet."[58] In this description, only Tecumseh is noted to be "giving a signal"; the "knives" and other weapons appear to be theirs and not his. But in the accompanying image, the figure presumed to be Tecumseh is facing away from his men; instead of "giving a signal to his warriors," his knife is uplifted.

Who, then, is Tecumseh in this scene? Complicating the question still further is the identical dress worn by the two figures: unlike any of the other Native men in Tecumseh's entourage, both figures have matching fringed leggings and belted tunics; both wear feathers in their hair and on their collars; and both wear what appear to be peace medallions around their necks. The conventional blocking of this scene in other visual representations of it uniformly depict Harrison and Tecumseh as facing adversaries; Tecumseh's arm is always raised, and is often (though not always) shown to be holding a weapon (see figure 3.2). That conventional iconography suggests that the figure in the Bowen lithograph, with knife raised, is indeed Tecumseh and not the signing figure at its center. Nevertheless, the peculiar interchangeability of their dress and accoutrements invites the recognition of a powerful form of ideological work at play here, a displacement of embodied political speech from Tecumseh to the interpreter and the substitution of violence (in the superimposition of the weapon for the "signal") for that speech. In the end, what is perhaps most clear is also what is most surprising. In the Bowen lithograph—nominally a depiction of the famous confrontation between Harrison and Tecumseh—the two famous principals play visually supportive roles, at the heads of two flanking phalanxes that serve also to frame the ambiguous true subject of the image at its center: a Native man in an act of signed speech.

Regarded individually, the sketchy accounts of the historical record perhaps betray little that is recoverable in the way of manual linguistic

Figure 3.2. John Reuben Chapin, *Genl. Harrison & Tecumseh*. Engraving by William Ridgeway. New York Public Library, Mid-Manhattan Picture Collection, PC AME-181, New York. In this more conventional view of the Council at Vincennes, Tecumseh and Harrison's confrontation is unmediated by any translator or interpreter; unlike the Bowen lithograph, this image depicts a gesture for Tecumseh but encodes it as an assertion of violent intentionality by redirecting it from his entourage (and toward Harrison) and correlating it to his upraised tomahawk.

content. But ultimately, the politically intertwined questions of what Tecumseh may have said and his unintelligibility for Harrison are perhaps less consequential than the broader grammars and networks of intertribal alliance, resistance, and claims of self-determination that are invoked by his gestures in and of themselves. In chapter 4, I return once more to the figures of Tecumseh and John Dunn Hunter and explore more deeply the political networks and communicative repertoires that connect Tecumseh's Great Lakes region to the massive, if quixotically doomed, effort of political coordination represented by the Fredonian Rebellion in east Texas in the 1820s. Throughout, the haunting literary presence of Indian sign languages—unclassified, misunderstood, yet still represented—persists as a means of reimagining political and social relations and contested identity formations, across the intellectual trade routes and cryptolinguistic archives of an early western borderlands that connected Canada to Mexico.

4

Connecting Borderlands: Native Networks and the Fredonian Rebellion

> The speech of the savages abounds in figurative expression and actions. In order to criticize a lack of truthfulness, they put two fingers on the edge of their lips and with very rapid movements they represent the volubility of the tongue. At the end of the action they say, "man with two tongues, or serpent's tongue." *Quippe domum timet ambiguam, tyrios que bilingues.* Virg[il].
> —From the diary of General Manuel de Mier y Terán, June 3rd, 1828

Circulations of Resistance

Although Tecumseh's diplomatic mission to the Osage ended in failure, John Dunn Hunter's publication of his speech ensured its longevity in print, even as it provided for Hunter an ideological template with which to frame his own acts of Native organization and resistance in Texas—an outcome that brings the complex alliance of Native and British interests on the U.S./Canadian border to bear on the even broader confederation of Native and U.S. extranational interests on the construction of the U.S./Mexico borderlands in the 1820s.[1] Sign languages and manual gesture, wampum, rumor, prophetic news, and a transatlantic war of words constitute some of the key "intellectual trade routes," as Robert Allen Warrior has theorized them (and which I first discussed in chapter 2) that bring these two borderlands histories into alignment. For Warrior, intellectual trade routes may cross time and space "across great geographical and cultural divides," enacting emancipatory intellectual geographies that unite indigenous knowledges and textualities with patterns of trade, human travel, and practices of reading on pathways that crisscross European and indigenous spaces.² Enlisting this term here elicits a sense of the multiform circulations of ideas that connected Tecumseh's Confederacy and his brother Tenskwatawa's religious movement to the U.S/Mexico borderlands, but it is particularly apt in this context for evoking also the consequential presence of the network itself, as independent of the ideas it conveyed, in the discourse of Pan-Indian resistance in the first half of the nineteenth century.

As the meeting between Tecumseh and William Henry Harrison at Vincennes discussed in chapter 3 demonstrates, a key measure of the political potency that nonoral and nonalphabetic Native communication systems carried was the level of threat they were perceived to embody by official U.S. audiences. Wampum exchange practices are another prime example. Intelligence recording the wide traffic of wampum belts advancing the cause of the Confederacy was sought and received with a great deal of trepidation; indeed, William Clark warned Harrison in the fall of 1810 of rumors he had heard that Tenskwatawa had sent wampum belts to tribes west of the Mississippi in advance of a planned attack on Vincennes.³ As scholars such as Matt Cohen, Phillip Round, and Birgit Brander Rasmussen have discussed in groundbreaking recent work, the multiform purposes of wampum exchange (identified commonly with Native peoples of the eastern seaboard and the Haudenosaunee but practiced also by the Shawnee and other tribes of the Great Lakes region) exemplify the incongruence of Native and alphabetic writing systems even as they illustrate, in Rasmussen's words, "the inter-animation between alphabetic and indigenous literacies."⁴ Functioning variously as information media in intertribal exchange, forms of currency, objects to solemnize promises, ritual mnemonic devices, and forms of personal surrogacy, wampum materializes the multisemiotic and changeable qualities of Native networks often felt to be most threatening to systems of federal management in western borderland territories. In particular, because wampum belts were not only a medium for conveying information but also a form of personal surrogacy—a means of supplying presence in the space of absence—news of their circulation west of the Mississippi would have been particularly ominous for Clark and Harrison. For his followers, Tenskwatawa himself was bearing his millennialist message of resistance on routes of circulation that could not be contained by control of his physical body.

John Tanner, the white captive and adoptive Ojibwe who coauthored (with Edwin James, compiler of the account of the Long Expedition) a highly important and ethnographically rich memoir of his life in and beyond captivity, provides a detailed account of an earlier reception of Tenskwatawa's wampum in his village in what is today Minnesota that illustrates this dynamic. An arriving stranger, by dress an Ojibwe, but marked by "something strange and peculiar in his manner," announced a list of injunctions, including prohibitions on dogs, flint and steel, alcohol, and other influences of settler colonialism. "The prophet himself is coming to shake hands with you," the stranger said.

> When the people, and I among them, were brought into the long lodge, prepared for this solemnity, we saw something carefully concealed under a blanket, in figure and dimensions bearing some resemblance to the form of a man. This was accompanied by two young men, who, it was understood, attended constantly upon it, made its bed at night, as for a man, and slept near it. But while we remained, no one went near it, or raised the blanket which was spread over its unknown contents. Four strings of mouldy and discoloured beans, were all the remaining visible insignia of this important mission. After a long harangue, in which the prominent features of the new revelation were stated and urged upon the attention of all, the four strings of beans, which we were told were made of the flesh itself of the prophet, were carried with much solemnity, to each man in the lodge, and he was expected to take hold of each string at the top, and draw them gently through his hand. This was called shaking hands with the prophet, and was considered as solemnly engaging to obey his injunctions, and accept his mission as from the Supreme. All the Indians who touched the beans, had previously killed their dogs; they gave up their medicine bags, and showed a disposition to comply with all that should be required of them.[5]

In this account of the wampum belt being transmitted and received as the transmuted body of Tenskwatawa, with whom one could shake hands, Tanner portrays an image of the person as the network itself. The equation is reflexive. More than endowing the person with the projective power of the circulating medium, this metempsychosis endows the very medium with the religious power and sacred presence of the Prophet. The potency of this chiasmus illustrates the force of Tenskwatawa and Tecumseh's reputations across vast distances, both for Native peoples and with the U.S. state actors who monitored their activities with alarm. It also underscores the immanent appeal of Tenskwatawa's unifying message for Indian peoples—enacting a form of political and spiritual selfhood that, in the mode of its wide circulations, constituted medially an experience of simultaneity and omnipresence that reinforced his message of common land, common worship, and collective political action.

A similar logic animates popular understandings of Tecumseh's mission to Alabama and Florida in 1811 and the role of indigenous media in inspiring the Red Stick War. Years later, Thomas McKenney and James Hall embellished Tecumseh's real organizational and political prowess with the trappings of myth by affixing posthumous credibility to the story that the "Red Sticks" faction of the Muskogee derived their name from a number of painted sticks supplied them by Tecumseh, from which they were to count down singly by days in order to synchronize a prearranged attack of conspiring British forces in order to acquire arms.[6] As Gordon Sayre has pointed out, for several reasons this story "is preposterous" on its face.[7] But even if this origin story for the "Red Sticks" name (and the promise of a British invasion) was a fabrication, it contained a grain of truth: Tecumseh's alliance with the British, however attenuated in the Southeast, was real; in Pensacola, British agents offered the Creeks a bounty of five dollars for every American scalp.[8] Indeed, what lent credence to this story for McKenney and Hall was not only the undeniable power Tecumseh embodied for Native peoples in the Southeast but also the military consequences of his reputation. According to George Stiggins, by marital and matrilineal kinship ties recognized as a full member of the Muskogee and Natchez tribes, and the Creek Indian Agent between 1831 and 1844, Tecumseh's spiritual credibility with the Muskogee rested on his prediction of the New Madrid earthquakes in 1811, which commenced in December and ended in February 1812:

> He stated to them the great supernatural power he possessed, he said if he was to beat the white people in his intended conflict with them and obtain his desire, they would know it by the following sign, That he would assend [sic] to the top of a high mountain *in about four moons* from that time.... And there he would whoop three unbounded loud whoops slap his hands together three times and raise up his foot and stamp it on the earth three times and by these actions call forth his power and thereby make *the whole earth tremble*.[9]

In Stiggins's account, the New Madrid earthquakes transpired approximately three months later, and "the earthquake happening so near the time that Tecumseh was to convince them of his power and truth, by his actions on the mountain to shake our globe, they were certain that the shaking was done by him, [and] their conviction of the event left no room to doubt anything he had said of the successful irruption of the Indians against the white people"[10] Though compiled in the 1830s, Stiggins's "Narration" is regarded as the most authoritative documentation of these events. In this version, Tecumseh's prophecy entails a form of supernatural speech in which the quaking earth is surrogate: whooping, clapping his hands, and stamping his hands three times on the earth will make *"the whole earth tremble."* In McKenney and Hall's version, the story is both more spectacular and more mundane. Their story puts Tecumseh's promise to "stamp on the ground with my foot, and shake down every house in Tuckhabatchee," on the day of his return to Detroit, as a refutation to skeptics who "do not believe the Great Spirit has sent me." To vouchsafe his word, accompanied by wampum and a war hatchet, Tecumseh again offers sticks to be counted down singly by days: "The morning they had fixed upon as the day of his arrival at last came. A mighty rumbling was heard—the Indians all ran out of their houses—the earth began to shake; when, at last, sure enough, every house in Tuckhabatchee was shaken down!" Anticipating and confronting the likely skepticism of their readers, McKenney and Hall declare that their sources are firsthand, that "the anecdote may, therefore, be relied on," and that these events transpired "on the very day on which Tecumthé arrived at Detroit, and in exact fulfillment of his threat."[11] What is most notable here is not their endorsement of the story of Tecumseh's prediction of the New Madrid earthquakes but their introduction of indigenous communicative media to that story. Fusing a famous story with an indigenous technology of calendrical coordination, McKenney and Hall imbue material networks of Native communication with a power of prophecy that endows them with extraordinary precision and projection over vast geographical distances, and they amplify that power still further in their own act of retelling in a print medium for a new arena of circulation and audience reception.

But by the time McKenney and Hall added printed substance to these stories, Tecumseh had been dead for twenty years; in that time, his enmity to the United States had been reimagined culturally as an exceptional patriotism that warranted national adulation, such that, in Richard White's words, "the paradoxical nativist who had resisted the Americans, became the Indian who was virtually white."[12] On one hand, the hagiographic reinvention of Tecumseh after his death effaced the fundamental legitimacy of Tecumseh's message of Pan-Indian grievance and resistance;

but on the other, preserving the memory of its former power remained vital to the political capital of several of his former military enemies, including William Henry Harrison, Andrew Jackson, and Lewis Cass.[13] Nevertheless, Tecumseh remained, even in the valedictory appraisal of McKenney and Hall, a powerful emblem who symbolized the possibility of future Native confederation and resistance. In McKenney and Hall's account, the divided status of White's "paradoxical nativist" is expressed concisely. Affirming "the real greatness of his character," McKenney and Hall introduce the Red Sticks story as one that "may serve to illustrate the penetration, decision, and boldness of this warrior-chief"; implicitly, but no less significantly, the story serves also to underscore the volatility and untrustworthiness of those Indians Tecumseh aspired to organize. Tecumseh's mastery of subtle stratagems and secret communication systems displays formidable cunning, personal charisma, and technological sophistication, but it is the aftermath of his reputed prediction of the New Madrid earthquakes for which "the effect was electric"—an effect that is hysterically amplified by the passion, fear, and superstition of the Creeks, Seminoles, and "portions of other tribes" through those same communication networks Tecumseh's genius had activated.

But despite his inspirational role, Tecumseh is not the thematic counterpart to McKenney and Hall's "Indians [who] took their rifles and prepared for the war" in the wake of the New Madrid earthquakes; rather, it is Tenskwatawa.[14] "Tecumthé was bold and sagacious—a successful warrior, a fluent orator, a shrewd, cool-headed, able man, in every situation in which he was placed. His mind was expansive and generous." By contrast, Tenskwatawa, though perhaps surpassing even Tecumseh in oratorical gifts, was fundamentally "sensual, cruel, weak, and timid. Availing himself of the superstitious awe inspired by supposed intercourse with the Great Spirit, he lived in idleness, supported by the presents brought him by his deluded followers." There is a breathtaking irony in this denunciation of Tenskwatawa, given that the previous paragraph exalts Tecumseh's estimable influence through the example of his claim to have summoned earthquakes, and the readiness of his followers to believe in his supernatural power.

If these elements are ironically similar in their retelling, one major difference remained between them: Tecumseh was dead; Tenskwatawa was not. Although McKenney and Hall close their chapter in a gesture of dismissal—"the prophet was living, when last we heard of him, west of the Mississippi, in obscurity"—the implication lingers past those lines that Tenskwatawa, however much they wished to confine him within aspersions of the cruelty, cowardice, and superstition he typified for Indians elsewhere, remained an unaccounted presence in the West.[15] McKenney and Hall's dismissal of Tenskwatawa is doubly ironic, though, given the influence that his teachings and the decades-long pattern of insurgencies of which they formed a part still held in the Great Lakes region and their central role in the ideological framing of Black Hawk's War, an episode both recent and prominent in the national dialogue at the time of their writing in 1834.[16] In his 1833 *Life*, Black Hawk's encounter with Tenskwatawa shortly before the Battle of Tippecanoe discloses his firsthand knowledge of the Prophet's insurgent message: "I remember well his saying—*'If you do not join your friends on the Wabash, the Americans will take this village from you!'* I little thought then that his words would come true!"[17] Tenskwatawa's words prove prescient; Black Hawk's failure to heed them in 1812; his eventual recognition of their truth through his alliance with the Winnebago Prophet, Wabokieshiek; and the development of his own style of natural-rights thinking about the inalienability of land describe the narrative arc of Black Hawk's political coming-to-consciousness in the book: "My reason teaches me that *land cannot be sold*. The Great Spirit gave it to his children to live upon, and cultivate, as far as it is necessary for their subsistence; and so long as they cultivate it, they have a right to the soil." Although Wabokieshiek is skeptical initially that the whites could or would displace Black Hawk's people from their land, "he at once agreed with everything I said, and advised me never to give up our village, for the whites to plough up the bones of our people." Having exchanged wampum and tobacco with Ottawas, Ojibwes, and Potawatomis, Wabokieshiek informs Ne-a-pope that "all the different tribes before mentioned would *fight* for us, if necessary, and the British would support us." Readers of the book would know that British promises were unavailing and that the outcome of Black Hawk's War was decided before the full impacts of a broad Native military alliance might be realized. But, speaking in the present tense of the book's moment of composition following that outcome, Black Hawk suggests that the alliance itself, and the enlarging intertribal diplomatic network upon which it relied, remains active—and extended as far south as Mexico: "Communication was kept up between myself and the Prophet. Runners were sent to the Arkansas, Red river and Texas—not on the subject of our lands, but a secret mission, which I am not, at present, permitted to explain."[18]

Even as words such as these gesture toward the future action of clandestine intertribal networks of Native resistance across the western borderlands, the framing of Black Hawk's *Life* works proleptically to contain them and unmask the worrying figure of Native political speech as a prelude to surrender. In the opening pages of the book, the image of Sauk speech is, in fact, quite literal. Immediately following a certification of the narrative's authenticity by Antoine Leclaire, who is identified by his official title, "U.S. Interpreter for the Sacs and Foxes," are two full pages of the Sauk language rendered phonetically in Roman alphabetic orthography. The reader must turn the page to arrive at a translation of what is revealed to be Black Hawk's dedication of the book to General Henry Atkinson. But before the pages are turned, the reader is confronted with an imposing edifice of Indian speech, surely incomprehensible to the overwhelming majority of those who encountered it, consisting of 170 Sauk words (see figure 4.1).

As Mark Rifkin has argued, the prominent notation of Leclaire's status as an official interpreter suggests that the narrative "is entering the public discourse through a process quite similar to that at work in treaty-making, positioning the text as a somewhat uncanny addendum to the administrative record."[19] Coming on the heels of Leclaire's certification, this "Dedication" in Sauk only enhances that impression, even as it performs a brief but elaborate fiction of its own. Here, it would seem, is the unmediated voice of Black Hawk himself. Black Hawk, though, was illiterate; the transliteration into alphabetic type was performed by Leclaire and, possibly, John A. Patterson (who wrote the narrative from Black Hawk's dictation to Leclaire). Moreover, "the non-native formal device" of the "Dedication," coupled with the awkward English translation that follows, in the assessment of Eric Cheyfitz, "in a strange way serves to undermine the appearance of authenticity, both by the distance it figures between Sauk and English and by the very need to have it in writing to assure genuineness."[20] Indeed, although most readers would have been unaware of it, the word rendered in Sauk as "Ne-Ka-Na-Wen," which Leclaire and Patterson translate as "Dedication," translates more simply as, "My Speech."[21]

But this graphic representation of Black Hawk's formal rhetoric—however obvious its flaws of linguistic sleight-of-hand may be to contemporary scholars—works nevertheless to fashion a compelling illusion of direct Native encounter, one that transports the reader from an accessible literary scenario to an imaginary oral scenario of diplomatic exchange on a western borderlands in political turmoil. Simulating a moment of linguistic exchange as experienced by Leclaire, the "Ne-Ka-Na-Wen" fashions

NE-KÁ-NA-WEN.

MA-NE-SE-NO OKE-MAUT WAP-PI MA-QUAI.

W<small>A-TA-SAI</small> <small>WE-YEU</small>,

Ai nan-ni ta co-si-ya-quai, na-katch ai she-ke she-he-nack, hai-me-ka-ti ya-quai ke-she-he-nack, ken-e-cha we-he-ke kai-pec-kien a-cob, ai we-ne-she we-he-yen; ne-wai-ta-sa-mak ke-kosh-pe kai-a-poi qui-wat. No-ta-wach-pai pai-ke se-na-mon nan-ni-yoo, ai-ke-kai na-o-pen. Ni-me-to sai-ne-ni-wen, ne-ta-to-ta ken ai mo-he-man tà-ta-que, ne-me-to-sai-ne-nc-wen.

Nin-à-kài-ka poi-pon-ni chi-cha-yen, kai kà-ya ha-ma-we pa-she-to-he-yen. Kài-nà-ya kai-nen-ne-naip, he-nok ki-nok ke-chà-kai-ya, pai-no-yen ne-ket-te-sim-mak o-ke-te-wak ke-o-che, me-ka ti-ya-quois na-kach mai-quoi, à-que-qui pà-che-qui ke-kan-ni tà-men-nin. Ke-to-tà we-yen, à-que-kà-ni-co-te she-tai-hai yen-nen, chai-chà-me-co kai-ke-me-se ai we-ke ken-ne-tà-mo-wàt, ken-na-wà-ha-o mà-co-quà-yeai-quoi. Ken-wen-na àk-che-màn wen-ni-ta-hài ke-men-ne to-tà-we-yeu, ke-kog-hài ke-ta-shi ke-kài nà-we-yen, he-na-cha wài-che-we to-mo-nan, ai pe-che-quà-chi mo-pen mà-me-co, mài-che-we-tà nà-mo-nan, ne-ya-we-nan qui-a-hà-wa pe-ta-

1*

Figure 4.1. The first page of Black Hawk's two-page dedication of his *Life* to General Henry Atkinson (U.S. Army), in a phonetic rendering of the Sauk language. From *Life of Ma-Ka-Tai-Me-She-Kia-Kiak or Black Hawk* (Cincinnati: J. B. Patterson, 1833), 5. Courtesy of the American Antiquarian Society, Worchester, MA.

that moment as one of vertiginous inscrutability, an experience of linguistic intimidation unrelieved (if only momentarily) by an unbroken stream of 558 exotic Indian phonemes. If the readerly experience to be counted on was one of dizzying incomprehension before an image of unassimilated Nativism, the trick, as it were, of that image's linguistic sleight-of-hand is provided on the following page in the translation of the "Dedication" itself. There, the discomfort of protracted incomprehension gives way to ideological reassurance: Black Hawk, once threatening, is disclosed in an attitude of surrender. "Sir,—The changes of fortune, and vicissitudes of war, made you my conqueror," the "Dedication" reads in opening:

> When my last resources were exhausted, my warriors worn down with long and toilsome marches, we yielded, and I became your prisoner.... I am now an obscure member of a nation, that formerly honored and respected my opinions. The path to glory is rough, and many gloomy hours obscure it. May the Great Spirit shed light on your's—and that you may never experience the humility that the power of the American government has reduced me to, is the wish of him, who, in his native forests, was once as proud and bold of yourself.[22]

What is notable here, beyond the revelation of formal and resigned capitulation behind a simulation of linguistically uncompromised Nativism, is the positioning of Black Hawk as disconnected from the networks of intertribal organization that made him such an imposing symbolic (if not, in real terms, military) threat to the scheme of westward expansionism—he is "now an obscure member of a nation, that formerly honored my opinions." In this light, the silent substitution by Patterson and Leclaire of the term "Dedication" for "My Speech" is perhaps most pointed in its linguistic shifting of a style of oratory indigenous to Native politics to an assimilated gesture of literary formality.[23]

In doing so, this substitution announces one form of ideological work the narrative aspires to perform. Whatever lingering alarm may reside in Black Hawk's statement in the narrative that Wabokieshiek had sent runners as far south as Arkansas and Texas on "a secret mission, which I am not, at present, permitted to explain," the "Dedication" announces that Black Hawk himself is fully disarticulated from the intertribal networks of the West. The conclusion of the book completes this figure, revealing him to be installed safely at last as an exhibit on a public tour of the eastern seaboard, harmlessly circulating aboard commercial networks of steamboats and railroads during which he is seen to marvel wondrously at feats of U.S. technological prowess and urban development.

The complexities of Tecumseh's and posthumous reputation, and their ongoing implications for the development of intertribal Native insurgency as would be exemplified by Black Hawk, provide perhaps the most salient context for explaining the vehemence with which John Dunn Hunter's authenticity was contested in the United States. Lewis Cass orchestrated the campaign to discredit him, working with Jared Sparks of the *North American Review* to solicit a collection of seemingly authoritative testimonials that rejected Hunter's claims to have resided amongst the Osage. The weight of this evidence, Cass writes in the January 1826, issue, reveals Hunter to be "one of the boldest imposters, that has appeared in the literary world, since the days of Psalmanazar," whose book is "a worthless fabrication . . . compiled, no doubt, by some professional book maker, partly from preceding accounts, and partly from the inventions of Hunter."[24] But the vigor of this attack may have been something of a smokescreen. Richard Drinnon has pointed out that letters Cass wrote prior to publication suggest that Hunter may only have been an incidental target; the real object to be kept in view was the "peculiar malignity" of John Murray's *Quarterly Review* from London, which is "so calculated to injure the character of our country abroad, that I have determined to prepare an article for the next *North American Review*, to contain a refutation of those calumnies."[25] For Drinnon, Cass's effort to discredit Hunter was, among other things, a proxy battle for a contest of national chauvinisms embodied in competing journals. Indeed, the section of Cass's review devoted to Hunter begins and ends with denunciations of the *Quarterly*'s gullibility, carelessness, and misrepresentations and "the ignorance, or perverseness, of British writers" more broadly.[26] But, however energetic Cass was in his partisanship against the mandarins of British culture, the primary emphasis for his printed vitriol was not the *Quarterly Review*, or even Hunter, but rather Tecumseh. Cass begins his exposé of Hunter by focusing on Hunter's account of Tecumseh's speech (he claims, incorrectly, that it could not have happened), which provides the occasion to comment on Tecumseh's role during the War of 1812; it is not until the eighth page of a thirteen-page section devoted ostensibly to Hunter that Cass pivots "to return once more to the book in question." What transpires in the interim is a calculated defamation of Tecumseh's posthumous character: "Tecumthé was a disaffected man, and had seceded from the '*legitimate*' authority of his tribe. All the chiefs, and almost all the warriors, were opposed to his plans. They saw, that these were fraught with ruin to their people, and believed them to have originated in a system of self aggrandizement."[27] Targeting the legitimacy of Tecumseh's leadership in this fashion serves to diminish the Pan-Indian movement he symbolized as merely the feverish projection of an isolated narcissist decisively at odds with a united and sober people. Tecumseh's alliance with the British presented another opportunity as well, allowing Cass to acknowledge the former's celebrity while dismissing its true basis (like Hunter's) as a propagandistic British fiction. But in devoting almost an equal number of words to the discrediting of Tecumseh as he does to Hunter, Cass effectively fashions them as mirrors for one another. That is, Hunter may provide a useful occasion to denounce Tecumseh here, but in expending such energy on the latter aim, Cass implicitly (if inadvertently) casts Hunter as Tecumseh's analogue and dangerous equal, the still-living proxy for a posthumous legacy whose self-presentations and national disloyalty must be contested as the extension of a Pan-Indian agenda into the present moment.

Ultimately, the question of John Dunn Hunter's possible imposture as it was contested publicly in the 1820s illustrates the strategic importance of a multinational print culture for controlling the political narrative of U.S. westward expansionism—a program that, as Cass and William Clark advised in an official report to the secretary of war in 1829, would require the perpetual removal of Native peoples beyond U.S. national boundaries, if not their extinction. Nominally, this is a question of competing story lines in a broadly circulating print arena. More fundamentally, what is at issue is an ideological contest of divergent institutional and cultural values, and the establishment of an authoritative epistemology concerning Native peoples, practices, and spaces whereby the truth-claims of competing narratives might be either established or rejected. This latter ideological contest was joined by a host of actors with divergent agendas: self-appointed official spokespeople like Cass; learned societies like the APS whose romantic presentiments (from Cass's point of view) were not always to be trusted to align with official policy; U.S. critics from across the Atlantic; and, finally, Native peoples themselves—whose enemies strove to confine the representation of Native interests to questionable figureheads like Hunter. As Jonathan Elmer has argued: "Whether Hunter was an imposter or not finally matters less than the fact that widespread doubt about precisely this issue kept his name before the public."[28] Yet if the extraordinary aspects of Hunter's autobiography presented an opportune target for the likes of Cass (and his protégé Henry Rowe Schoolcraft,

William Clark, and others), he also represented a multipronged threat to their bid for narrative control of a program of westward expansion. On one hand, the vehemence of Cass's attack on Hunter and Tecumseh tacitly acknowledges the real and persistent threat of Pan-Indian resistance to a developing program of western territorial expansion. But Hunter also represented the publication of that threat—embodied in the printed record of Tecumseh's speech, the Native communication networks through which Tecumseh's legacy might yet be realized, and in Hunter's own spirited defense of Native rights—within a transatlantic literary discourse that Cass recognized lay beyond his or any coordinated national control. It is telling in this sense that Cass's indictment of Hunter took place within a long essay that took aim at so many different authorities and institutions, and specifically the program of American Indian linguistics advanced by John Heckewelder and identified with the American Philosophical Society. But in the goal of discrediting a rogue figure like Hunter, Cass found common cause with Peter Du Ponceau and the leadership of the APS. Cass's accusations decisively shifted public opinion against Hunter, but the most authoritative judgment against him was provided by Du Ponceau, America's foremost linguist. Having learned of Hunter in New York, in 1822, Du Ponceau subjected Hunter to a series of linguistic "tests" and, as it was later publicized, declared him incompetent in Osage—a verdict heralded by Robert Walsh, the former secretary of the APS, as a triumphant vindication of "the soundness of those philological studies which have engaged some of our profoundest scholars."[29] As Richard Drinnon has argued, Hunter's apparent inability to provide consistent answers in his attempted translation of Osage words was not proof of imposture by any means and may well have stemmed from the fact that Du Ponceau (who did not speak Osage) was testing Hunter's vocabulary against a rigidly defined lexicon; weighing in on the matter in response to a query by Drinnon on the subject, the eminent linguist Mary Haas affirmed Drinnon's conclusions.[30] In one sense, the particular outcome of this linguistic test masks a larger point. Hunter's "failure" of Du Ponceau's test may have satisfied the latter that Hunter was an imposter, but had Hunter passed the test, the authenticity of his self-representation would not have been vindicated. Linguistic "passing" was not, and could not be, evidence of Indian identity or personhood from Du Ponceau's perspective. For all of the cultural allure of the mythology of the "White Indian," whiteness and Indianness entailed nontransferable kinship assumptions in Euro-American culture that, as Gordon Sayre has pointed out, did not correspond to a Native model of kinship, which, "unlike Euro-American custom, regarded . . . adoptees as real kin and did not define identity phylogenetically."[31]

The Red and White Republic of Fredonia

Following the publication of the Philadelphia edition of his book, Hunter traveled to London in the spring of 1823, where, as he prepared the English editions of his book, his growing celebrity ushered him into the society of such notable figures as the Duke of Sussex, the botanist James Smith, the newspaper editor Cyrus Redding, and the socialist reformer Robert Owen. It would be another year before Owen developed his plan for an experimental community at New Harmony, Indiana, but Owen's communitarian ideals made a strong impression on Hunter (and some evidence suggests that Hunter may have inspired elements of Owen's aspirations for New Harmony).[32] For his part, Hunter soon began to develop his own scheme to organize a mission of civilizing outreach among the Quapaws that would be organized around a homestead on land Hunter had purchased in the Arkansas Territory.

Hunter published that scheme first in a pamphlet and then later appended it to the second edition of his *Memoirs*. The plan was vaguely Jeffersonian in conception and was to proceed by his personal demonstration of the benefits of agriculture, education, and industry in order to convert as many Indians as possible from a nomadic way of life that he perceived to be unsustainable owing to "the ravages of the white man." Hunter outlined his plan with optimism that seems almost unimaginably naïve: "It is easy to conceive what would be the result: the Indian wigwam would be soon supplied by a lasting dwelling, and the bountiful fruits of the field supply the exertions of the chase. The roaming tenant of the woods would soon be the ornament of civil society. I have no assistant to accompany me with my designs, though I have many friends in the country. I have much to perform, and but little beyond personal exertion with which to accomplish it."[33] To say Hunter's plan was lacking in particulars is something of an understatement. Yet from his point of view, the circumstances that impelled action were urgent and inexorable. The Indians of North America faced oblivion, owing to four primary causes: first, "the rapid approach of the white settlements on the Indian borders, and the purchase of their lands" was forcing Native peoples into greater conflict with one another and would leave them either to "perish contending against superior powers, or gradually decline into significance"; second, "the incredible destruction of their game since the whites have entered their country" gravely threatened traditional means of subsistence; third, "loss of national pride of character, from being duped out of their lands," the consequence of which being "all manner of dissipation and vice, disease and poverty"; and, fourth, "the introduction of ardent spirits among them."[34] In these reflections, the example of Tecumseh was strongly on Hunter's mind, but primarily as a emblem of collective resistance that was no longer possible: "Not until within a very few years, have the brave Indians believed that all the powers of the earth combined could conquer them. The brave and gallant Tecumpseh [sic] was of that opinion," he wrote; "his fall has damped the ardour, and crushed the hopes of many; and now, the wise and experienced are conscious they must either become tenants of the soil, or be soon lost in the sea of forgetfulness!"[35] The tone here is resigned and elegiac, but the conditions Hunter discovered upon his return to United States territory led to the transformation of a vision of tragic accommodation to one of defiance, and the revival of a Pan-Indian agenda of armed resistance. The territory in which that revival was mounted was not the United States but Mexican Texas. Following a final visit to Jefferson at Monticello in the fall of 1824, Hunter traveled with William Owen by steamboat down the Mississippi to New Orleans. Journeying west into Arkansas, Hunter discovered that the Quapaws were already undergoing removal farther west and had begun to move into Mexican territory along with an unfolding diaspora of Native peoples displaced from the territorial borders of the United States, including Cherokees, Choctaws, Osages, and Caddoes from the southeast and Missouri region, and Delawares, Kickapoos, Miamis, and Shawnees from the Old Northwest. Joining the exodus, Hunter traveled with them across the Red and Sabine Rivers seeking lands for permanent Native settlement.

Demographically transformed by waves of Anglo-American colonists and displaced Native peoples from the United States and politically redefined by the Mexican Revolution of 1821 and again with the ouster of Iturbide in 1823, northeastern Texas (after 1824, Texas y Coahuila) was a borderland zone in the middle of a decade of almost perpetual upheaval. By 1830, Anglo-American colonists, squatters, and filibusters outnumbered Mexican Tejanos perhaps six to one, and the Native American population in eastern Texas was extremely diverse.[36] A young trader named J. C. Clopper, who was traveling with Josiah Gregg on a commercial trip through Texas in 1828, found the experience of San Antonio de Bexar to be disorienting, a cacophony of voices: "The traveler hears around him a confusion of unknown tongues: the red natives of the forests in their different guttural dialects; the swarthy Spaniard of a scarce brighter hue; the voluble Frenchman; a small number of the sons of Green Erin; and a goodly few of Uncle Sam's Nephews or half expatriated sons. He feels himself for the first time in his life a stranger truly in a foreign land."[37] In Clopper's journal, Bexar is a canvas of foreignness so deep it verges on the surreal: languages, races, ethnicities, and nationalities converge and then separate into unsettling ambivalence, as in the "goodly few of Uncle Sam's nephews or half expatriated sons." The Fredonian Rebellion and the conflicts it generated reflect a similar oscillation of voices and ambiguous national affiliations. Joining millennialist language to the rhetoric of the American Revolution, the Fredonians declared independence from Mexico in the name of Red and White solidarity; they were countered by Stephen F. Austin, who borrowed from the same patriotic stockpile of U.S. revolutionary rhetoric in order to assert his loyalty to Mexico and reassert racial hierarchies that were threatened by the demographic transformation for which the Fredonian alliance was an unsettling symbol.

Although it is usually cast in Texas history as an Anglo affair conceived and prosecuted by Haden and Benjamin Edwards, the roots of the Fredonian Rebellion are Cherokee and pre-date by several years the advent of the contested Edwards grant.[38] Western Cherokees led by Duwali (also known as Bowles, or Bowl) and the Anglo-Cherokee Chief Richard Fields had been among the first Native Americans displaced from their traditional homelands in the United States to cross the Red River into what was still Spanish territory in 1819 and 1820, settling north of Nacogdoches by 1822.[39] Initially, the Spanish government and the post-Revolutionary imperial government under Iturbide welcomed Cherokee immigration along with Anglo *empresarios* as a means of buffering northern Mexico against both the territorial ambitions of the United States and the perpetual threat of greater Comancheria.[40] Seeking land grants under terms of the same colonization law through which Stephen Austin updated the *empresario* status granted originally to his father under Spain, Fields traveled to Mexico City in early 1823 but was only able to elicit a resolution that promised noninterference for Cherokees already in Texas but that deferred recognition under the new Colonization Law and proscribed further Cherokee immigration.[41] Fields, who was a skillful diplomat, continued his negotiations with the Nacogdoches *alcalde* to fortify the standing of the Cherokee by agreeing to serve as security against Comanche and

Lipan raids and surreptitiously generated another form of counterbalancing political capital for his people through a series of shrewd alliances forged with Shawnees, Delawares, Senecas, and Chickasaws. This effort of confederation was not limited to Texas. In September 1823, the interim governor of the Arkansas Territory, Robert Crittenden, wrote to Secretary of War John C. Calhoun to warn of a Cherokee alliance "headed by the most daring and intelligent man in the nation," who had "recently made a tour to their Northern brethren on the White River and in the name of the Cherokee Nation made an offensive and defensive alliance"—an alliance that now consisted of upward of ten thousand Shawnees, Delawares, Piankeshaws, Kickapoos, Potawatomis, and Senecas.[42]

With Hunter's arrival in 1825, this offensive and defensive alliance included the Quapaws as well with Hunter serving as their representative. Much like Tecumseh in his leveraging of alliances alternately with Great Britain and the United States, Fields (and, after 1825, Hunter) masked this project of Pan-Indian organization in eastern Texas by strategic professions of alliance and cooperation. Writing to Jefe Político Saucedo in San Antonio, in August 1824, Fields declared the Cherokee would "have nothing to do with the Anglo Americans here, and we will not submit to their laws, or dictates"—squatters were a growing problem, and Mexican officials feared their collusion with Indians—"but we do, and always will, submit to the laws and orders emanating from the Mexican nation."[43] Hunter echoed this profession of allegiance in his own diplomatic trip to Mexico City in March 1826, when he pledged to General Victoria the loyalty, defensive power, and Christian conversion of thirty thousand Native Americans (including many en route but not yet in Texas from United States territory) in exchange for a permanent grant of lands sufficient to enable their conversion to agriculture subsistence.[44] In light of the events that followed shortly thereafter, it is not hard to detect the threat implicit in Hunter's formal request: grant Indian lands, and you will have their loyalty and force of defensive arms of thirty thousand citizens; refuse, and you will have thirty thousand enemies on hand in the distant precincts of Texas, with more on the way.

The request was refused. That year, in 1826, two other catalyzing factors converged and brought the situation to a point of crisis. First, the Haden Edwards *empresario* grant near Nacogdoches, established for the purpose of bringing in eight hundred families from Louisiana, was at risk of unraveling. Edwards had been assigned land by Mexico City that was already claimed by Hispanic Tejanos for generations; the local *alcalde*, appealed to in order to resolve the issue, found against Edwards's interests. Second, the Native American diaspora from the United States into Texas hit a peak and numbered in the thousands.[45] That summer, addressing an alliance now composed of twenty-three tribes, Fields and Hunter called for action. Fields proclaimed: "I am a Red man and a man of honor and can't be imposed on this way we will lift up our tomahauks and fight for land with all those friendly tribes that wishes land also If I am Beaton I then will Resign to fate and if not I will hold lands By the forse of my Red Warriors."[46] The assembled delegates of the alliance assented, and Hunter and Fields negotiated with Benjamin Edwards an agreement whereby virtually all of what became the state of Texas would be divided and declared independent by fiat.

The Fredonian Republic was born on December 21, 1826, when they solemnified their pact with a formal Treaty of Union, League and Confederation modeled on the U.S. Declaration of Independence "in order to prosecute more speedily and effectually the War for Independence." The treaty was authored by Benjamin Edwards, Herman Mayo, Fields, and Hunter. It was ratified by the "Agents of the Committee of Independence" (the white people), which included, in addition to Mayo and Benjamin Edwards, Haden Edwards and three others. Ratifying for the "Committee of Red People" were Fields, Hunter, Ne-Ko-Lake, John Bags, and Cuk-to-Keh. They adopted a flag that bore a red and a white stripe to signal their union.[47] Article 2 of the Treaty of Union, League and Confederation designated what the new boundary would be:

> The Territory apportioned to the Red people, shall begin at the Sandy Spring, where Bradley's road takes off from the road leading to Nacogdoches to the Plantation of Joseph Dust, from thence West by the Compass, without regard to variation, to the Rio Grande, thence to the head of the Rio Grande, thence with the mountains to the head of Big Red River, thence north to the boundary of the United States of North America, thence with the same line to the mouth of Sulphur Fork, thence in a right line to the beginning.
>
> The territory apportioned to the White people, shall comprehend all the residue of the Province of Texas, and of such other portions of the Mexican United States, as the contracting parties, by their mutual efforts and resources, may render Independent, provided the same shall not extend further west than the Rio Grande.[48]

Successive articles of the Treaty affirmed the existing rights of *empresarios* and other established settlers; pledged the "Red people" opportunity to move north of the boundary, with any improvements on vacated lands to be compensated fairly; and affirmed the openness of all channels of conveyance in both territories to the free travel of the inhabitants of each.

But what is perhaps most striking is article 1, which bound the contracting parties to a pact of mutual defense of independence from an entity labeled "the Mexican United States"—a minor, but nevertheless revealing, moment of national geopolitical conflation that only underscores how radical (and, perhaps, how rapidly executed) this undertaking was.[49] On one level, the label is simply an error—an obvious transposition of the conventionally recognized English name "United Mexican States," or "United States of Mexico" (for Estados Unidos Mexicanos), which was established in 1824 after the overthrow of Emperor Iturbide. Yet given the response of Stephen Austin to the Treaty of Union, League and Confederation, who perceived the Fredonian Rebellion as an unforgivable violation of U.S. national and racial identity, the label has a peculiar resonance that indicates a political act that was internationally transgressive in a fundamental way. A "Mexican United States" would be, in the most literal and grammatical sense, one in which the latter is the possession of the former (as, for example, an object of political, military, or cultural conquest or appropriation). From this perspective, a new "Mexican United States" would be one in which the traces of that possession are somehow legible (beginning with a revised national title)—a United States that has been "Mexicanized" somehow. Situated from the standpoint of widespread anti-Mexican prejudice among Anglo colonists and squatters in Texas (about which I will have more to say below), such a transformation evokes panics over purity that highlight a set of racialized assumptions about the respective bodies politic of the United States and Mexico, and the implicit hierarchy of difference in the relationship of those national bodies. In this light, a Red and White Fredonian Declaration of Independence *from* that troubling national hybrid would announce a republic that refuses those hierarchies of racial embodiment.

In a letter to Captain Aylett C. Buckner of Austin's Colony, Benjamin Edwards articulates a political cause that evolves rhetorically to express something akin to this logic. Paraphrasing Thomas Paine ("this is the time to try the souls of men"), Edwards announces that "the flag of *liberty* now waves in majestic triumph on the heights of Nacogdoches," and states: "We are Americans, and will sooner die like freemen, than to live like slaves."[50] Such language works the main line of American revolutionary rhetoric, but shortly thereafter Edwards's announcement of the nature of the Fredonian treaty rhetorically transforms the implicit racial constitution of the patriotic "We" (and the "flag of *liberty*") to include Native Americans as well. "That treaty was signed by Doctor John D. Hunter and Richard Fields as the Representatives of the United Nations of Indians, comprising twenty-three tribes," Edwards writes. "They are now our tried friends, and by compact as well as interest are bound to aid us in effecting Independence of this country."[51] Edwards's language here represents a remarkable shift to a more racially inclusive view of U.S. revolutionary heritage, even as the irony of the use of the term "freemen" in this context is more pronounced and makes clear that the terms of that inclusion were not thought to be universal. Nevertheless, where the United States Declaration of Independence and Constitution announce freedom and equality for all in language that masks a fundamentally unequal racial, social, and economic order that relied on black chattel slavery, the Fredonian Treaty of Union, League and Confederation eschews a rights-based language of universalism and makes the racial underpinnings of political union explicit, forging a sense of republican purpose solely on the basis of contract. This is not to say that the Fredonians achieved in their expressed intention anything like a fully emancipatory model of human freedom or justice that the rights-based Declarations of the United States and United Mexican States lacked (in Mexico, of course, slavery had been abolished formally with the Plan of Iguala in 1821); after all, the Fredonians, both Red and White, practiced slavery and other forms of captive bondage. But in elevating race to the fundamental organizing principle of political union, the Fredonian Treaty of Union, League and Confederation holds up an obverse mirror to U.S.-style rights-based constitutionalism that exposes the fiction of the latter's claims to universality of personhood, even as the rhetoric of "freemen" that surrounds the Fredonian treaty reinscribes blackness as an exclusionary category.

Following the Treaty of Union, League and Confederation, the Fredonians empaneled a "Committee of Correspondence" to compose a series of circulars, to be distributed both within Texas and in the United States, to rally potential supporters and future settlers to a revolutionary cause now evoked in a newly fatalistic rhetoric. One such document, copied for distribution among Austin's Colony, begins by announcing that "the clouds of Fate are fast gathering over our heads, full of portentous import." Another, addressed inclusively "To the citizens of the United States of North America," adds an element of apocalypticism, opening with a pledge of faith that "what is passing, and what has passed" evidences "the beneficent desires of an Almighty Providence," and expressing the belief "that a political millennium is approaching, when the thrones of despotism shall be prostrated, the fetters of mankind unbound, and slaves, by a resurrection as miraculous as that which shall raise our moulded dust to eternal life, be exalted to freemen."[52] The escalating millennialism of this rhetoric speaks both to the presence of actual crisis and an evolving recognition that the political future announced by the Fredonian Republic was not a return to the spirit of 1776 but betokened the "miraculous" prospect of a world fundamentally transformed. As these documents circulated across and beyond Texas, rumors of Hunter's activity in various precincts were widespread, including the farfetched notion that he pegged the success of the rebellion on the intervention of the British. As colonist James Kerr anticipated to Austin on January 24, 1827: "Hunter would act on the frontiers; stimulating to action our red Bretheren, while the British would land on the Coast and over power all opposition."[53] However outlandish the expectation of a British invasion of Texas was, there was legitimate reason to suspect some degree of British interference. While making his petitions to General Victoria on behalf of the Cherokee in Mexico City in March 1826, Hunter had enlisted the support and assistance of the British chargé d'affaires in Mexico, Henry George Ward, a fact noted and reported by Joel Roberts Poinsett, the U.S. minister to Mexico. But, not unlike Tecumseh's and Black Hawk's respective overestimation of British commitment to their causes, Hunter appears to have overplayed his hand in the announcement that he expected a five-hundred-man British force to invade via the Brazos under General Wavell.[54] But Hunter had one last part to play. On January 4, 1827, Samuel Norris, the local *alcalde* previously ousted by Haden Edwards, with a force composed of a small contingent of *empresario* loyalists and sixty Mexicans, took up assault positions under the flag of the Mexican Republic at the Old Stone Fort in Nacogdoches, which served as the Fredonian headquarters. Preemptively, Hunter led eight Cherokee warriors and three white Fredonians on a charge that scattered the Mexican force, killing one and wounding perhaps a dozen more. The victory was decisive, but brief; by the end of January 1827, the alliance had collapsed under political pressure applied by Stephen Austin and the arrival of Mexican troops. By the end of February, both Fields and Hunter had been assassinated by Cherokees loyal to their traditional Chief, Duwali (Bowl), who was acting in concert with the Indian trader and borderland provocateur Peter Ellis Bean.[55]

Before moving on to discuss the later implications of the Fredonian Rebellion for the Mexican government, I want to explore more fully the interrelations of national and racial identity precipitated by the rebellion and to consider some additional echoes of Tecumseh's model of Pan-Indianism in the work of Fields and Hunter's Native confederation. If the erroneous phrase "Mexican United States" hints obliquely at the racial construction of rights-based constitutionalism, it also figures a kind of international hybridity that underscores a complex of allegiances for Anglo-American *empresarios* who had exchanged their U.S. citizenship (and many, like Austin, their Protestantism) for Mexican citizenship, land, and Catholicism. In a series of (very effective) open letters to the inhabitants of the District of Victoria, dated from Austin on January 1, 1827, Austin denounced the Fredonian Union and challenged all Texans to recognize their overlapping duties: as Mexicans, to defend their adopted country; as men, to suppress vice, anarchy, and massacre; and their evidently unelapsed duty as Americans to repudiate those who "are our countrymen no longer," but who have "by a solemn treaty united and identified themselves with Indians, made common laws with savages, and pledged their faith to carry on a war of murder and plunder against the peaceable inhabitants of Texas."[56] Caught in a web of obligations in which race, filiation, nationality, and masculinity overlap, Austin asserts that "common laws with savages" is, on its face, "unnatural" (as he elaborates his sentiment slightly later), and in so doing inadvertently expresses another racial fiction of U.S. constitutional law—namely that the contractual basis of the U.S. treaty system implicitly recognizes the sovereign autonomy and equal rational capacity of Native peoples. This passage recalls a letter he wrote to Hunter earlier in the month that offers another echo of the world of treaty making in the northern borderlands of Tecumseh and Harrison in the Old Northwest:

> My dear sir, let us examine this subject calmly, let us suppose that the Indians overrun the country and take possession of it for the present as far as the Rio Grande and drive out and massacre all the honest inhabitants, what will they gain? What kind of government will they establish? How will they sustain themselves? You know the Indians well enough to know that so many different tribes, and habits and languages cannot be organized into anything like a regular government, or government of any kind, and would not long agree among themselves. When the Spaniards and Americans are driven out and there is no common enemy to contend with, *they would fight* amongst themselves, and nothing but confusion and massacre and plunder would be the consequence. As to the miserable Americans who might

remain and form a part of such a combination, they would be too insignificant both as to character, or property, or numbers to effect anything or to have or deserve to have any influence in anyway. All would be Indian.⁵⁷

Asserting inevitable Indian anarchy as a function of the supposedly natural basis of oral linguistic fragmentation, Austin voices the identical line of reasoning presented by Harrison to Tecumseh at the famous 1810 meeting at Vincennes. And in the closing line quoted here, Austin again makes the panic of his racial ideology explicit: the consequence of "unnatural" alliance with savages unequipped by nature to form enduring political union is degeneracy, a return to primitivism: "All would be Indian." But, unlike the multiple records of Tecumseh at Vincennes, there is no record of Hunter's reply. Indeed, there is no direct written testimony from Hunter at all concerning his time in Texas beyond his coauthorship of the Fredonian treaty itself. There are only reports, scattered mentions, and the rare testimonial appraisal, such as the one by Fredonian cosignatory Herman Mayo I quoted in chapter 3 in reference to Hunter's knowledge of sign language: "When his feelings were raised . . . at times, his high excitement would render him masterless of himself, and while it made him eloquent in gesticulation, frequently deprived him of all command over words. Any discussion relative to the situation and character of the Indians would rouse the level of calm in his ordinary manner into a storm that agitated his entire soul."⁵⁸ Again, the record is too nonspecific to know if Mayo is describing Hunter employing sign language here when, "masterless of himself," he became "eloquent in gesticulation" but lost "all command over words." Is this sign language being described, or are these the "gestures" of a practiced fabulist, the practiced theatrics of a white man who had been "playing Indian" for his entire adult life? Mayo did believe in Hunter and defended him posthumously, even if this description seems to reach for trite literary conventions of embodied Indian emotionalism. But there is one last thing to consider in this light: wherever one falls on the question of John Dunn Hunter, sign language was beyond doubt a key tool in the political organization of the Pan-Indian alliance Fields and Hunter built between 1823 and 1827. No fewer than twenty-three separate tribes formed part of the short-lived Red and White Republic of Fredonia, representing a minimum of six separate language families. This incredibly diverse linguistic environment coalesced in what is recognized now as the cradle of Indian sign language in North America; and in 1806, William Dunbar and John Sibley had confirmed that PISL was the predominant common language throughout the region.⁵⁹ Sign language was, in other words, the only eligible medium through which so many voices could be brought together to forge a political consensus (even one this precarious and short-lived).

Tejas as Carthage: Manuel de Mier y Terán and the Comisión de Límites

If the Fredonian Rebellion is largely remembered in the United States as a quixotically doomed enterprise, a preliminary tremor that briefly anticipates the Texan Revolution, its aftermath was felt with significant alarm in the United States of Mexico. Writing to President Guadalupe Victoria from San Antonio de Bexar on March 28, 1828, General Manuel de Mier y Terán noted that "with the recent example of the revolution of Nacodoches [sic] . . . there is constant fear of an upheaval, and the traveler hears talk of little else."⁶⁰ As head of the Comisión de Límites, Terán had been appointed by President Victoria and charged with assessing the natural and human conditions of Coahuila y Tejas in the wake of the Adams–Onís Treaty of 1819—nearly a decade after the treaty had been ratified by the United States and the new international boundary along the Red and Arkansas Rivers had been surveyed and mapped by his U.S. counterpart, Major Stephen Harriman Long with the United States Exploring Expedition.⁶¹ The Adams–Onís Treaty had been negotiated between the United States and Spain, but its ratification was delayed by the Mexican Revolution of 1821, the imperial ascension of Iturbide, and the 1824 establishment of the democratic United States of Mexico. Now, in 1828, the Comisión de Límites was tasked with cataloguing the natural resources of Texas, mapping the new Sabine River boundary in the northeast, and, certainly most urgently, assessing the impact and implications of the heavy influx of North American Indian tribes and Anglo-American settlers, squatters, fugitives, and *empresarios* who had been flooding into Texas from United States territory for a decade.

For his counterpart, Major Long, the territory of the southern Great Plains bordering Texas had been rugged, inhospitable, and largely devoid of human interest—a "Great American Desert" unfit for permanent habitation. By contrast, for Terán, the landscape in Tejas seemed overcrowded, even claustrophobic at times. By the time he arrived in Nacogdoches, in June 1828, he had seen enough. In his diary of the expedition,

Terán recounts his obligation upon his arrival to receive emissaries from a range of tribes both traditionally indigenous to the region and recently emigrated from the territorial United States—among them the Delaware, Kickapoo, Shawnee, Cherokee, and Caddo, who had lately been involved in the Fredonian Rebellion—whose "harangues" he found "very annoying" and whose excessive numbers made his room, he wrote, "an insufferable oven":

> My lodgings are regularly frequented by considerable numbers of [Indian] men, and sometimes women as well. They all shake hands in greeting, and their gesture of politeness is to give a rough jerk to one's entire arm. Their hands, of course, are filthy and hard, like those associated with wild men: since the women do all the tasks and labor, their hands are rougher and dirtier. The ceremonial handshake is required even for children, and they have not excused me from it, even when some of them have scabies. This act concluded, they sit on the trunks and even on the bed—if I have not taken the precaution of preventing it—when there are not enough chairs. Others sit on the floor, and they all form a circle.[62]

Close proximity and physical contact with Native peoples inspire in Terán something close to disgust that nevertheless magnifies his sense of the relationships between Native gesture, culture, gender, and disease. Gesture forms one part of the ceremonial language of exchange here in the form of obligatory handshakes; rather than civility, what Terán perceives is the rough filthiness of "wild men," the underlying physical truth of an expressive cultural practice he correlates to degrading gender relations and a form of contagion he perceives on some children's hands.

The physical discomfort Terán expresses here in his journal corresponds to his ambivalence about the ultimate entitlement to the lands he is charged with surveying for the Mexican government; indeed, in his diary, he also gives voice to the notion that the fate of Tejas had already been written against Mexico's favor. In the same daily entry quoted above, Terán records his meeting with the venerable Caddo chief Dehahuit, who wore epaulettes and a medallion bearing the portrait of King Carlos III of Spain: "I asked him 'whether he and his tribe were in the Mexican part or in that of the North [the United States],' and when he fully understood what was being asked, he replied that he was not in Mexican territory nor in that of the North Americans, but in his own land, which was nothing else but his."[63] Terán closes his entry for that day with these lines: "The speech of the savages abounds in figurative expression and actions. In order to criticize a lack of truthfulness, they put two fingers on the edge of their lips and with very rapid movements they represent the volubility of the tongue. At the end of the action they say, 'man with two tongues, or serpent's tongue.' *Quippe domum timet ambiguam, tyrios que bilingues.* Virg[il]."[64] This brief depiction of Plains Indian Sign Language, the common use of which he had noted in his journal the previous month, seems driven less by ethnographic aims than by the ironic thematic pertinence of the particular sign he describes, "to lie," to his larger circumstance as a representative of the Mexican government. Terán was deeply aware of the history of broken promises of accommodation by the Mexican government to the Native peoples in the vicinity of Nacogdoches, including Dehahuit's people—the very lies that had given rise to the Fredonian Rebellion, on the site of which he now penned these lines. The frequency with which he must have encountered this sign on the day's presentations of grievance from different tribal emissaries was clearly noteworthy. But what is most suggestive is the closing Latin passage that implicitly comments on the entry it concludes, "*Quippe domum timet ambiguam, tyrios que bilingues.* Virg." This line comes from book 1 of *The Aeneid*, following the arrival of Aeneas to Dido's Carthage.

> But in her breast the Cytherean ponders
> new stratagems, new guile: that Cupid, changed
> in form and feature, come instead of sweet
> Ascanius and, with his gifts, inflame
> the queen to madness and insinuate
> a fire in Dido's very bones. For Venus
> is much afraid of the Tyrians with their double tongues.
> (bk. 1, lines 918–25) [65]

In its wider epic context, the passage speaks to the perilous journey of Aeneas to Italy following the Trojan War, upon his shipwreck in Carthage (present-day Tunisia) and his incipient relationship with the widowed Queen Dido; at the same time, it reveals the stratagem of that relationship in a proxy conflict of the Gods. Venus (the Cytherean) is anxious to protect her son Aeneas, the destined founder of Rome, from jealous Juno, whose favorite city, Carthage, is destined to be destroyed by the Romans. Aeneas receives refuge from Dido in the temple of Juno, but Venus mistrusts "the Tyrians with their double tongues" and enlists Cupid to make

Dido fall in love with Aeneas; their affair ends with Aeneas's secret departure, Dido's aggrieved and eternal pledge of enmity between Carthage and Rome, and her suicide. For Terán, the geopolitical parallels to his situation in Tejas might have seemed only too apt. Dido, the widowed queen from Tyre (present-day Lebanon), rules Carthage but is induced by fate and higher powers to offer hospitality to the figure destined to destroy it. Terán, emissary of a Mexico recently independent from Spain, presides over lands that, as Dehahuit has reminded him, are not indigenously his own and must play reluctant host to Native peoples and *norteamericanos* whose presence is the result of the United States unmistakable expansionist ambitions into Mexican territory.

But if he confesses in his diary an instinct to recoil from physical contact with Native Americans and a sense of epic fatalism about his larger undertaking, Terán is also highly dutiful in his resignation to the conflict. In his official dispatches, he is consistent in recommending the garrisoning of northern towns and outposts more heavily against the possibility of further U.S. incursions and expresses a preference for a national policy that would evacuate Native Americans from Tejas altogether. Writing to the minister of foreign relations a week later, he concluded: "I would argue against permitting the introduction of any [tribes] into Mexican territory, where there are plenty of savages on which the nation may exercise its tolerance and human sentiment." Instead, he suggested that the best (though, by now, impracticable) solution would be to "do with them what the North Americans have done with their savages: subjugate them and send them beyond their borders."[66]

As Terán's counterparts in the United States recognized, any policy aimed toward Indian Removal depended extensively on ethnographic intelligence of Native peoples. This was, in fact, a part of his formal charge as head of the Comisión de Límites, and throughout his writings Terán evinces keen interest in recording his observations of Native customs and character and also his impressions of Indian racial performance. Noting that "they all like to highlight their faces with vermilion red," Terán states that they "call themselves red men, creating in this color a race, like that of the whites and of the blacks. Perhaps from these vain notions of race and lineage comes the pleasure the American savages take in red hues, because, even though they apply different colors to their faces, they prefer red over all others."[67] Although he finds "notions of race and lineage" to be "vain" (indicating, perhaps, a view that he finds them lacking in essential merit, and not only preening), Terán seems also to emphasize such moments that highlight difference among the peoples he encounters as a compensation for the dissolution of those differences from the standpoint of the *norteamericanos* who exercise outsize cultural and political influence. The Anglo-Americans, he finds, seem not to see meaningful boundaries where the bodies of Hispanic Mexicans are concerned. In a letter to President Victoria, he writes: "I must disturb you in the same way I was disturbed to see the foreign colonists' attitude toward our nation. Most of them . . . think that [Mexico] consists of nothing more than blacks and Indians, all of them ignorant."[68]

Indeed, the writings of Terán, José Maria Sánchez (a draftsman who wrote a memoir of his experience while composing valuable sketches of the scenes and people encountered), and Jean-Louis Berlandier (a young French botanist attached to the Comisión de Límites) betray a collective sense of unease that previously reliable boundaries of racial, ethnic, and national difference had become dangerously unsettled. Across these texts (and in Berlandier particularly) there is an extraordinary level of attention and detail devoted to recording the populations, religious practices, social conditions, and economic and military cultures of the many tribes they encountered. In their discussions of Native American character, these efforts resemble in their descriptions of Native Americans levels of bias and prejudice that were common in the works of many U.S. writers, finding in Native Americans a common stock of invidious stereotypes: a readiness to treachery; rapaciousness; vengefulness; vanity; habitual laziness, and so on. The persistence of these tropes is hardly surprising; what interests me here is the frequent echo of these "Indian" racial attributions in descriptions of the Anglo colonists and *empresarios* at San Antonio, the Austin's Colony, and Nacogdoches. Terán performs this rhetorical alignment in a letter to President Victoria dated March 28 from Bexar:

> Alongside these savage men who everywhere assault the Mexican frontier, arrogating to themselves the rights given them by the need to survive [and] sustained by their weapons, invaders of another kind are seen to arrive carrying the tools of a very advanced industry. Without respect for borders or boundaries of pure convention, they choose the best land. Nature tells them that [the land] is theirs, because, in effect, everyone can appropriate what does not belong to anyone or what is not claimed by anyone.[69]

Although immigrant Indians from the United States and Anglo colonizers in Texas differ in their methods (one is "sustained by their weapons";

the other by "the tools of a very advanced industry"), Terán presents them as invaders alike, both acting on the "rights" of nature in defiance of the political boundaries of human civilization. Beyond this broad equation, perhaps the most notable specific analogue expressed in these works is the frequency with which American Indian women are described as the "*slaves*" of indolent American Indian men—indeed, the term "slave" is employed by all three of these writers, across multiple tribal contexts.[70] Whether or not the metaphor carries explanatory power with respect to the circumstances they specifically describe, the term "slave" resonates forcefully across these texts in descriptions of the mistreatment of African American slaves by Anglo colonizers. For instance, José Maria Sánchez describes the "common vices" of the Comanche as "vengeance, pride, and excessive laziness," the latter quality guaranteeing that "the women are real slaves to the men, who occupy themselves with war and hunting only." Consider, in this light, his description of the North Americans in Stephen Austin's colony, as "lazy people of vicious character. Some of them cultivate small farms by planting corn; but this task they usually entrust to their negro slaves, whom they treat with considerable harshness."[71] This style of rhetorical coordination serves at once mutually to disqualify both Anglo colonists and Indian settlers from prospective incorporation into the body of Mexican nationhood. But it also serves to reclassify the status of Mexican Tejanos living in regions dominated by Anglo settlers. Throughout the descriptions of Laredo, San Antonio de Bexar, and Austin's Colony, Hispanic Mexican nationals are described by Sánchez as "ardently fond of luxury and leisure," "little inclined to work," corrupt, ineffectual, and ignorant. In Nacogdoches, Terán finds them "dissipated" and reduces all inhabitants to a common savagery:

> The men of either nation on this frontier are notable for the diversity of their origins and the present similarity of their customs. Descendants of the French founders of Louisiana, of the Spanish in Mexico, and of the English race, which lately has spread from Virginia to the Gulf of Mexico, and the tribes of savages, and among all, the blacks and their different mixture: all these men have the same rural tasks, skill at hunting, and the cunning and instincts that guide the savage in natural life. (80)

These characterizations perform an Indian racialization of Mexican Tejanos on the northern frontier. More specifically, they constitute a form of national reassignment of Tejanos from Mexico to the threatening border presence of the United States, one that draws on an existing catalogue of racial attributes used elsewhere to characterize indigenous peoples as essentially and irremediably savage, promiscuous, and marginal.

* * *

By way of transition into the following chapter, I will point to a striking exception to this pattern. Away from the enervating and destabilizing coordinates of the towns and *empresario* colonies, in rural settings on individual Anglo farms and homesteads, the Comisión de Límites experienced moments of hospitable accord with Anglo settlers that prompted clear examples of sympathetic identification. In his record of one such setting, which he describes as an "illusory Arcadia," Sánchez departs from his pessimistic reportage to engage an American family in a moment of conspicuous sentimental reverie. I quote the passage in full:

> On seeing the tranquillity which these peaceful inhabitants enjoy in contrast to the passions that wreck our souls in the populous cities, an involuntary sigh escaped my breast just as one of the girls, who was barely more than ten years old, and whose beauty made her attractive, came out to offer me a seat with that charming grace that only innocence can lend. Her kindness, so rare among those of her nationality, the sight of her roselike face and her bare little feet, and the recollection of human misery which at this moment crowded my mind, moved me strangely, as I thought that perhaps some day a daring hand would pluck rudely this flower of the desert, and then tears would come to wither the face where now joy and smiles dwell. These thoughts permitted me only to thank her and I returned to our camp to wait for slumber to come and deaden the bitter thoughts of the afternoon.[72]

Tinctured bitterly with a fantasy that this vision of sublime tranquility must one day be spoiled, Sánchez's tragic romanticism might seem to be a poor model for imagining lasting forms of cross-racial understanding in ill-defined border regions. But, as I transition to another boundary survey of the U.S./Mexico border, and John Russell Bartlett in 1851, I want to note one other dynamic at play here: an experience for which words are impossible (he can only voice thanks in the moment) but also superabundant in an act of retelling. If the extension of romantic and U.S. patriotic sentiment to Native Americans is possible for rogue figures like Hunter—and, even if only briefly—within the context of rogue movements like the

Fredonian Rebellion, it would appear seldom to have been extended by official agents of the Mexican and United States governments (or, in the case of Tecumseh, was only extended posthumously). But romantic sentiment, for Sánchez and, as we shall see, with Bartlett, did occasionally offer a style of sympathetic identification between Anglo-American and Hispanic-Mexican peoples in unsettled borderlands environments in which boundaries of national difference remained undefined.

5

John Russell Bartlett's Literary Borderlands: Ethnology, the U.S-Mexico War, and the United States Boundary Survey

Reading "Indian Sign"

On October 24, 1850, on the banks of the South Concho River, in the vicinity of Fredericksburg, Texas, John Russell Bartlett had his first "official" encounter with an American Indian—or, as he would put it, in his habitual blend of scientific and romantic lexica, his "first specimen of the wild denizens of the prairie."[1] As the recently appointed United States boundary commissioner, Bartlett headed a 120-man expedition—comprised of surveyors, astronomers, and topographical engineers, sketch artists and cartographers, mechanics, laborers, cooks, servants, and teamsters, translators, doctors, geologists, zoologists, and botanists—all collectively charged under his authority with establishing the international border between the United States and the Republic of Mexico pursuant to article 5 of the 1848 Treaty of Guadalupe-Hidalgo. This first "specimen of the wild denizens of the prairie" in question was Chipota, a chief of the Lipan Apache, who "suddenly appeared from behind a clump of bushes, and the next moment was in the midst of the camp," and who, according to several witnesses from the expedition presumably in a position to judge, bore an uncanny likeness to Lewis Cass, Democratic senator from Michigan (76–77). Although the suddenness of Chipota's arrival came as a surprise, an encounter had not been unexpected. Three days prior, scouts from the expedition had discovered within a mile of their trail what Bartlett termed "Indian sign": "It is not necessary that the savage should be seen, to judge of his presence," he writes. "He always leaves marks behind him, which are soon understood by the sagacious travelers of the prairie, and are as unmistakable as his own red skin" (72). Deriving knowledge of American Indians within an evidentiary framework in which their presence is unnecessary, Bartlett fashions the "reading of signs" as an interpretive activity that finds presence in a scene of absence and rewards "sagacious travelers" with the "unmistakable" signs of racial difference.

Ironically, the actual presence of an American Indian would prove insufficient to manifest reliable knowledge of his status. When Chipota arrived in the Survey's camp on the 24th, his identity was unknown to Bartlett. Here, presence was again a superfluity; the "Indian sign" that begged to be read, in this instance, were documents Chipota carried that had been issued by the military officers and the local Indian agent certifying the bearer as a Lipan chief and requesting his friendly treatment of any Americans who should pass through his territory. Although his actions in the camp were outwardly hospitable, it was not those actions themselves but, curiously, the production of official U.S. documents requesting from their bearer such hospitable behavior that seemed to verify for Bartlett and his company that Chipota's friendliness was, in fact, friendly. Following their preliminary introductions, Bartlett invited Chipota into his riding carriage for the next leg of their journey. There, Bartlett records, "contrary to the custom of his race, he manifested much curiosity respecting all he saw"—in particular, with respect to the large collection of revolvers and rifles that lined the interior of the carriage (77–78). Chipota picked up Bartlett's telescope, assuming it to be another firearm, and asked how it was fired: "The instrument was adjusted, and a distant tree pointed out, which he was told to look at with the glass. His credulity had been overtasked, and it was hard to convince him that it was the same far-off tree. I told him that we used that to see the Indians at a distance, and could always tell when they were about or had stolen any mules" (78). In a moment that echoes a New World history of "marvelous possessions" held by imperial claimants dating to John Smith and his magical compass, Bartlett conscripts this piece of optical technology into an object-lesson that promotes U.S. dominance as a function of its epistemological superiority.[2] Fashioning a fantasy of U.S. omniscience through the warning that he may see without being seen, Bartlett seizes on Chipota's misrecognition of a scientific instrument as an object of war and presents knowledge as a tool of conquest. In this sense, Bartlett's message to Chipota is similar to his message to the reader regarding "Indian sign": for the "sagacious traveler," physical proximity to the Indian is unnecessary to produce a correct knowledge of him (indeed, proximity may inhibit understanding); instead, specialized techniques of viewing (including the lens of government documents) are seen to leverage power and knowledge most effectively at a distance.

In its broadest sense, this chapter argues that John Russell Bartlett's fascinating but seldom discussed *Personal Narrative of Explorations and Incidents in Texas, New Mexico, California, Sonora and Chihuahua* represents a key, yet equivocal, literary consolidation of the work of empire and ethnology in the American Southwest. I open with this vignette because it evokes a style of collusion of agendas of U.S. empire and scientific knowledge production that governs central aspects of Bartlett's literary project, a project that culminates a backstory of scientific opportunism by prominent amateur ethnologists in New York eager to capitalize on U.S. efforts to annex Mexican territory in the Southwest. The pages that follow investigate the manner in which a burgeoning ethnological project continued to participate in the larger national and imperial enterprise of boundary creation and discuss the relationship of cultural epistemology, political speech acts, and literary form. More specifically, I explore the complex interplay of ethnological research motives between the American Ethnological Society and the War Department, unforeseen technical challenges arising from the Boundary Survey itself, and formidable legal and political issues in shaping the techniques of Bartlett's literary representation. Bartlett attempts to reconcile these diverse elements in the *Personal Narrative*, but this project is troubled throughout by the lingering memory of political controversy. Having been charged with the duty of surveying and inscribing a politically binding international border across a vast expanse of inhospitable terrain, Bartlett's efforts were disastrously undermined by contradictory treaty instructions and an erroneous map—untenable conditions that led eventually to his ouster as boundary commissioner in 1853. The *Personal Narrative* was, in one sense, Bartlett's bid to vindicate his own actions as commissioner, but the displacement of Bartlett's authority from official spokesman to private individual underscores throughout his text a failure of ideological coordination between the overlapping projects of ethnological research and national inscription. In the end, Bartlett's fractured embodiment of national authority—intact as the events described are played out, yet compromised at the moment of literary authorship—is reflected in the *Personal Narrative* in a set of amorphous boundaries between competing modes of sentimental and scientific representation and is most keenly legible in discussions of racial and national difference. Turning throughout on the shifting textual terrain of "the personal" within an ambiguously determined borderlands territory, this textual dynamic culminates in Bartlett's depiction of the Boundary Commission's liberation of two sets of Mexican captives held by the Apache in the vicinity of the Gila River in New Mexico.

Bartlett, Gallatin, and the American Ethnological Society

At first blush, John Russell Bartlett would appear to have been an unlikely candidate for the appointment of commissioner of the U.S. Boundary Survey. A Rhode Island Whig of a serious and decidedly bookish temperament, Bartlett was an amateur ethnologist, talented sketch artist, bookseller, and accomplished lexicographer who landed the position due to savvy political connections established during the Polk and Taylor administrations—and not, that is, due to a résumé of actually relevant experience, a fact that led the eminent historian William Goetzmann to dismiss Bartlett as "the very epitome of visionary impracticality."[3] In his life prior to his tenure with the Boundary Survey, Bartlett had been a fixture of the literary and scientific circles of Providence, Rhode Island; upon moving to New York, he opened a bookshop with the Englishman Charles Welford on the ground floor of the Astor House Hotel in New York City that became a gathering place for such prominent figures as James Fenimore Cooper, Henry Rowe Schoolcraft, John Lloyd Stephens, and Edgar Allan Poe.[4] During these years, Bartlett established himself as an important member of the intellectual circle surrounding the venerable Albert Gallatin, joining Gallatin in the resurrection of the then-moribund New-York Historical Society while serving as his part-time amanuensis and intellectual kindred spirit. He achieved his greatest renown in 1848, with the publication of his *Dictionary of Americanisms*, a lexicon of U.S. colloquialisms that went through several editions in his lifetime and that remains a valuable scholarly resource on nonstandard American English. But like his mentor Gallatin, his chief passion was ethnology.

When Bartlett arrived in New York in 1836, the emergent study and practice of ethnology in the United States was at an early crossroads. Not yet established as a formal academic discipline, ethnological study was largely a sideline of state historical and antiquarian societies, library societies, and athenaeums; it was advanced most vigorously by an ad hoc constellation of well-heeled amateurs whose philosophical investments and methods of inquiry were frequently at odds. In 1842, Bartlett and Gallatin cofounded the American Ethnological Society (AES), the first such society of its kind in the United States and still active today as the oldest professional anthropological organization in the country. The society was organized into three membership rolls—the Core Membership (largely comprised of doctors, lawyers, and men of leisure on-site in New York); a larger Corresponding Membership (which was international in its scope); and a list of Honorary Members, containing an international roster of luminaries (including James Alexander, Alexander von Humboldt, James Pritchard and Leopold Ranke, among others). A quick review of the Society's first membership roll offers a concise view of the professional demographic of a still-inchoate research discipline. Of thirty-six local members, only five held formal appointments at universities; among the Corresponding Membership, which numbered forty-two, only two had academic appointments. Instead, among the Corresponding Membership one finds chiefly diplomats, missionaries, military officers, Indian agents, and bibliophiles—a diverse pool of amateur scientific enthusiasts who were to be counted on to send in dispatches from their far-flung locations.[5]

As president of the American Ethnological Society in New York, Gallatin was acknowledged as the leading figurehead of a Jeffersonian school of ethnological thought that traced its philosophical roots to the Enlightenment and transatlantic eighteenth-century debates over Buffon's degeneracy theory. Committed to the principle of human political equality and a progressive view of history, Gallatin assumed a monogenetic origin to the human species as a matter of course and asserted that the phenomenon of human diversity was attributable to environmental factors.[6] To substantiate this position, he committed himself to philological inquiries into Native American dialects with the goal of mapping the evolutionary relationships between the language families of North America. Combining data compiled from grammar surveys, available missionary dictionaries, and tribal vocabularies collected by Lewis Cass, William Clark, and others, Gallatin produced the first extensive map of Native American language families in 1826 and published his definitive statement on American Indian tribes, human origins, and philological methods in the second volume of the *Transactions* of the American Antiquarian Society, under the title "A Synopsis of the Indian Tribes of North America" (1836).[7]

Gallatin's "Synopsis" is a landmark work in the fields of Native American ethnology and comparative philology; it also stands as a landmark of scientific collaboration between the War Department and a private individual, and as such illustrates with unusual force the material and ideological relays between the projects of U.S. empire and ethnological knowledge production prior to the U.S.-Mexico War. As Gallatin later reflected, his massive project of assembling all available Indian grammars and vocabularies had been "greatly assisted" by the War Department, which, at Gallatin's request, had circulated blank vocabulary forms and questionnaires devised by Gallatin to Indian agents nationwide in 1826.[8] As I have explored in previous chapters, this history of systematic collaboration between learned societies on the eastern seaboard and the War Department exposes the interlocking ideological and epistemological agendas of a widening scientific discourse that was itself taking shape according to the shifting political and geographical boundaries of the United States. Conceived broadly as an Enlightenment-style knowledge project devoted to the establishment of neutral historical truths concerning the relations of kinship between human groups, the practice of ethnological linguistics at midcentury was nevertheless committed to exploiting the institutional capillaries of the federal apparatus—a relationship modeled by the American Philosophical Society with the Lewis and Clark and Long Expeditions. By the mid-1840s, more dedicated institutional frameworks had been established for the gathering and circulation of ethnological data between learned societies like the APS and AES and military expeditions in the Southwest. Central to this network of developing intelligence was the Army Corps of Topographical Engineers, founded in 1838 to survey and map accurately American interests west of the Rockies and headed by Colonel John James Abert, a charter Corresponding Member of the American Ethnological Society. Over the course of several expeditions spanning tens of thousands of miles, the scientific teams of Abert's Topographical Corps made detailed topographical maps and scrupulous geodetic calculations fixing the positions of travel routes in the Rockies, the Great Basin, Oregon, California, and New Mexico. Promoted vigorously by the westward expansionist Thomas Hart Benton on the floor of the U.S. Senate, these expeditions also produced extensive narrative reports, which were widely reprinted, describing significant land features, native populations, and other practical considerations to facilitate transcontinental travel and western resettlement (water and food sources, the passability of remote terrain, and so on).[9]

In key respects, the philosophy of mission publicized by the American Ethnological Society at its founding echoes the agenda of the War Department to manage and control Native populations in the process of westward expansion. Building on his work as corresponding secretary of the AES, Bartlett published a volume titled *The Progress of Ethnology* in 1847, a global survey of current research in the field that likewise reflects this posture. The tone Bartlett adopts throughout this book is forward-looking and optimistic. The recent fieldwork of E. G. Squier, respecting the Indian burial mounds of the Mississippi Valley, and John Lloyd Stephens concerning the ancient civilization of the Maya, had brought, he wrote, a "new impulse... to the study of American Antiquities"—one that had begun to eclipse the armchair researches of an early generation of ethnological inquiry with field researches that were presented in compelling narratives of travel and exploration.[10] The tremendous popularity of Stephens's books catalyzed a new direction of American ethnological inquiry into ancient civilizations and Indian tribes of the Southwest and Mexico—an area of research emphasis nowhere more prominently visible than in the agenda of the AES, which imagined itself as embarking on ground "unoccupied by any institution in the United States."[11] From Bartlett's point of view, the excitement generated by the current status of ethnology was not fully explained by these discrete inquiries into local archaeological and anthropological formations, however significant those inquiries might have been. Instead, *Progress* illustrates that Bartlett's vision of ethnology was of an abidingly synthetic enterprise that aspired toward totality—yoking anthropology, archaeology, linguistics, philology, geography, and history into one imperial discipline that promised to elucidate the entire physical history of humankind. More immediately, the discoveries of Squier and Stephens, among others, represented triumphs of a personally affecting nature, as he counted them both among his friends at his Astor House bookshop and had, in fact, first suggested to Stephens the great potential of exploring the Mayan ruins of Mexico and Central America. Following Bartlett's advice, Stephens had accepted the post of U.S. minister to Central America in 1839 with the hope of using the appointment as a springboard for field research and publication, a hope that was realized in 1841 with his *Incidents of Travel in Central America, Chiapas, and Yucatan*.

With the advent of the U.S.-Mexico War, the AES and the War Department jointly perceived an unprecedented opportunity to upgrade and enlarge their collaborative research network. In a packet Bartlett conveyed personally to Secretary of War William Marcy, in March 1846, Gallatin enclosed multiple copies of his "Notes on the Semi-Civilized Nations of Mexico, Yucatan, and Central America," and appealed to

Marcy's sense of patriotism on the basis of that text's national literary prestige.

> The work has been favorably received, principally in Germany and France, and has, we are told, added something to the literary reputation of our country. But that which is naturally expected of us, and should be the principal object of our next volume, is to collect all the knowledge that can be obtained respecting our own Indians. The annual reports of your agents will probably afford that which relates to the social state and apparent progress of civilization of those people. But the most difficult branch of the subject, and that to which the attention of our society is naturally drawn, is a much more complete knowledge of the grammar or structure of the several languages, or rather families of languages. This differs so much from the grammatical system to which we are used that it cannot be acquired without much time and labor.[12]

Gallatin's presentation of such research obstacles illustrates a powerful and enduring tension in the development of ethnological practice, one in which the epistemological necessity of decentralization (that is, the geographically dispersed data points necessary for the collection and comparison of discrete grammars and vocabularies) sits uneasily with the ideological necessity of centralization (both for the collection and interpretation of data and vis-à-vis the political uses to which those interpretations are placed in service). Adding further that the execution of this research was far beyond the local means of the American Ethnological Society in New York, Gallatin suggested to Marcy that a new generation of Indian agents, missionaries, and educators at Indian schools enjoyed the best resources and opportunity to enact a more comprehensive survey of indigenous vocabularies and grammars. Gallatin's earlier "Synopsis" had focused on indigenous languages east of the Rocky Mountains; the new direction of the research proposed would endeavor westward, "and the analysis of the Mexican and other languages, contained in our first volume"—that is, in the volume Bartlett presented to Marcy with Gallatin's letter—"would point out the direction to be pursued in the investigation of the structure of the languages of our own Indians" (627). The key word here is "Mexican." Indeed, what is most striking overall in this letter is Gallatin's and Bartlett's crafty sense of political opportunity in applying for Marcy's assistance in March 1846—two months after President Polk had ordered General Taylor's forces south to the Rio Grande and barely a month prior to a formal declaration of war with the Republic of Mexico. Pointedly, Gallatin proposed that Marcy use the authority of the War Department to conscript a roster of eligible individuals (the list of whom was to be furnished by Gallatin and Bartlett) to participate in this new research survey by issuing an official departmental request that they "comply with our wishes."[13] Such a program would be supplemented by the circulation of subsequent publications of the AES, for which Gallatin made a further appeal for additional financial assistance (Gallatin and Bartlett had largely borne the costs of publication to that point, the latter publishing the Society's *Transactions* from his bookselling firm). He closed the letter by referring Bartlett as the party to engage for further discussion and action. This design appears to have gained significant traction. As Bartlett subsequently reported to General Caleb Cushing: "All the departments at Washington as well as the officers of the army have tendered to Mr. Gallatin of the Ethnolog. Soc. any papers, maps, &c in their power."[14] To Cushing himself, who marched with his regiment of Massachusetts volunteers to Mexico City after its capture, Bartlett appealed for another bounty of Mexican conquest—printed dictionaries and grammars of Mexican languages from the seventeenth and early eighteenth centuries, along with any ancient manuscripts or antiquities that still existed "in the convents & museums of the country and may be obtained under certain circumstances" (407). Cushing himself had expressed the desirability of a broad scientific survey of northern Mexico. Anticipating his own work as the boundary commissioner, Bartlett wrote, "*Nothing would please me better than to engage in such an expedition* and when the proper time comes, we must see what can be done" (408, emphasis in original).

Of the various forms of assistance from the War Department pursued by the American Ethnological Society to advance the work of ethnological linguistics, none would have greater specific import to Bartlett and the work of the Boundary Commission than the correspondence between Gallatin and William Emory of the Topographical Engineers in the fall of 1847. At that time, Gallatin was in the process of composing a magisterial introduction to Horatio Hale's "Indians of North-West America, and Vocabularies of North America" for the second volume of the AES *Transactions*.[15] In research for this work, Gallatin's elusive object was to establish a basis of linguistic comparison between the geographically insulated and little-known tribes in the vicinity of the Gila River (in present-day southeast Arizona and southwest New Mexico) and those languages from Mexico and Central America he had been able to classify already, specifically

Nahuatl (which he referred to in his writings alternately as "Mexican," or "Aztec"), Huastec, Otomi, Maya, and two partial dialects from Guatemala.[16] Gallatin had determined in 1836 that the sixty-one languages and dialects he had examined east of the Rockies in United States and British territories constituted only eight "great families" and that these eight families shared a fundamental consonance of grammatical structure—a discovery that led him to assert an ancient commonality of origin for all indigenous peoples surveyed.[17] If he were able to establish a complementary basis of common grammatical structure between the tribes of the Gila and those languages obtained from points south, he would be able to add a powerful empirical bulwark to his theory of hemispheric commonality of origin—one that would bolster strongly the monogenetic lynchpin theory of a primordial migration of peoples across the Bering Strait.

In this design, Gallatin was frustrated by the limitations of available source material, having to rely primarily on the sketchy details of Pedro Castañeda's firsthand account of the 1540–42 Coronado expedition (which itself had only recently come into his possession).[18] Struggling to adduce salient and reliable geographical and cultural data relative to the Pima, Maricopas, and Apache, Gallatin wrote to General Stephen Watts Kearny of the Army of the West in the wake of his 1846–47 wartime expedition through New Mexico to California to inquire into recent geographical and ethnological information obtained in the field. Kearny referred Gallatin to Lieutenant William H. Emory, who served in the Topographical Corps unit attached to Kearny's expedition as the chief astronomer. (Emory would later serve in a similar capacity on Bartlett's Boundary Survey before assuming the post of commissioner following Bartlett's dismissal in 1853.) In a series of letters exchanged with Emory during the fall of 1847, Gallatin sought to corroborate geographical aspects of the Castañeda account and inquired further after structures of habitation as well as the availability of botanical samples of agricultural products (in a speculative effort to establish historical patterns of trade with Mexican tribes to the south). Emory responded with detailed geographical information, a draft of a regional map, and general cultural details concerning the Pima, Coco Maricopas, and Apache, which Gallatin incorporated into his work. Gallatin's keenest interests, though, concerned matters of language. In response to Gallatin's detailed inquiries, Emory also provided a vocabulary of the Coco Maricopas, which Gallatin reported was "quite a new language" that bore "no resemblance" to the four Mexican languages or the thirty-two minor language families of North America in his possession.

One detail, though, he found particularly suggestive: "*Apache* is the word for *man*; and judging by analogy from several other Indian languages, [the Coco Maricopas] should be Apaches or belonging to that family."[19] Given that the tribal names of the Illinois and Lenni Lenape were both evidently derived from the common Algonquin word *Linno*, for man, this parallel derivation was suggestive, but however intriguing this line of conjecture might be, Gallatin was forced to acknowledge that "the accounts, by report, of the Indians to the mouth of the Gila are conflicting and of an indefinite character," as Emory had reported. "This observation applies to every information derived from other sources. We have as yet only vague rumors."

As it would turn out, the imminence of Gallatin's publication schedule for the AES prevented him from including the full range of information that Emory's report, once completed, would be able to provide. But Gallatin did not write too late for Emory to make use of him in his own work. Included as the first appendix in Emory's *Notes of a Military Reconnaissance from Fort Leavenworth, in Missouri, to San Diego, in California, Including Parts of the Arkansas, Del Norte, and Gila River*, is the text of Gallatin's letter of October 1, 1847, along with the full text of Emory's reply. An executive document of the Thirtieth Congress, Emory's *Notes* was printed in a large edition of ten thousand copies by the Washington firm of Wendell and Van Benthuysen in 1848 and distributed widely—an act of print appropriation that (in mirrored reverse to the Gallatin/Bartlett proposal to Marcy two years earlier) effectively conscripted Gallatin's scientific project into the service of a state discourse of wartime military action. Both of these texts were promoted with excitement by ethnologists in the East who were quick to perceive new areas of research opportunity in the Southwest. One of these was E. G. Squier, who speculated both on the suitability of recently conquered southwestern lands for white settlement while heralding the important new findings of Emory and Gallatin, among others, in an article for the *American Review* in November 1848. "Within the habitable regions here indicated, and which have hitherto been very imperfectly known," he writes, "are a number of Indian tribes, in many respects as remarkable as any on the continent," adding that, "the recent war against Mexico, however unsatisfactory its results in other respects, has indirectly contributed in enlightening us very materially in regard to some of these singular aboriginal families."[20]

Against this background, it is easy to appreciate the eagerness with which Bartlett pursued his application for the position of United States Boundary

Survey commissioner and the opportunity it could afford to conduct original field research into Indian languages and culture—particularly concerning those tribes of New Mexico's Gila River. Bartlett's own later recollection, recorded in his autobiography, substantiates this design, albeit in a language in which his earlier enthusiasm was subdued by the retrospective knowledge that his project would prove ultimately unsuccessful: "Although my life and pursuits had always been of a sedentary character I always had a great desire for travel, and particularly for exploring unknown regions. I had also ever felt a deep interest in the Indians, and was glad of an opportunity to be thrown among the wild tribes of the interior. I saw, too, that there would be a wide field for new exploration and that if the government would permit these, I would prefer the office of Commissioner to any other."[21] The route from bookseller to being "thrown among the wild tribes of the interior" was a circuitous one. The rising expense of conducting business in New York had prompted Bartlett, in 1849, to dissolve his partnership with Charles Welford in their Astor Hotel bookshop and remove his family to his hometown of Providence. Around this time, armed with a letter of introduction from Albert Gallatin to John C. Calhoun, Bartlett made a series of forays to Washington to pursue a government appointment abroad—setting his sights at first on the Mission to Denmark, which Bartlett hoped would afford financial and geographical opportunity to furnish European educations for his children.

As Nathaniel Hawthorne discovered to his singular dismay at the Custom House in Salem, however, the presidential election of General Zachary Taylor in 1848 conjured a swarm of Whig Party hangers-on seeking sinecures at home and abroad; despite Bartlett's own developing retinue of political supporters, he was unable to secure the position in Denmark. Other shifts in the political winds, though, soon played out in Bartlett's favor. In execution of article 5 of the Treaty of Guadalupe-Hidalgo, President Polk had appointed the Ohioan John B. Weller (succeeding the suddenly deceased Ambrose Sevier) as boundary commissioner, who was discharged of his duties by President Taylor in December 1849. For a short period, the vaunted explorer and disgraced hero of the U.S.-Mexico War John C. Frémont had been designated as Weller's successor to the post of commissioner. Frémont regarded his appointment as vindication following his 1847 court-marital for insubordination during the U.S.-Mexico War but resigned abruptly to become the first United States senator from the newly chartered state of California. In the midst of this climate of political upheaval, Bartlett made his play. Enlisting the favor of those allies he had already begun to cultivate the year before, Bartlett lobbied for the further support of Jefferson Davis of Mississippi, Thomas Hart Benton of Missouri, Stephen A. Douglas of Illinois, and his long-standing acquaintance John C. Clarke of Rhode Island, the latter making a speech on the floor of the Senate in favor of Bartlett's appointment.

From the scene of these political maneuverings, Bartlett wrote cryptically of recent developments ripening to his favor in a letter to his friend Evert Duyckinck in January 1849. The position of boundary commissioner now a concrete possibility, he predicted boldy to Duyckinck in January 1849,:"If I can carry out a scheme which is now on the carpet, I shall be able to do more for American Ethnology, than has been done by any one, not even excepting Humboldt or Squier."[22] Bartlett formally accepted his appointment on June 19, 1850, at an annual salary of three thousand dollars and lost little time in orchestrating the logistics of the endeavor to optimize his opportunities for ethnological field research. Having conferred personally with Secretary of the Interior Thomas Ewing to advocate for a "through exploration of the wide district about to be traversed, in connection with the survey of the Boundary," Bartlett composed the first draft of his own official instructions, "which being in accordance with [Ewing's] own views he authorized me to give him ... and my instructions were prepared accordingly, not varying in the least from my own draft."[23] If so, the reach and complexity of those instructions would constitute a formidable burden. In addition to the encouragement of "every opportunity afforded by your passage through the unexplored regions of Texas, New Mexico, and California, to acquire information as to its geography [and] natural history," they conveyed special instructions to survey an eligible southern route for a transcontinental railroad, and to collect information "relative to the precious metals, quicksilver, and the various minerals, ores, and other substances, useful in the arts ... as well as the locations of mines formerly worked by the early settlers in California and New Mexico, and since abandoned, owing to the incursions of the Indians" (*Personal Narrative*, 2:590). In this light, Bartlett's agenda as the U.S. commissioner was subject to multiple, sometimes conflicting agendas: establishing the borderline; prospecting for precious metals; surveying a railroad; advancing knowledge of the natural history of the region; and, finally, his own long-deferred ambition to realize a substantive and original contribution to the field of ethnology in print.

At the end of June, the latter aim was strongly on his mind. Within a week of Bartlett's appointment, Henry Rowe Schoolcraft informed him that, on behalf of the Indian Bureau, he had recommended to the secretary of the interior a supplemental appropriation in the amount of twenty-five thousand dollars "to collect by a special agent statistical & historical facts of the tribes north of the Gila & east of the Colorado," advising him further that Secretary Ewing was fully supportive of this plan.[24] Given that the region identified for this special research expenditure was specifically the area that carried such compelling linguistic interest for Gallatin in his communications with Emory in 1847, its designation here surely followed Bartlett's personal recommendation. Moreover, considering that the initial appropriation for the Boundary Survey itself was fifty thousand dollars (a figure that would soon prove grossly inadequate), this proposal of a supplemental expenditure of twenty-five thousand dollars indicates concretely the degree of emphasis devoted by the federal government to the cause of ethnological investigation—in addition to the confidence it placed in Bartlett as the party to conduct it.[25] To execute his plan, Bartlett proceeded by surrounding himself with men who shared his passion for literary and scientific matters. Bartlett first approached his friend George H. Moore, librarian of the New-York Historical Society, to serve as the commission secretary, the position vested with the responsibility of documenting the work of the commission in the field. Owing to problems of health and ongoing family concerns, however, Moore was obliged to refuse. Bartlett then approached an old friend, the physician Dr. Thomas H. Webb, now secretary of the Massachusetts Historical Society, to serve in that post. Bartlett had been a close scholarly associate of Webb for many years, both having been among the original founders of the Providence Athenaeum in 1831 (Webb began as secretary; Bartlett, treasurer). In addition, they were both involved in the Franklin Society in Providence, the Rhode Island Historical Society, and, among other joint projects, had traveled to document the inscriptions on Dighton Rock at the request of the Royal Society of Northern Antiquaries in Copenhagen in 1834.

Word of Bartlett's appointment spread quickly, and he was feted with letters of congratulation and advice from an international coterie of ethnological researchers and amateur theorists, among them Squier, the anatomist Samuel George Morton, the linguist William Wadden Turner, and Meriwether Lewis Clark Sr. Charles C. Rafn, of the Royal Society of Northern Antiquaries in Copenhagen, offered congratulations on Bartlett's appointment and heralded his unique opportunity "to collect important facts toward the enrichment of ethnological, philological, and archaeological science," requesting further that Bartlett act as an agent of the Royal Society in collecting "Mexican antiquities and ethnographical objects" for their collections and propose for membership "active and eminent individuals" he should encounter from the Southwest.[26] Captain James Edward Alexander of the British army, author of numerous well-regarded works documenting his travels in Asia, Russia, and the Middle East, and honorary member of AES, wrote to Bartlett in the field in 1851 to suggest, in a similar vein, that "your position will be one much to be envied, if you complete, satisfactorily, all you intend," adding that he had been sending newspaper clippings tracking Bartlett's progress to the Royal Ethnological Society in London. Rafn and Alexander shared another prediction: enormous and unfailing success. In Rafn's words, "the interesting discoveries you cannot fail to make" would be gratifyingly received by him and the Royal Society; as Alexander put it, "I only fear you will have so much material 'to work up at the end of your enterprise, that you will have difficulty in selecting what will make [the] most interesting tomes."[27]

Problems of Inscription: Geographies and Narrative

As things would turn out, the literary and scientific fame predicted by Bartlett, Alexander, and Rafn did not materialize in the form envisioned. On April 24, 1851, in the desert near what is now Doña Ana, New Mexico, John Russell Bartlett buried a sarsaparilla bottle in the sand and, with it, unwittingly, the possibility that he might realize his long-held dream of becoming the American Humboldt. Present also on this occasion was Bartlett's Mexican counterpart, General Pedro Garcia Condé, and other members of the Mexican delegation. At the time, April 24 was celebrated jointly by the bilateral Boundary Commission as an important moment of accord; by mutual agreement, Bartlett and Condé had established Doña Ana as the "initial point" of the international boundary—the point, that is, at which the border between the United States and Mexico was to depart from the physical course of the Rio Grande and proceed westward according to the virtual terrain of latitude, along what Bartlett and his team called "the imaginary line." Placing a document delineating the "initial point," effected as binding by their signatures and those of the two surveyors appointed to the respective commissions, inside the sarsaparilla bottle along with a pebble chipped from the Washington Monument, the physical burial of the bottle at the site burnished with the trappings of ritualistic ceremony a performative speech act—here is Mexico; here is the

United States—that would prove highly consequential, as well as personally costly to Bartlett.[28]

Amid a host of alternately tragic and squalid events straining the early work of the commission in its first year under Bartlett's tenure (murders, insubordination, inebriate incapacity), Bartlett's actions in determining the boundary line between Chihuahua and New Mexico generated (certainly unfairly) a lasting and notorious reputation of incompetence, recklessness, and vanity. At principal issue was an ambiguous determination of the Treaty of Guadalupe-Hidalgo itself. Article 5 of the treaty stipulates that the new international boundary, to be delineated cooperatively by a joint binational commission,

> shall commence in the Gulf of Mexico, three leagues from land, opposite the mouth of the Rio Grande, otherwise called Rio Bravo del Norte, or opposite the mouth of its deepest branch, if it should have more than one branch emptying into the sea; from thence, up the middle of that river, following the deepest channel, where it has more than one to the point where it strikes the Southern Boundary of New Mexico; thence, westwardly along the whole Southern Boundary of New Mexico (which runs north of the town called *Paso*) to its western termination.[29]

The "southern boundary of New Mexico" had been predetermined by the plenipotentiaries to the treaty and laid down on the official map of the treaty—the so-called "Disturnell Map" of 1847. However, when Bartlett met with the Mexican Boundary Commission, headed by his counterpart, General Pedro Garcia Condé, in El Paso del Norte (present-day Ciudad Juárez, Chihuahua), in November 1850, they discovered two significant errors: whereas the Disturnell Map locates El Paso at 32 degrees, 15 minutes north latitude, its true position was found to be 31 degrees, 45 minutes—some 40 miles south of its indicated position on the map; second, the Disturnell Map locates the Rio Grande well over one hundred miles east of its actual terrestrial course (see figure 5.1). Rather than recalibrating the boundary according to the actual, physical location of El Paso, which was invoked by name in the treaty (and which strikes most as the commonsense solution), Bartlett and Condé fashioned a compromise based on the Disturnell Map's erroneous calculations of latitude. The result was to extend the southern boundary of New Mexico west from the Rio Grande from an "initial point" of 32 degrees, 20 minutes, at Doña Ana—approximately 45 miles north of present-day El Paso, Texas (see

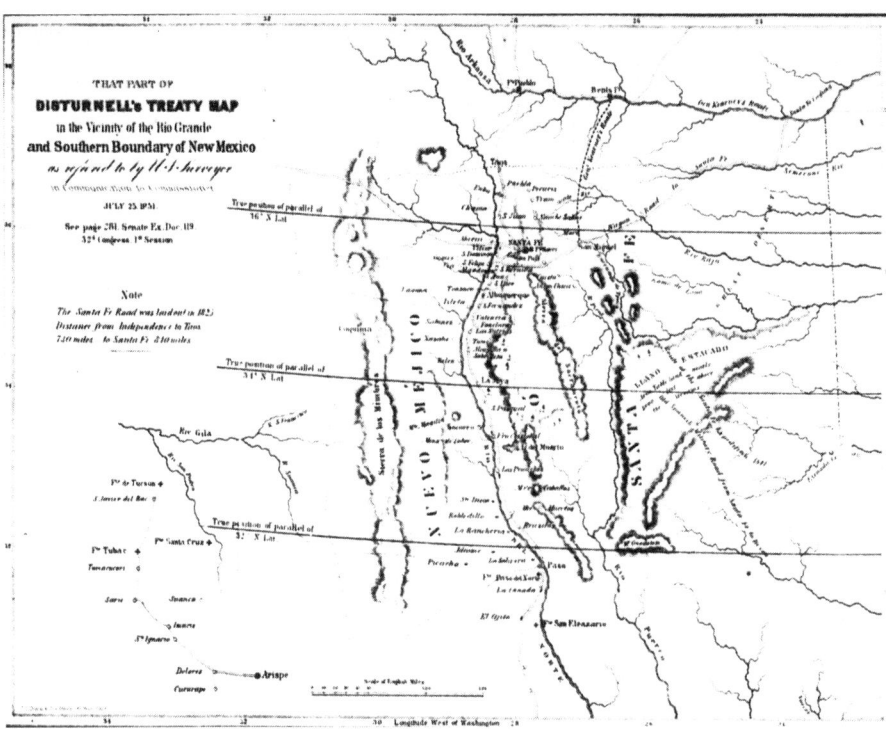

Figure 5.1. "That Part of Disturnell's Treaty Map in the Vicinity of the Rio Grande and Southern Boundary of New Mexico, as referred to by U.S. Surveyor in Communication with Commissioner. July 25, 1851." Sen. Exec. Doc. 119, 32nd Cong., 1st Sess. Washington, 1852. Source: Proquest U.S. Serial Set Digital Collection (Historical Full Text). April 1, 2011. Copyright ProQuest, LLC. All rights reserved. Reprinted with permission.

figure 5.2). News of Bartlett's compromise prompted widespread accusations of cowardice, perfidy, and incompetence—particularly among congressional Democrats (among them John B. Weller, who had been dismissed from the position of boundary commissioner by Zachary Taylor, and who was now a senator from California), who accused Bartlett of treacherous collusion with antislavery interests in the North (Bartlett was a Whig and had opposed the U.S.-Mexico War to begin with). From one point of view, their outrage was not without cause. In effect, Bartlett's compromise determination of the "initial point" of the southern New Mexico boundary at Doña Ana conceded back to Mexico an area of land roughly the size of Massachusetts and Rhode Island combined, including

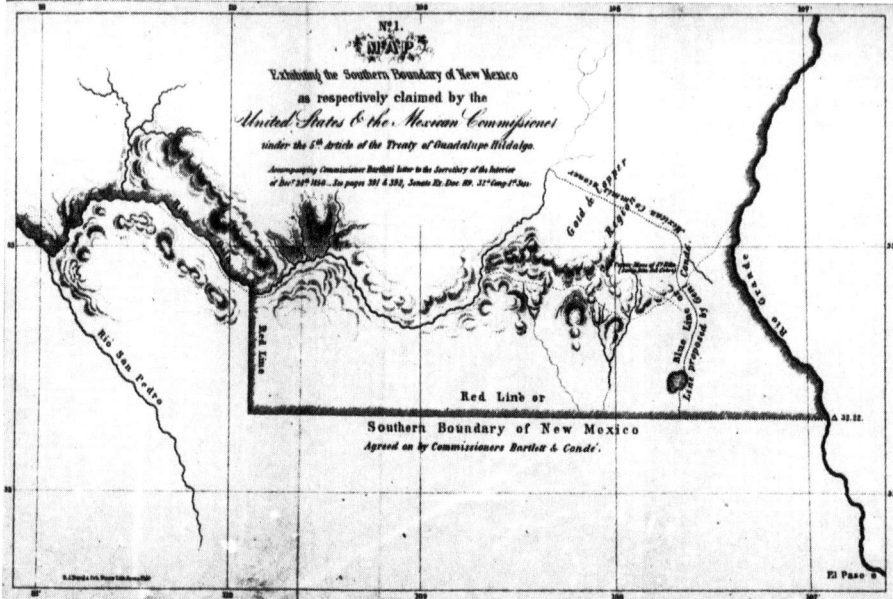

Figure 5.2. "No. 1 Map Extending the Southern Boundary of New Mexico as respectively claimed by the United States & the Mexican Commissions under the 5th Article of the Treaty of Guadalupe-Hidalgo." Sen. Exec. Doc. 119, 32nd Cong., 1st Sess. Source: Proquest U.S. Serial Set Digital Collection (Historical Full Text). April 1, 2011. Copyright ProQuest, LLC. All rights reserved. Reprinted with permission. The "initial point," on the Rio Grande at Doña Ana (32.22), is marked at the eastern terminus of the "Red Line"; the Santa Rita Copper Mines are marked here just west of the 108th latitude, south of the 33rd parallel.

the Mesilla Valley, considered by many to offer the most promising route for the construction of a southern transcontinental railroad (Bartlett, *Personal Narrative*, vi–x).[30]

Although an argument can be made that Bartlett's actions were the best interpretation of the letter of the treaty (this, at least, was the opinion of Nicholas Trist, who had negotiated the Treaty of Guadalupe-Hidalgo),[31] his concession to Condé secured his lasting infamy, and he was eventually forced to resign his post and dissolve the commission in January 1853. After two-and-a-half years of fieldwork in the borderlands, Bartlett's greatest ambition had been to publish an account of his service and the fruits of his research into natural history and ethnology under the august imprimatur of the United States Congress. In addition to his field notes and numerous fine sketches and drawings, Bartlett had compiled twenty-five vocabularies of American Indian tribes during his time on the border, consisting of two hundred common words.[32] Although his cause was advanced by Sam Houston in the Senate, this hope was dashed by congressional Democrats who regarded Bartlett as a disgrace and feared he would use such an opportunity to air his grievances against those who had maligned him. Denied the official sanction of the government, Bartlett arranged subsequently with the New York publishing firm of D. Appleton and Company to recast his field notes within the framework of a "personal" rather than "official" record. The publication, in two volumes, is titled *Personal Narrative of Explorations and Incidents in Texas, New Mexico, California, Sonora and Chihuahua, Connected with the United States and Mexican Boundary Commission, 1850–53.*

The lengthy title of Bartlett's *Narrative* might easily be overlooked, but what begs closer scrutiny manner in which the title displaces the multiple, overlapping agendas of the commission and of the ethnological project onto the category of "the personal." Reconstituted as a "narrative" according to the spatial and temporal horizons of "explorations" and "incidents," the sphere of "the personal" is suspended on an ambiguous authorial boundary line with respect to the conspicuous metonymy that comprises the last part of the title, *Connected with the United States and Mexican Boundary Commission.* In this sense, the publication of the *Personal Narrative* under the Appleton imprint, and the complex semantics of its title, register the text's genealogy as a rejected official history. At the same time, the letter of Bartlett's text itself manifests repeatedly the representational dynamics of displacement, dislocation, and ambiguous association embedded in the book's title. Having already been definitively frustrated in his effort to establish an imaginary boundary line as the U.S. commissioner, Bartlett-as-author finds that the boundaries that define his literary project are no less difficult to locate. This is most acutely visible in Bartlett's efforts to navigate the interface between empirical data and the literary conventions of narrative form. Indeed, throughout the narrative, Bartlett avows repeatedly that the limited mandate of "the personal" requires him to suspend the "objective" stance of scientific reportage; yet it is precisely at these moments that his ethnological agenda emerges most prominently as an organizing principle of his "narrative" and colludes most explicitly with the official agenda as the boundary commissioner.

Following the establishment of the problematic "initial point" at Doña Ana, the Boundary Commission encamped at the Santa Rita Copper Mines in May 1851. Located roughly 140 miles northeast of El Paso del Norte, the mines had been intermittently productive for more than a half century; as such, a careful evaluation of their continued viability would be highly relevant to Bartlett's instructions to ascertain "locations of mines formerly worked by the early settlers in California and New Mexico, and since abandoned, owing to the incursions of the Indians" (*Personal Narrative*, 1:325). What was more, the Copper Mines were within reach of that vicinity of the Gila River that had focused Gallatin's attentions four years prior and that (as we have seen) had been designated explicitly for a special survey of local tribes following Bartlett's appointment. There, Bartlett's team encountered the Mimbreño band of the Apache, who encamped near the commission's headquarters and were daily visitors during the three months of the commission's initial residence at the mines. They were led by the redoubtable chief Mangas Coloradas (or "Red Sleeves," as he was sometimes called)—a figure who would soon assume a prominent role both as Bartlett's political adversary and as a subject of his ethnological speculations.[33] Upon introducing them to the *Narrative*, Bartlett alludes first to their appearance, traditional homelands, and patterns of gender relations, then interrupts his narrative to suggest that, "there is much to be said relative to them all, which the limits of this work will not admit of, nor does it seem proper in a 'personal narrative' of incidents, to enter into the broad field of ethnological investigation which presents itself west of the Rocky Mountains" (1:325). Following this declaration, however, Bartlett immediately embarks on just the sort of ethnological disquisition he has just disavowed as improper—delineating their similarities and differences from the Navajo and advancing the argument, on grounds of linguistic similarity, that the Apache are the southernmost descendants of the Athapaskan speakers of Alaska. It is here that new conceptual boundary lines begin to emerge:

> The Apaches with which we have had intercourse must rank below the Indian tribes east of the Rocky Mountains, dwelling on the tributaries of the Mississippi and Missouri Rivers. They are without dignified bearing, and those noble traits of character, which characterize the latter; and as they perform no labor, not even that of hunting, their physical developments are greatly inferior. Mangus Colorado [*sic*], and a few other prominent chiefs, who live pretty well, and have the lion's share of their plunder, are rather good-looking; and a finer set of children than those of Mangus, of Dalgadito, and Poncé, are not often seen. But beyond these few exceptions, the Apaches are an ill-formed, emaciated, and miserable looking race. (1:326–27)

Bartlett then goes on to correlate their physical malformation to a culture of immorality, emphasizing the commonplace view of a notorious Apache propensity to thievery. He attributes this general condition of depravity to their want of agriculture—from his point of view the prerequisite of moral civilization—and the signal characteristic he uses to differentiate the Apache from the Navajo. And yet, here too, the categorical borders of ethnological classification fail him in his efforts to locate boundaries between the peoples he encounters. When a band of Navajo arrive at their encampment, he finds that their similarities of dress, customs, and habits of treachery make them virtually indistinguishable from the Apache of Mangas Coloradas's band. Even the famous and distinctive Navajo blanket, which he esteems as being "superior to any native fabric I have ever seen" and finds to be "quite equal to the best English blankets," is not a reliable index of cultural difference—instead, he voices uncertainty about their comparative quality by mentioning a rumor that the "richer colors" of their blankets may in fact be threads unraveled from cloths of English manufacture and woven into their own (1:330).

Borders, Persons, and Literary Representation

Such anxieties about the permeability of ethnic and national boundaries repeatedly trouble the surface of Bartlett's narrative, doubling his own anxieties about the boundaries of "the personal" even as the work of the commission reflects the technical difficulty of enforcing boundary lines drawn on a faulty map. As Alex Hunt has argued in his discussion of William Emory (Bartlett's eventual successor as boundary commissioner), "the production of geographical space [hinges] on the relationship of imaginative, scientific, and political constructions," one that, "in romantic fashion attempts to unify cartography with biology and other natural sciences to map the space of the nation in such a way that it confirms the ideology of manifest destiny."[34] Bartlett's actions in the field, and the literary representation of those acts that followed them, clearly aspire to this unifying sense of ideological confirmation. But Bartlett's account is haunted throughout by the disastrous political compromise over the "initial point." Throughout the *Personal Narrative*, the epistemological and ideological dimensions of romantic science, cartography, and imperial power do not cohere, and the imaginative completion of a newly inscribed national space is never fully realized. Instead, boundary lines between science, persons, and nations persist—and, in their unreconciled persistence, suggest the degree to which the interlocking components of national space rely upon a construct of authoritative national personhood to organize and unify them all in the field of representation. The ideal version of national personhood entails a virtual disappearance of individuality, a disavowal of personal agency in favor of legal protocols and institutional procedures that may speak through the person. But when science, cartography, and power fail to unify into a coherent national image, that form of personhood is destabilized as well. In this concluding section, I want to explore the shifting contours of personhood Bartlett projects for himself in the *Personal Narrative* in two parallel episodes involving Indian captivity: one, involving negotiations with the Apache band led by Mangas Coloradas, in which Bartlett strives to maintain a stance of neutral objectivity that might unify the joint prerogatives of ethnology and nationhood in a careful orchestration of speech acts; and the second, a scene of reunion between the rescued captive Inez Gonzales and her Mexican family, in which Bartlett's neutral objectivity vanishes in favor of a style of intimate personal engagement in which classifiable speech acts are supplanted by the wordless, emotional parameters of literary sentimentality.

The first episode begins with a dramatic confrontation between Bartlett and a group of Apache chiefs, led by Mangas Coloradas, in which Bartlett, as commissioner, was called upon to execute his enforcement powers as the ranking United States agent of the Treaty of Guadalupe-Hidalgo respecting new proscriptions on American Indian actions against citizens of Mexico. Given the significance of Mangas Coloradas as a party to these events, a brief delineation of his background is warranted. His reputation was formidable. In his 1868 memoir of expeditionary life in the Southwest, *Life among the Apaches*, John Cremony, Bartlett's official translator on the Boundary Commission, evoked him with a mythic combination of transcendent and terrible qualities: Mangas Coloradas was "the greatest and most talented Apache Indian of the nineteenth century," with a "subtle and comprehensive intellect," and whose "sagacious counsels partook more of the character of wide and enlarged statesmanship than those of any other Indian of modern times"; yet his life, "if ever it could be ascertained, would be a tissue of the most extensive and afflicting revelations, the most atrocious cruelties, the most vindictive revenges, and widespread injuries ever perpetrated by an American Indian."[35] Renowned both for his abilities of military strategy and political skill in coordinating with the Chiricahua Apache and Navajo across wide stretches New Mexico and

Arizona, Mangas Coloradas forcefully resisted first Mexican, then U.S. incursions into the traditional homelands of the Mimbreño Band of the Apache in the vicinity of the Santa Rita Copper Mines and Gila River in southwestern New Mexico.[36]

In the wake of the U.S.-Mexico War, Mangas Coloradas developed a powerful military and political alliance with Cochise of the Chiricahua Apache and ramped up coordinated actions against white settlers and travelers moving west to California—movements that escalated the urgency of U.S. Calvary efforts to subdue him. He died shortly after being captured, under a false flag of truce, by Captain Edmond Shirland of the California First Volunteer Cavalry in January 1863 and conveyed quickly to Fort McLean, in Arizona. There, as has been widely documented, he was tortured and then murdered by two sentries during the night of his arrival, who pressed hot bayonets against his flesh before shooting him for attempting to "escape" their treatment.[37] Following his death, Mangas Coloradas was decapitated and the flesh boiled from his skull by Captain D. B. Sturgeon, the fort physician; Sturgeon shipped his skull to the futurist and phrenologist Orson Squire Fowler, in New York, who proclaimed that Mangas Coloradas's skull was "monstrous" in size, exhibiting unprecedented endowments of "Secretion, Caution, [and] Destruction," and evidenced "Cunning" that "far exceeds any other development of it I have ever seen, even in any and all Indian heads. It is simply monstrous."[38] When Mangas Coloradas met John Russell Bartlett in May 1851, his gruesome dismemberment and posthumous enlistment in a macabre phrenological pageant would be more than a decade away. Nevertheless, Fowler's magical production of unprecedentedly "monstrous" qualities of "Secretion, Caution, Destruction... [and] Cunning" in Mangas Coloradas's skull—not unlike the fantasy of a "hive of subtlety" within the decapitated head of Babo at the end of Melville's *Benito Cereno*—offers an uncanny coda to a sequence of events that would play out at the Santa Rita Copper Mines involving the rescue of two captive Mexican boys and a captive Mexican girl.

On a hot afternoon late in June, more than a month after the commission's arrival, two naked and terrified Mexican boys named Savero Aredia (approximately thirteen years old) and José Trinfan (between ten and twelve years old) rushed into the tent of the translator John Cremony and begged for his protection. The boys were prisoners of the Mimbreño Apache (Aredia for six months; Trinfan, six years), both having been captured from their homes in the State of Sonora (with which the Apache had been in a state of war for several years). In Cremony's version of events, he quickly armed himself with four revolvers, outfitted his assistant with a carbine rifle and double-barreled shotgun, and then proceeded slowly, the men back to back with the boys shielded on either side, from the peripheral location of his tent to Bartlett's headquarters—all the while surrounded by "thirty or forty" Apache, who, "with menacing words and gestures, demanded the instant release of their captives."[39] Article 11 of the Treaty of Guadalupe-Hidalgo declares, "It shall not be lawful, under any pretext whatever, for any inhabitant of the United States, to purchase or acquire any Mexican or any foreigner residing in Mexico, who may have been captured by Indians inhabiting the territory of either of the two Republics"; moreover, the treaty requires that, "in the event of any person or persons, captured within Mexican territory by Indians, being carried into the territory of the United States, the Government of the latter engages and binds itself, in the most solemn manner, so soon as it shall know of such captives being within it's [sic] territory, and shall be able so to do, through the faithful exercise of it's influence and power, to rescue them, and return them to their country, or deliver them to the agent or representative of the Mexican Government."[40] As the U.S. commissioner in charge of enforcing those aspects of the treaty connected to boundary disputes, Bartlett was obliged to act. Cognizant of the legitimate possibility that the Apache (who, now split between two camps, surrounded and outnumbered the commission and its small military detachment) would mount a retaliation and attempt to recapture the boys, Bartlett conveyed Aredia and Trinfan to General Condé's encampment the same evening and awaited further developments. Following a tense interval, a delegation of the Apache headed by Mangas Coloradas, and including the chiefs Dalgadito and Ponce, approached the commission headquarters a few days later to state their grievances and demand the restoration of the boys to their custody.

The negotiations with Mangas Coloradas, Dalgadito, and Ponce that followed reveal extraordinary incongruities in the legal constitution of an ill-defined borderlands, in which nonconsenting agents (the Apache, who were neither party to the negotiation of the treaty, nor accorded legal autonomy by it) are made subject to the ambiguous jurisdiction of an area of land yet persisting in national territorial limbo (the set of cartographical and signatory acts constituting the work of the binational Boundary Commission had not, after all, completed its enactment of the international border). These negotiations are likewise accorded extraordinary formal treatment in Bartlett's representation of them in the *Personal Narrative*. Abandoning the literary technique of first-person narrative that otherwise carries the book, Bartlett chooses at this point to represent negotiations in the form of dramatic dialogue, a conspicuous departure of method that throws into relief the layered ironies of their interaction. This choice, Bartlett suggests, stems from the intrinsic ethnological interest of the episode, and he offers it "therefore at length, as the arguments used by my opponents display to good advantage their natural shrewdness of character":

> *Mangus Colorado* [sic]: Why did you take our captives from us?
> *Commissioner*: Your captives came to us and demanded our protection.
> *Mangus Colorado*: You came to our country. You were well received by us. Your lives, your property, your animals, were safe. You passed by ones, by twos, and by threes, through our country; you went and came in peace. Your strayed animals were always brought home to you again. Our wives, our children, and women, came here and visited your houses. We were friends! We were brothers! Believing this, we came amongst you and brought our captives, relying on it that we were brothers, and that you would feel as we feel. We concealed nothing. We came here not secretly or in the night. We came in open day and before your faces, and we showed our captives to you. We believed your assurances of friendship, and we trusted them. Why did you take our captives from us?
> *Commissioner*: What we have said to you is true and reliable. We do not tell lies. The greatness and dignity of our nation forbids our doing so mean a thing. What our great brother has said is true, and good also. (1:312–13)

Mangas Coloradas presses the legitimacy of his grievance according to two modes of argument. The first is political, premised on a claim of sovereign occupancy—"you came into our country"—a point Bartlett does not explicitly challenge. The second follows from the unwritten obligations of hospitality; because the Apache had not encroached upon the lives or property of the commission (and had, in fact, taken steps to protect them), a reciprocity of noninterference was expected. Embedded in this is a discourse of sympathetic identification, a trust that "you would feel as we feel." Although this trust would appear to have been unavailing in this circumstance, it is worth noting here in light of Bartlett's own valorization of the power of sympathy in a contrasting episode regarding the Indian captive Inez Gonzales (discussed below). Bartlett eschews Mangas Coloradas's bid for emotional kinship here, promoting instead a myth of U.S. incapacity for mendacity. Explaining to the Apache delegation the background of the commission's treaty obligations (while the Apache were at war with Sonora, the United States was at war with the nation of Mexico, which, now peacefully concluded, obligates protection), Bartlett pledged friendship and protection to the Apache, "and we will give it to you. If we had not done so to Mexico, you could not have believed us with regard to yourselves. We cannot lie" (1:313). Bartlett is then interrupted by the chief Ponce, who accompanied Mangas Coloradas's delegation:

> *Ponce*: Yes, but you took our captives from us without beforehand cautioning us. We were ignorant of this promise to restore the captives. They were made prisoners in lawful warfare. They belong to us. They are our property. Our people have also been made captive by the Mexicans. If we had known of this thing, we should not have come here. We should not have placed that confidence in you.
>
> *Commissioner*: Our brother speaks angrily, and without due reflection. Boys and women lose their temper, but men reflect and argue; and he who has reason and justice on his side, wins. I have no doubt but that you have suffered much from the Mexicans. This is a question in which it is impossible for us to tell who is right, or who is wrong. You and the Mexicans accuse each other of being the aggressors. Our duty is to fulfil [sic] our promise to both. This opportunity enables us to show to Mexico that we mean what we say; and when the time comes, we will be ready and prompt to prove the good faith of our promises to you.
>
> *Ponce*: I am neither a boy nor a squaw. I am a man and a brave. I speak with reflection. I know what I say. I speak of the wrongs we have suffered and those you now do to us. (Very much excited.) You must not speak any more. Let some one else speak (addressing himself to Mr. Cremony, the interpreter).
>
> *Commissioner*: I want you to understand that *I* am the very one to speak; the only one here who can speak (peremptorily). Now do *you* sit down. I will hold no more talk with you, but will select a *man* (beckoning to Dalgadito.) Do you come here and speak for your nation. (1:315–16, emphasis in original)

Like Mangas Coloradas, Ponce is clear in his argument: the boys were prisoners captured in the course of lawful military engagement and held the status of property. As synecdoches of the body of the Mexican nation, the boys stood thus in precisely the same relation to the Apache as the greater Southwest stood then to the United States—bodies taken by right of force and accorded the status of legal possession by virtue of that force. Whether Bartlett was sensitive to this irony is unclear; what is clear is that he responded to Ponce's challenge with a hyperbolic attack on his masculinity, drawing on his ethnologically informed assumptions about equations of honor, sobriety, and rationality in idealized forms of male Apache identity. In his forceful dismissal of Ponce and enlistment of Dalgadito as a proper "*man*," however, Bartlett inadvertently acknowledges both the Apaches' right and ability to participate in a mode of deliberative rationality that promises to ensure a fair outcome to an open and neutral contest of arguments ("he who has reason and justice on his side, wins"). This is a remarkably bold fiction given: (*a*) neither the Apache nor any other Indian tribe was accorded autonomous recognition in the treaty that "ended" what had been and still was, in fact, a multilateral conflict; and, (*b*) the outcome of this particular contest with respect to the custody of the boys ("reason and justice" notwithstanding) was already decided.[41] In order to resolve the conflict finally (and to preserve the illusion of open-ended negotiation), Bartlett then offered up a Mexican man to buy the boys (which would not violate the treaty) and negotiated then on the man's behalf; in response, Dalgadito eventually proposed the figure of twenty horses as compensation. Bartlett replied: "The Apache laughs at his white brother! He thinks him a squaw, and that he can play with him as an arrow! Let the Apache say again" (1:316). What seems notable, even astonishing, is the brazenness of Bartlett's ethnic pantomime in this reply (which was, it should be noted, delivered to Cremony in English, who then translated it into Spanish, not Apache). As if pressing the rhetorical advantage gained by his previous insult of Ponce as a "squaw," Bartlett escalates his approximation of Apache oral style by deploying the word again, this time in a compressed form of diction that seems lifted from one of the Cooper novels he had loved in his youth.[42]

Bartlett's scrupulous transcription (and crude imitation) of Apache speech casts them simultaneously as the objects of a linguistic model of ethnological speculation (their "natural shrewdness of character" is legible in speech acts) and as potent political adversaries (whose "natural shrewdness" and unmasculine emotionalism might be countered through active rationality and adroit use of rhetoric). Like his previous encounter with Chipota, the Lipan chief, in which Bartlett relies on the agency of government documents to frame the terms of Indian encounter, the Treaty of Guadalupe-Hidalgo serves here as a legal foundation from which ethnological observation and the rhetoric of imperial power are coordinated and leveraged most powerfully. The combination of these elements is important, and it contrasts markedly (both in content and manner of representation) to a parallel episode of Indian captivity that occurred just a few days earlier and that would "long awaken the finest sympathies of our nature; and by its happy result afforded a full recompense for the trials and hardships attending our sojourn in this inhospitable wilderness" (1:303). On the evening of June 27, 1851, a party of New Mexican traders stopped at the commission's headquarters to acquire provisions; accompanying the party was a young Mexican girl named Inez Gonzales. Interviews with this company and their leader, a man named Peter Blacklaws, established her identity as Inez Gonzales of Santa Cruz, in Sonora, who had been captured ten months prior by a band of Piñal Indians (a tribe related to the Apache, located north of the Gila) on a raid into Sonora while she traveled with her family to the town of Madelena; she had been purchased subsequently by Blacklaws, who asserted his right of possession by virtue of his Indian trading license and planned to convey her to Santa Fe for profit. Acting on the authority of article 11 of the Treaty of Guadalupe-Hidalgo, Bartlett directed Lieutenant Colonel Lewis S. Craig, ranking officer of the commission's eighty-five-man military escort, to liberate Gonzales and place her in the protective custody of the commission. Bartlett and the commission were highly solicitous toward their "fair captive," who, as Bartlett described her, "was young, artless, and interesting in appearance, prepossessing in manners, and by her deportment gave evidence that she had been carefully brought up" (1:304). Having been provided with such new clothes as the commission could furnish in the field, "she received many presents from the gentlemen of the Commission, all of whom manifested a deep interest in her welfare, and seemed desirous to make her comfortable and happy" (1:309). Gonzales remained with the commission for nearly three months, while the survey of the Gila River was completed, and embarked with them on a journey south in September, where Bartlett had arranged to meet his counterpart, General Garcia Condé at Santa Cruz, with a corollary plan to restore her to her family.

Not unlike his rendition of his negotiations with the Apache, Bartlett's depiction of the reunion of Inez Gonzales with her family stands out in the text as a significant departure from the literary protocols that otherwise govern the *Personal Narrative*. But, whereas Bartlett eschews first-person narrative and representations of interiority in his transcription of the Apache negotiation, Bartlett commits here to the conventions of literary sentimentality to evoke the effusive emotional dynamics of the scene of reunion. Upon their approach to Santa Cruz, the commission encountered Gonzales's father and uncle by chance among a large party of Mexican workers hunting wild cattle near the San Pedro River. Bartlett here records the scene of the reunion of daughter and father, who had not yet learned of her rescue, in the following manner:

> The joy of the father and friends in again beholding the face of her whom they supposed was forever lost from them, was unbounded. Each in turn (rough and half naked as many of them were), embraced her after the Spanish custom; and it was long ere one could utter a word. Tears of joy burst from all; and the sun-burnt and brawny men, in whom the finer feelings of our nature are wrongly supposed not to exist, wept like children, as they looked with astonishment on the rescued girl. She was not less overcome than they; and it was long before she could utter the name of her mother, and ask if she and her little brothers yet lived. The members of the Commission who witnessed this affectionate and joyful scene, could not but participate in the feelings of the poor child and her friends; and the big tears as they rolled down their weather-beaten and bearded faces, showed how fully they sympathized with the feelings of our Mexican friends. (1:399)

A number of details stand out at this moment. Making explicit the fact of racial difference of Mexican people in a manner that echoes conventional tropes concerning American Indians, Bartlett emphasizes the "rough and half naked" appearance of the "sun-burnt and brawny men, in whom the finer feelings of our nature are wrongly supposed not to exist." But if the supposed difference of Mexicans from "our nature" is disavowed, their natural difference from the Apache is asserted clearly. Possessed even at this charged and unguarded moment of a commendable attention to Old World manners (they embraced "after the Spanish custom"), they have lost utterly the power of speech. In Apache speech, character is made manifest; here, character is revealed by its absence. Moreover, Gonzales's surge of authentic emotion conscripts Bartlett and his company into a posture of complete sympathetic accord that affirms fundamental identity. The cultural meanings of this episode are reinforced by their repetition four days later, at the reunion of Inez with her mother (Inez, now accompanied by her father, remained with the commission for the conclusion of their journey). Within two miles of Santa Cruz, the commission encountered a small party "partly on mules and partly on foot," consisting of "the fair captive's mother, brothers, and uncle," who had been advised of her imminent return. Here is the relevant passage in full:

> As we drew nearer, Mr. Cremony helped Inez from the saddle, when in perfect ecstacy she rushed to her mother's arms. Words cannot express the joy manifested on this happy occasion. Their screams were painful to hear. The mother could scarcely believe what she saw; and after every embrace and gush of tears, she withdrew her arms to gaze on the face of her child. I have witnessed many scenes on the stage, of the meeting of friends after along separation, and have read highly-wrought narratives of similar interviews, but none of them approached in pathos the spontaneous burst of feeling exhibited by the mother and daughter on this occasion. Thanks to the Almighty rose above all other sounds, while they remained clasped in each other's arms, for the deliverance from captivity, and the restoration of the beloved daughter to her home and friends. Although a joyful scene, it was a painfully affecting one to the spectators, not one of whom, could restrain his tears. After several minutes of silence, the fond parent embraced me, and the other gentlemen of the party, in succession, as we were pointed out by her daughter; a ceremony which was followed by her uncle, and the others, who had by this time joined us. We then remounted our animals and proceeded towards the town in silence; and it was long before either party could compose themselves sufficiently to speak. (402–3)

Here, speech is again made superfluous by a rising crescendo of sentiment, with the exception of "thanks to the Almighty, which rose above all other sounds." What binds the episode instead is pain—from the screams of joy that "were painful to hear" to the "painfully affecting" experience of ungovernable tears for the spectators. In this retrospective reconstruction of the scene, Bartlett is notably self-conscious of its seemingly melodramatic cast. Indexing this reunion according to a catalogue of literary models, Bartlett finds that neither experiences of the theater nor "highly-wrought narratives of similar interviews . . . approached in pathos the spontaneous burst of feeling" to which he is here both witness and participant. In this Bartlett qualifies literature as an inadequate prototype for the emotional life of an exotic borderlands setting. Yet by inviting readers of the *Personal Narrative* to gauge their appreciation of this episode in terms of melodramatic literary convention, Bartlett effectively domesticates the exotic within the realm of the familiar. In this he stages a model of sympathetic identification for which his 1850s readers were well conditioned, one in which the gaps of racial and linguistic difference are effectively bridged by shared understandings for which words are an unwelcome intrusion ("it was long before either party could compose themselves sufficiently to speak").

In each of these two sets of examples—negotiations with the Apache; and the scenes of reunion with Inez Gonzales's family—speech acts organize and distinguish parallel projects of racial classification. Undergirding each are Bartlett's long-standing investments as an ethnological researcher, for whom comparative linguistics represented the premier method of inquiring into human relations. Although Bartlett, like his mentor Gallatin, was a monogenist who believed that the findings of philology would vindicate a philosophical vision of human equality, the literary project of representing speech acts under the category of "the personal" ironically produces signs of racial difference. If reading "Indian sign" entails a rigorous attention to the manner in which Apache speech reveals their true character, it also provides a rationale for rejecting Apache overtures of sympathetic understanding, such as those offered by Mangas Coloradas. Residing somewhere beyond the explicitness of language, such understandings are not subject to the protocols of classification and review proper to Bartlett's reflexive scientific positivism and hence to be rejected. By contrast, Bartlett's emphasis on the fundamental sympathy of Mexican character in moments in which speech is conspicuously absent effectively cordons off Mexican peoples as objects of scientific classification. But here the erasure of boundaries of racial difference masks the inscription of boundaries of national difference. To exempt the Mexicans he encountered from acts of positivistic classification outwardly and significantly affirms their humanity, even as it elides the imperial context of territorial conquest represented by the work of the commission itself.

Where geographies (both physical and human) are uncertain, acts of national inscription are provisional, subject always to further recalculation. In Bartlett's narrative, the space of "the personal" fills the vacuum of national uncertainty. This illustrates, on one hand, a climate of failure—a displacement of conquest by compromise, national destiny by human error, and scientific confidence by uncooperative facts encountered in the field. But there is also a logic of compensation at work here, a literary substitution of personal sensibility for a national logic that is suddenly no longer self-evident or complete. Far from being an act of self-aggrandizement, Bartlett's emphasis on the space of "the personal" expresses a double-edged capitulation: discredited by Congress, he may no longer claim for his literary voice the finality of an embodied position of federal authority; but, lacking an adequate publishing opportunity to offer a comprehensive ethnological study, neither can his record of personal observations claim fully the mantle of scientific objectivity. Yet the space that remains is deeply connected to both. If Bartlett's *Personal Narrative* is neither fully national nor scientific in its authority, its oscillating styles of literary representation illustrate the degree to which American romantic personhood was already mapped onto the emotional cartographies of manifest destiny.[43] In the wordless reunion of Inez Gonzales with her family, Bartlett's affecting literary sensibility eclipses a scenario of national conquest, fostering a remarkable sense of personal immediacy with his readers. But here, deep in the Mexican territory of Sonora, Bartlett's triumphant story of family reunion physically moves beyond the contested territories of the U.S./Mexico borderlands, suggesting for his readers that the natural impulses of human justice—guaranteed by the upright conduct of heroic Americans—cannot be contained by arbitrary national borders but inevitably follow the course of manifest destiny to overspread the continent.

Indian Passports

> Hereafter other Indians from the East called Sarah's people "Say-do-Carah"—conquerors, because they had conquered and annihilated these terrible enemies. It is difficult to acount [sic] for the name "Piutes" that we gave the Say-do-carahs. It does not appear to be a word originating with the tribe itself. Fremont named their chief "Truckee," which signifies, "All right."
>
> —General Oliver O. Howard, "Causes of the Piute and Bannock War"

In closing, I want to return to the anecdote that opened chapter 5, in which Chipota, a chief of the Lipan Apache, encountered John Russell Bartlett in central Texas in 1850.[1] Chipota carried with him a collection of United States government documents, a passport of sorts, that certified the bearer's identity, social and political standing, and friendly status in relation to the United States and its citizens. Such documents, widely referred to as "Indian passports" in nineteenth-century literatures of encounter, served as an ad hoc and quasi-formal system through which Native identity was often classified and managed locally, within scenarios of white encounter and settler colonialism on the western borderlands. In returning to this figure for one final act of investigation, I want both to interrogate and to extend it—to reverse "Indian passports," in a sense, from their historical purpose and direction as a means of exploring the textual and performative relays between scenarios of borderlands encounter and schemes of literary representation that might suggest new pathways for reading and interpretation. To do so, I turn to Sarah Winnemucca's 1883 memoir, *Life among the Piutes: Their Wrongs and Claims*, a text in which such "passports" figure prominently and explore the manner in which Winnemucca's text renders explicit the bureaucratic protocols through which the legitimacy of Native identity, and the legitimacy of Native political dissent, were established in the national commons of print discourse. More specifically, I want to suggest that the protocols of literary authentication Winnemucca establishes for her memoir textually reenact the production and circulation of "Indian passports" across wide frontier spaces and reveal important connections between the formalisms of political sovereignty and the conditions of political recognition for nineteenth-century Native self-representations in literary discourse.

What drew me initially to this set of concerns is the striking if uncanny resemblance between her grandfather Truckee's "rag friend" (a personal testimonial from John C. Frémont he bore proudly, which is prominent in the early portion of the book and much discussed by scholars) and the sequence of testimonials from U.S. military officers vouching for Sarah Winnemucca's good service and loyal conduct during the 1878 Bannock War that form the text's appendix. That appendix—so reminiscent of the conventional attestations by white authorities for the authenticity of African American authorship (the other class of domestic persons required to bear passports in the nineteenth-century United States)—is full of interesting problems but also ripe with interpretive possibility for thinking about what Jace Weaver, Craig Womack, and Robert Warrior have termed "Native intellectual sovereignty" in nineteenth-century Native and U.S. national discourses.

Life among the Piutes exemplifies that subgenre of Native memoir that A. Lavonne Browne Ruoff termed "ethnoautobiography"—a work combining "myth, history, and contemporary events with tribal ethnohistory and personal experience."[2] Sarah Winnemucca, or Thocmetony, was born "somewhere near 1844," as she puts it in the opening lines of the book. The memoir covers some major events of her childhood in Nevada and California; the criminal mistreatment of the Northern Piutes by white settlers and Indian agents at Malheur and Yakima; the events of the Bannock War, during which time Winnemucca served as a guide and interpreter for General Oliver. O. Howard; and the onset of her political activism and lecturing career following the forced relocation of the Northern Piutes to the Yakima Reservation. The book was edited by, and published with the assistance of, Mary Peabody Mann, in 1883, who announced in its preface that it represents "the first outbreak of the American Indian in human literature"—a spirited assessment that, if not remotely accurate as a reflection of Native publication history, is remarkable for its evocatively combative tone (as in an "outbreak of Indian hostility") that also suggests that the emergence of an Indian literary voice may be contagious.[3] The early chapters of the book revolve around Sarah's grandfather, "Truckee," and his naïve welcome and adoration of the white settler colonists and military officers who will later author the "wrongs" of the book's title. Central to his character is his pride in a testimonial letter bestowed upon him by John C. Frémont for his role as a guide and fellow combatant against Mexican Californios during the U.S.-Mexico War. In Truckee's view, his "rag friend" possesses magical qualities that cannot be overestimated: "It was a paper, which he said could talk to him. He took it out and he would talk to it, and talk with it. He said, 'This can talk to all our white brothers, and our white sisters, and their children . . . [and] can travel like the wind and it can go and talk with their fathers and brothers'" (18–19). Throughout the early portions of the book, Truckee uses Frémont's letter as a "passport," furnishing it to every white person he meets to recommend his own character and to win gifts and safe passage for himself and his people. It becomes his most precious possession. Holding it up to heaven at one point and kissing it "as if it was really a person," he says, "Oh, if I should lose this . . . we shall all be lost"; on his deathbed, his last words are to request that his "rag friend" be placed on his breast at his burial (22).

Andrew McClure has suggested that Winnemucca's depiction of her grandfather's faith in the power of Fremont's "passport" is "pathetically" rendered; but Truckee's overestimation of the stability of the written word and the promise of good faith by the whites it represents is also, I think, the central trope of the book—one that invokes widespread practices for the textual marking of Native persons across the West throughout the mid-nineteenth century and, in that wider context, one that provides important clues to the ironic character of Winnemucca's own reliance on written testimonials to conclude her book.[4] In his 1859 emigrant guide, *The Prairie Traveler*, Captain Randolph Marcy speaks of the prevalence of such passports as that borne by Truckee across the southern Great Plains. The Indians, he writes, "are always desirous of procuring, from whomsoever they meet, testimonials of their good behavior, which they preserve with great care, and exhibit upon all occasions to strangers as a guarantee of future good conduct." As a specific example, Marcy cites his 1849 encounter with Senaco, a chief of the southern Comanches, near Abilene, Texas. Senaco, he writes,

> exhibited numerous certificates from the different white men he had met with, testifying to his friendly disposition. Among these was one that he desired me to read with special attention, as he said he was of the opinion

that perhaps it might not be so complimentary in its character as some of the others. It was in these words: "The bearer of this says he is a Comanche chief, named Senaco; that he is the biggest Indian and best friend the whites ever had; in fact, that he is a first-rate fellow; but I believe he is a damned rascal, *so look out for him*."[5]

Marcy plays this out for comedic effect, but the punch line makes a serious point: the joke is on Senaco; he is to be regarded warily, and the "passport" accomplishes its end. To cite another example, an almost identical experience is recorded by the German explorer Julius Froebel in his book, also published in 1859, *Seven Years' Travel in Central America, Northern Mexico, and the Far West of the United States*. Encountering the formidable chief of the Chiricahua Apaches, Mangas Coloradas, Froebel is presented with documents that proclaim:

> "The possessor of this paper is the *Red Sleeve*, a celebrated chief of the Apaches, who is on friendly terms with the whites. Travellers will do well to show him kindness and respect, but they must at the same time be on their guard." Under this is written the *visa* of travelling traders: "The *Red Sleeve* has visited our camp, and conducted himself, with his followers, respectably." Further on: "Do not trust this fellow—he is a rascally Indian." When such a voucher is presented to you, with that taciturn gravity of which an Indian only is capable, you are obliged to control your features like an Indian not to betray the humour of the thing,—an indiscretion which might have disagreeable consequences.[6]

Like Marcy, then, Froebel finds such documents worth little more than laughter and contempt. But Froebel's overall assessment of their purpose, though dismissive, is striking: they are, he says, "a ludicrous reverse of the passport system of the Old World, being at the same time the only passports met with in the United States."[7] In this characterization, significant underlying questions about the nature of sovereignty, literacy, indigenous self-representation, and political recognition emerge in explicit relief. The "Old World" passport system invoked by Froebel works by ritualizing and performing acknowledgments of mutual political sovereignty between states, summoning for the passport bearer the privileges of citizenship in foreign, yet commensurable, territories also marked as sovereign. Granting its bearer an official verification of identity, the traditional passport also reciprocally exercises the power of the state as the official entity endowed with the means to confer and guarantee an identity deserving of political and legal recognition by others.

How, then, by contrast, does the "ludicrous reverse" of the Indian passport operate in politically volatile borderlands regions, in settings of settler colonialism, wars of conquest, and projects of extermination and removal? If the "passport system of the Old World" performs mutual acknowledgments of sovereignty, Indian passports perform only a pantomime of political recognition. Capitalizing on Native illiteracy, the ad hoc system of Indian passports granted to their possessors only the threat of open-ended revision in which classifications of "peacable" may be converted by future travelers (official or unofficial) to "hostile," proper names to jeering epithets. In documents that converted their possessors into unwitting bearers of personalized graffiti, the examples of Seneco and Mangas Coloradas demonstrate the fundamental emptiness of Truckee's letter of commendation from John C. Frémont as recounted by Winnemucca. Indeed, "Truckee's" very name, as Oliver Howard writes in the epigraph to this epilogue, answers to an identical purpose, also having been bestowed by Frémont and meaning "All right." More than this, the very redundancy of these examples concisely illustrates the very *conventionality* of this informal protocol of colonial action—its utterly commonplace and hatefully routine *banality* across the indigenous borderlands of the nineteenth century. As such, they recall a passage from Diana Taylor I quoted in the opening example of this book, in which she speaks of her conception of "scenarios as meaning-making paradigms that structure social environments, behaviors, and potential outcomes" in reiterative colonial settings since the arrival of Columbus. For Taylor, colonial scenarios "make visible, yet again, what is already there: the ghosts, the images, the stereotypes."[8] They structure understandings even as they occlude histories and haunt the present. Marcy and Froebel invoke the scenario of the Indian passport for a stock comedic effect—as if they were merely acting out a familiar script, or repeating a popular joke, a tale twice-told. That kind of comedy, of course, depends on an erasure of context. Indeed, the very portability of the colonial scenario, its reiterability, is in this sense its most insidious generic feature: they tend to play out as if they have no meaning beyond the script itself. The real story of the informal "Indian passport" system, the one that should haunt us, is a political one, a denial of Native sovereignty so routine it may serve as a punch line of nineteenth-century literatures of encounter—but one that invokes the wider circuits of military reconnaissance, commercial traffic, linguistic collection, textual inscription, and diplomatic corruption through which such decentralized encounters administered the U.S. territorialization of Native lands and peoples.

By the same token, of course, the "Indian passport" system also illustrates the precariousness of Sarah Winnemucca's reliance on similar testimonial documents in her appendix to guarantee the reliability of her own text. Indeed, Winnemucca's own acquisition of literacy and assimilation into systems of frontier textual documentation only underscore the ambiguity and liminality of indigenous claims to self-representation and political recognition in national print discourse. On one hand, Winnemucca's literacy and command of English confer on her unique social capital among the Piutes (for example, Chiefs Egan and Oytes, who ally themselves with the Bannocks, defer to her with the honorific of "mother" because of this ability). At the same time, her literacy and multilingualism generate unique political and economic power among the whites and provide the means of gaining the confidence of professional soldiers like General Howard. On the other hand, Winnemucca's literacy also exposes her to great personal risk: after pleading with her to address their grievances against the Indian agent at Malheur, William Rinehart, in writing, Egan and Oytes suspect her literacy is a prelude to mendacity and tribal disloyalty and plot to kill her after joining the Bannocks in war. Similarly, her literacy and access to the public stage mark her as a threat to Father Wilbur at Yakima and Secretary of Interior Schurz in Washington, and she is often threatened by them with violence and imprisonment.

How, then, does Winnemucca's text negotiate this space of liminality—an acquisition of literacy that dislocates her from her tribe, one that empowers her uniquely but that also reveals the vulnerability of her claims of sovereign self-representation? And what lessons might her text provide here in closing, for readers of this book? The composition of the appendix provides one salient, if still ambivalent, answer. In yoking the reliability of her text to written testimonials from the likes of Generals Howard and McDowell attesting to her faithful service to the army during the Bannock War, Winnemucca perhaps opens herself to charges of Native disloyalty and betrayal in a time of crisis for her people—charges that have dogged her reputation for more than a century, as if she is finally no less naïve than her grandfather Truckee, another too-trusting tool of white conquest and, like the name he bore, "All right." I think this reading underestimates the literary qualities of Winnemucca's text and fails adequately to consider the subversive potential of an ironic repetition of Truckee's "passport" in the appendix. Indeed, the abundance of U.S. military testimonials, coupled with the words and actions of her detractors, serve primarily to underscore the *threat* she continued to embody for the U.S. government—marking her explicitly, at text's end, as a persistent *problem* for overlapping schemes of federal classification as "hostile" or "peaceable" within a broader frontier bureaucratic and social network that included the War Department, the agency system run through the Department of the Interior, local white settler colonial communities, and that extended to the white stage and print audiences that often received her public lectures and performances with hostility. Invoking, but not fully relying upon, the textual protocols through which Indian identity was officially established and administratively managed, this framing device pointedly illustrates the terms of recognition for the airing of Native "wrongs" and "claims" in the virtual geography of print culture and the embodied geographies of public performance—a coordinated spatiality in which authorship is coded as sovereign possession of body and story-making self and the meaning of Mann's claim for "the first outbreak of the American Indian in human literature" is made legible.

Within the main body of her book, Winnemucca invites her readers into that self-coordinating space of print and embodied public performance to offer an allegory of genocide, assimilation, and undying enmity—and with it, a powerful assertion of her own intellectual sovereignty that awaits acknowledgment. In chapter 4, titled "Captain Truckee's Death," Winnemucca presents what she calls "one of the traditions of my people" concerning a tribe of barbarous cannibals who inhabited the Humboldt River region hundreds of years ago. They were warlike and fierce and killed Winnemucca's ancestors in great numbers; their ghastly practices included the exhumation and consumption of their own buried dead. After a period of tense coexistence, punctuated by violent conflict between them, Winnemucca relates that the Piutes prosecuted a war of extermination against the cannibals. Surrounded with a wall of fire, the cannibals retreat to a cave on the east side of Humboldt Lake. At this stage, Winnemucca relates, her people offered an ultimatum to those cannibals who emerged: assimilate or die. "My people would ask them if they would be like us, and not eat people like coyotes or beasts. They talked the same language, but they would not give up" (73–74). Twice more the ultimatum is repeated, and twice more met with silence; eventually, Winnemucca's ancestors build the fire into the mouth of the cave, and the tribe of cannibals is exterminated: "This tribe was called people-eaters, and after my people had killed them all, the people round us called us *Say-do-carah*. It means conqueror; it also means 'enemy.' I do not know how we came by the name of Piutes. It is not an Indian word. I think it is misinterpreted. Sometimes we are called Pine-nut eaters, for we are the only tribe that lives in the country where Pine-nuts grow" (74–75, emphasis in original). Winnemucca's story ends here, in a lesson about false etymologies that serves as a brief corrective supplement to her own ethnographic self-representations in the text. The name of her people, she tells us, has been "misinterpreted": "Piute," which may indicate their classification by outsiders as eaters of pine-nuts, is "not an Indian word"; they are, instead, "*Say-do-carah*," conquerors, enemy. It is only with her subsequent disclosure immediately following these lines that the political import of this "tradition" is revealed as allegory: "My people say that the tribe we exterminated had reddish hair. I have some of their hair, which has been handed down from father to son. I have a dress which has been in our family a great many years, trimmed with this reddish hair. I am going to wear it some time when I lecture. It is called the mourning dress, and no one has such a dress but my family" (75). While the revelation of "reddish hair" suggests her people's adversaries were (or are) in fact white; their assignment in her story to the fate of the exterminated, barbarians who could not or would not assimilate into the dominant way of life reverses the roles of the Piute people in their relationship to contemporary Anglo-American domination. Such a transposition may have carried an implicit sympathetic appeal to her alert white readers (ones that might, perhaps, be more ready to identify with the terrible suffering of an uncivilized people if they are similarly complected). If so, the oppositional force of such an equation nevertheless resides with the "*Say-do-carah*," whose identity as "conquerers," "enemy," is still preserved in the traditional beliefs of a people perpetually misrecognized as being something they are not. More compelling still is her promise to mobilize this figure from the storybook setting of the printed page to the site of her body in performance of that traditional identity.

With this ending to her traditional story, Winnemucca invites her readers to project that story onto a theater setting in their imaginations: casting her in the role of the defiant barbarian faced with assimilation or extinction, beyond the flickering limelight and below a cavernous proscenium arch, as one who offers eloquent expression of the wrongs and claims of her people "in the same language" as her captive audience. Here, in an allegorized setting of theatrical performance, the scalps she surreptitiously bears on her "mourning dress" powerfully emblematize the traditional basis of a sovereign political identity forged in war and acknowledged "by the people round us" in a name that defines a relation of resistance. More so even than the attestations that compose her appendix, Winnemucca's sovereign possession of her family's mourning dress is her most powerful counterpart to her grandfather's "rag friend." A passport of her own creative self-fashioning for performative display in the public arena, Winnemucca's mourning dress persists as a powerful figure of what Gerald Vizenor has called "survivance," even as it functions as a material "counter-memory" that registers, as Joseph Roach writes, "the disparities between history as it is discursively transmitted and memory as it is publicly enacted by the bodies that bear its consequences."[9] Yet for all of the fatalistic militancy this aspect of her performance symbolizes and entails, Winnemucca's public enactment of a Native voice is finally a bid for public recognition of Piute sovereignty as a site of legitimate and enduring difference not a repudiation of that public. In this sense, Winnemucca's literary recasting of "Indian passports" and her remarkable figuring of "*Say-do-carah*" as a site of personal and political identification approach what Jace Weaver, Craig S. Womack, and Robert Warrior define as the production of Native intellectual sovereignty:

> After more than five hundred years of ever-consolidating colonialism and conquest, the last thing Natives can be sure of sovereignty over is words, thoughts, compositional strategies. Yet even these abstractions are not without practical efficacy. Political philosopher Hannah Arendt taught us all that, in the final analysis, the only freedom is the freedom to discipline oneself. In other words, as Seneca elder John Mohawk said, "If you want to be sovereign, you have to act sovereign." "Thinking sovereign" is a necessary precondition.[10]

Less a posture of tragic surrender than a political strategy of voluntary and contingent affiliation, Winnemucca's literary and performative engagement with U.S. national discourse models a style of embodied sovereign thinking, even as her readiness to cross boundaries separating peacemaker from enemy and back again expresses a straightforward and enduring hope that some colonial scenarios and story lines, in spaces of sovereign reenactment, may find different endings.

Notes

NOTES TO THE INTRODUCTION

1. Lewis H. Garrard, *Wah-to-Yah and the Taos Trail; Or Prairie Travel and Scalp Dances, with a Look at Los Rancheros from Muleback and the Rocky Mountain Campfire* (1850; Norman: University of Oklahoma Press, 1955), 59–60. Garrard reversed his first and middle names in the construction of his authorship. In his introduction to the University of Oklahoma Press edition, A. B. Guthrie Jr. notes that Garrard's "lack of a stout constitution" may have been a factor in his parents allowing him to undertake the journey (x).

2. Diana Taylor, *The Archive and the Repertoire: Performing Cultural Memory in the Americas* (Durham: Duke University Press, 2003), 28.

3. Garrard, *Wah-to-Yah and the Taos Trail*, 60.

4. Taylor, *The Archive and the Repertoire*, 26.

5. Laura Murray argues that the extant archive of Native American vocabularies deserves to be treated as a distinct literary genre, one organized by its representation of the unique "I-Thou" relationship of transcriber to linguistic subject. See her excellent essay "Vocabularies of Native American Languages: A Literary and Historical Approach to an Elusive Genre," *American Quarterly* 53.4 (December 2001): 590–623.

6. Joseph Roach, *Cities of the Dead: Circum-Atlantic Performance* (New York: Columbia University Press, 1996), 26.

7. On the early development of ideas about indigenous languages and the emergence of the field of Native American linguistics in America, see Julie Tetel Andersen, *Linguistics in America, 1769–1924* (London: Routledge, 1990); Edward G. Gray, *New World Babel: Languages and Nations in Early America* (Princeton: Princeton University Press, 1999); Edward G. Gray and Norman Fiering, eds., *The Language Encounter in the Americas, 1492–1800: A Collection of Essays* (New York: Berghahn, 2000); Sarah Rivett, *The Science of the Soul in Colonial New England* (Chapel Hill: University of North Carolina Press, 2011), esp. chap. 3; Patrick Erben, *A Harmony of the Spirits: Translation and the Language of Community in Early Pennsylvania* (Chapel Hill: University of North Carolina Press, 2012); Sarah Rivett, "Learning to Write Algonquian Letters: the Indigenous Place of Language Philosophy in the Seventeenth-Century Atlantic World" *William and Mary Quarterly* 71.4 (2014): 549–88; and Sean P. Harvey, *Native Tongues: Colonialism and Race from Encounter to the Reservation* (Cambridge: Harvard University Press, 2015).

8. E. G. Squier, "American Ethnology: Being a Summary of Some Recent Results Which Have Followed the Investigation of This Subject," *American Review*, n.s., 3 (April 1849): 385–98.

9. "Preface," *Transactions of the American Ethnological Society*, vol. 1 (New York: Bartlett and Welford, 1845), ix.

10. The so-called "spatial turn" in Americanist scholarship has explored many of these questions about space, regionality, borderlands, and transnationality in recent years. See in particular, Hsuan L. Hsu, *Geography and the Production of Space in Nineteenth-Century American Literature* (Cambridge: Cambridge University Press, 2010); Rachel Adams, *Continental Divides: Remapping the Cultures of North America* (Chicago: University of Chicago Press, 2009); Martin Brückner and Hsuan L. Hsu, eds., *American Literary Geographies: Spatial Practice and Cultural Production, 1500-1900* (Newark: University of Delaware Press, 2007); Martin Brückner, *The Geographic Revolution in Early America: Maps, Literacy and National Identity* (Chapel Hill: University of North Carolina Press: 2006); Bruce A. Harvey, *American Geographics: U.S. National Narratives and the Representation of the Non-European World, 1830–1865* (Stanford: Stanford University Press, 2001); and José David Saldívar, *Border Matters: Remapping American Cultural Studies* (Berkeley: University of California Press, 1997).

11. John Russell Bartlett to Evert Duyckinck, January 12, 1850, Box 1, Duyckinck Family Papers, New York Public Library

12. Benjamin Smith Barton, *A Comparative Vocabulary of Indian Languages* (extracted from his *New Views*), with Additions by Peter S. Du Ponceau, Mss.497.B28, American Philosophical Society, Philadelphia.

13. My approach here builds on that of several important literary and cultural studies of U.S. empire in the nineteenth century that place the U.S.-Mexico War and U.S./Mexico borderlands squarely at the center of national development. See Saldívar, *Border Matters*; John Carlos Rowe, *Literary Culture and U.S. Imperialism: From the Revolution to World War II* (New York: Oxford University Press, 2000); Shelley Streeby, *American Sensations: Class, Empire, and the Production of Popular Culture* (Berkeley: University of California Press, 2002); Kirsten Silva Gruesz, *Ambassadors of Culture: The Transamerican Origins of Latino Writing* (Princeton: Princeton University Press, 2002); Amy Kaplan, *The Anarchy of Empire in the Making of U.S. Culture* (Cambridge: Harvard University Press, 2002); David Kazanjian, *The Colonizing Trick: National Culture and Imperial Citizenship in Early America* (Minneapolis: University of Minnesota Press, 2003); Stephanie LeMenager, *Manifest and Other Destinies: Territorial Fictions of the Nineteenth-Century United States* (Lincoln: University of Nebraska Press, 2004); Martin Padget, *Indian Country: Travels in the American Southwest, 1840–1935* (Albuquerque: University of New Mexico Press, 2004); Amy S. Greenberg, *Manifest Manhood and the Antebellum American Empire* (New York: Cambridge University Press, 2005); Mark Rifkin, *Manifesting America: The Imperial Construction of U.S. National Space* (New York: Oxford University Press, 2009); Rachel Adams, *Continental Divides: Remapping the Cultures of North America*; and Marissa K. Lopez, *Chicano Nations: The Hemispheric Origins of Mexican American Literature* (New York: NYU Press, 2011).

14. "The Exploring Party," *New York Globe* 1.5 (May 1819): 268

15. Michel Foucault, *The Order of Things: An Archaeology of the Human Sciences*, trans. A. M. Sheridan Smith (1971; New York: Vintage, 1994), 297.

16. Gilles Deleuze and Félix Guattari's deployment of the figure of the rhizome is found in the introduction to *A Thousand Plateaus: Capitalism and Schizophrenia*, trans. Brian Massumi (Minneapolis: University of Minnesota Press, 1987), 3–28.

17. Ibid., 23.

18. Jodi A. Byrd, *The Transit of Empire: Indigenous Critiques of Colonialism* (Minneapolis: University of Minnesota Press, 2011), 13. For another valuable enlistment of Deleuze and Guattari in discussion of western regionality and theories of space, see Neil Campbell, *The Rhizomatic West: Representing the American West in a Transnational, Global, Media Age* (Lincoln: University of Nebraska Press, 2008).

19. Bruno Latour, *Reassembling the Social: An Introduction to Actor-Network Theory* (New York: Oxford University Press, 2005), 5, emphases in original.

20. Mark Rifkin, *Manifesting America*, 7.

21. Pekka Hämäläinen and Samuel Truett, "On Borderlands," *Journal of American History* 98.2 (September 2011): 338–61; the lines quoted are on pages 338 and 340. Some exemplary models of borderlands history that have particularly informed me here include Richard White, *The Middle Ground: Indians, Empires, and Republics in the Great Lakes Region, 1650–1815* (New York: Cambridge University Press, 1991); James F. Brooks, *Captives and Cousins: Slavery, Kinship, and Community in the Southwest Borderlands* (Chapel Hill: University of North Carolina Press, 2002); Kathleen DuVal, *The Native Ground: Indians and Colonists in the Heart of the Continent* (Philadelphia: University of Pennsylvania Press, 2006); Hämäläinen, *The Comanche Empire* (New Haven: Yale University Press, 2008); Samuel Truett, *Fugitive Landscapes: The Forgotten History of the U.S.-Mexican Borderlands* (New Haven: Yale University Press, 2008); Brian DeLay, *War of a Thousand Deserts: Indian Raids and the U.S.-Mexican War* (New Haven: Yale University Press, 2008); Andrés Reséndez, *Changing National Identities at the Frontier: Texas and New Mexico, 1800–1850* (New York: Cambridge University Press, 2004); Ned Blackhawk, *Violence over the Land: Indians and Empires in the Early American West* (Cambridge: Harvard University Press, 2006); David J. Weber, *Bárbaros: Spaniards and Their Savages in the Age of Enlightenment* (New Haven: Yale University Press, 2005); and Rachel St. John, *Line in the Sand: A History of the Western U.S./Mexico Border* (Princeton: Princeton University Press, 2011).

22. In writing this sentence, I have hazarded to quote from three separate texts written by Mignolo spanning more than a decade; nevertheless, the supplementary layering of his thought in the development of a coherent analytical framework justifies, I think, this pastiche as an attempt to delineate a key concept threaded throughout. Walter D. Mignolo, "Colonial and Postcolonial Discourse: Cultural Critique or Academic Colonialism?," *Latin American Research Review* 28.3 (1993): 126; "The Movable Center: Geographical Discourses and Territoriality during the Expansion of the Spanish Empire," in *The Latin American Cultural Studies Reader*, ed. Ana Del Sarto, Alicia Ríos, and Abril Trigo

(Durham: Duke University Press, 2004), 262; and *Local Histories/Global Designs: Coloniality, Subaltern Knowledges, and Border Thinking* (Princeton: Princeton University Press, 2000), 11.

23. Mignolo, *Local Histories/Global Designs*, 12; on gnosis and gnoseology, see ibid., 10–15 and passim. Mignolo projects these interrelated concerns as something of a manifesto for future scholarly and critical work that I find compelling: "Transimperial, transcolonial, and transnational (and by *trans* I mean beyond national languages and literatures as well as beyond comparative studies and presuppose national languages and literatures) cultural studies could serve as a new inter- and transdisciplinary space of reflection, in which issues emerging from Western expansion and global interconnections since the end of the fifteenth century might be discussed and linguistic and literary studies redefined" (ibid., 221). For another groundbreaking model of transcultural work that has inspired much of the best scholarship in the historiography of several related disciplines, see Mary Louise Pratt, *Imperial Eyes: Travel Writing and Transculturation* (London: Routledge, 1992).

24. In this design, I have taken inspiration from a host of important Native and Native-allied scholars now transforming Native American studies at the intersection of literary and history of the book studies, and their work to recover and theorize the material and social practices of Native textuality and performance in conjunction with early American media and print culture, the treaty system, and the federal policy of Indian Removal through the age of nineteenth-century U.S. imperialism. See Walter Mignolo, *The Darker Side of the Renaissance: Literacy, Territoriality, and Colonization* (Ann Arbor: University of Michigan Press, 1995); Gordon Sayre, *Les Sauvages Américains: Representations of Native Americans in French and English Colonial Literature* (Chapel Hill: University of North Carolina Press, 1997); Germaine Warkentin, "In Search of 'The Word of the Other': Aboriginal Sign Systems and the History of the Book in Canada," *Book History* 2 (1999): 1–27; Shari Huhndorf, *Going Native: Indians in the American Cultural Imagination* (Ithaca: Cornell University Press, 2001), particularly the introduction and chap. 1; Hillary Wyss, *Writing Indians: Literacy, Christianity, and Native Community in Early America* (Amherst: University of Massachusetts Press, 2003); Joanna Brooks, *American Lazarus: Religion and the Rise of African American and Native American Literatures* (New York: Oxford University Press, 2003); Robert Allen Warrior, *The People and the Word: Reading Native Non-Fiction* (Minneapolis: University of Minnesota Press, 2005); Maureen Konkle, *Writing Indian Nations: Native Intellectuals and the Politics of Historiography, 1827–1863* (Chapel Hill: University of North Carolina Press, 2004); Gordon Sayre, *The Indian Chief as Tragic Hero: Native Resistance and the Literatures of America, From Moctezuma to Tecumseh* (Chapel Hill: University of North Carolina Press, 2005); Lisa Brooks, *The Common Pot: The Recovery of Native Space in the Northeast* (Minneapolis: University of Minnesota Press, 2008); Matt Cohen, *The Networked Wilderness: Communicating in Early New England* (Minneapolis: University of Minnesota Press, 2010); Phillip H. Round, *Removable Type: Histories of the Book in Indian Country, 1663–1880* (Chapel Hill: University of North Carolina Press, 2010); Joshua David Bellin and Laura L. Mielke, eds., *Native Acts: Indian*

Performance 1603–1682 (Lincoln: University of Nebraska Press, 2011); Byrd, *The Transit of Empire*; Mark Rifkin, *When Did Indians Become Straight? Kinship, the History of Sexuality, and Native Sovereignty* (New York: Oxford University Press, 2011); Birgit Brander Rasmussen, *Queequeg's Coffin: Indigenous Literacies and Early American Literature* (Durham: Duke University Press, 2012); and Matt Cohen and Jeffrey Glover, eds., *Colonial Mediascapes: Sensory Worlds of the Early Americas* (Lincoln: University of Nebraska Press, 2014); see esp. Sarah Rivett's essay in that volume, "The Algonquian Word and the Spirit of Divine Truth: John Eliot's Indian Library and the Atlantic Quest for a Universal Language" (376–408).

25. Evert Duyckinck to John Russell Bartlett, November 19, 1849, Correspondence, 1847–1849, Box 3, John Russell Bartlett Papers, John Carter Brown Library, Providence, RI.

26. William Wadden Turner to John Russell Bartlett, February 25, 1851, Correspondence, 1850–53, Box 4, Bartlett Papers, John Carter Brown Library, Providence, RI.

NOTES TO CHAPTER 1

1. Epigraph: Peter Stephen Du Ponceau, "Notebooks on Philology," 9 vols., 6:78–81, Mss.410.D92, Box 2, Peter S. Du Ponceau Papers, American Philosophical Society, Philadelphia.

2. S[amuel] P[eter] Heintzelman to John Russell Bartlett, April 19, 1851, Folder 2, Box 1, John Russell Bartlett Papers, Rhode Island Historical Society, Providence.

3. J. Hammond Trumbull, "On the Best Method of Studying North American Languages," *Transactions of the American Philological Association*, vol. 1 (Hartford: Case, Lockwood, and Brainard, 1869–70), 57, 63, emphases in original.

4. John Heckewelder, *An Account of the History, Manners, and Customs, of the Indian Natives who once Inhabited Pennsylvania and the Neighbouring States*, in *Transactions of the Literary & Historical Committee of the American Philosophical Society*, vol. 1 (Philadelphia: Abraham Small, 1819), 317.

5. James Fenimore Cooper, *The Last of the Mohicans* (1826; New York: Penguin, 1986), 1. All subsequent references are to this edition and are cited parenthetically.

6. It should be noted that, although Cooper took special pride in the development of his fictional method of "keeping" as he called it in the "Preface" to *The Pioneers* (as in "keeping" faithfully to the model of documented nature), prominent early critics of the first two Leather-Stocking novels found his depiction of Native Americans to be the most romantic, and least believable, aspects of his work. See, for example, the *North American Review* 23.52 (July 1826): 150–98.

7. See Paul A. W. Wallace, "John Heckewelder's Indians and the Fenimore Cooper Tradition," *Proceedings of the American Philosophical Society* 96.4 (August 22, 1952): 496–504. For a discussion of Cooper in conjunction with Wilhelm von Humboldt's theory of language hierarchy, see Susan Kalter, "*The Last of the Mohicans* as Contemporary Theory: James Fenimore Cooper's Philosophy of Language," Cooper Panel, American Literature

Association Annual Convention, Baltimore, 1999, http://external.oneonta.edu/cooper/articles/ala/1999ala-kalter.html. In his recent monumental biography of Cooper, Wayne Franklin presents evidence that Cooper encountered Heckewelder prior to W. H. Gardiner's famous review of *The Spy* in the July 22, 1822, issue of the *North American Review*, widely assumed previously to have been the source in which Cooper first read Heckewelder's name (Franklin, *James Fenimore Cooper: The Early Years* [New Haven: Yale University Press, 2007], 473).

8. James Fenimore Cooper, *The Pioneers; Or, the Sources of the Susquehanna. A Descriptive Tale* (1823; New York: Penguin, 1988) 452. All subsequent references are to this edition and are cited parenthetically

9. Cooper, *The Last of the Mohicans*, 5. In a different vein, Nancy Ruttenburg reads Cooper's metatextual discussion of language in *Mohicans* as a representation of American innocence (Ruttenburg, *Democratic Personality: Popular Voice and the Trial of American Authorship* [Stanford: Stanford University Press, 1998], 313–17).

10. Du Ponceau responded specifically to Humboldt on this question in his "Translator's Preface" to Zeisberger's *A Grammar of the Language of the Lenni Lenape or Delaware Indians*," trans. Du Ponceau, *Transactions of the American Philosophical Society*, vol. 3, n.s. (Philadelphia: APS–James, Kay, Jun & Co., 1830), 77–78. For an excellent overview of Du Ponceau's linguistic contributions that includes discussion of the polysynthesis/agglutination distinction, see Pierre Swiggers, "Americanist Linguistics and the Origin of Linguistic Typology: Peter Stephen Du Ponceau's 'Comparative Science of Man,'" *Proceedings of the American Philosophical Society* 142.1 (March 1988): 18–46, esp. 28–30.

11. Like his correspondent Heckewelder (and Cooper, who derived his theories from him), Du Ponceau accepted the theory of an Asiatic origin for American Indians. Unlike Cooper, Du Ponceau's comparison of Native American languages to those of Asia revealed striking differences. American Indian languages, he writes, "are the very opposite of the Chinese, of all the languages the poorest in words, as well as in grammatical forms, while these are the richest in both. In fact, a great variety of forms, necessarily implies a great multiplicity of words; I mean, complex forms, like those of the Indians; compound words in which many ideas are included together, and are made to strike the mind in various ways by the simple addition or subtraction of a letter or syllable. In the Chinese much is understood or guessed at, little is expressed; in the Indian, on the contrary, the mind is awakened to each idea meant to be conveyed, by some one or other of the component parts of the word spoken. These two languages, therefore, as far as relates to their organization, stand in direct opposition to each other; they are the top and bottom of the idiomatic scale, and as I have given to the Chinese and its kindred dialects, the name *asyntactic*, the opposite name, *syntactic*, appears to me that which is best suited to the languages of the American Indians" (Peter S. Du Ponceau to John Heckewelder, July 31, 1816, "Correspondence between Mr. Heckewelder and Mr. Duponceau, on the Languages of the American Indians," letter 16, *Transactions of the Historical & Literary Committee of the American Philosophical Society*, vol. 1 [Philadelphia: Abraham Small, 1819], 401, 401–2).

12. Peter S. Du Ponceau, "Report of the Corresponding Secretary to the Committee, of his Progress in the Investigation committed to him of the General Character and Forms of the Languages of the American Indians," *APS Transactions*, 1:xxx–xxxi.

13. One can sense Du Ponceau's bounding enthusiasm for the novelty of these discoveries in the following rhetorical summation: "When we cast our eyes for the first time on the original structure of the languages of the American Indians, and consider the numerous novel forms with which they abound, it is impossible to resist the impression which forces itself upon us, that we are among the aboriginal inhabitants of a *New World*. We find a *new* manner of compounding words from various roots so as to strike the mind at once with a whole mass of ideas; a *new* manner of expressing the cases of substantives by inflecting the verbs which govern them; a *new* number, (the particular plural,) applied to the declension of nouns and conjugation of verbs; a *new* concordance in tense of the conjunction with the verb; we see not only pronouns, as in Hebrew and some other languages, but adjectives, conjunctions, adverbs, combined with the principal part of speech, and producing an immense variety of verbal forms. When we consider these and many other singularities which so eminently characterise the American idioms, we naturally ask ourselves the question: Are languages formed on this model to be found in any other part of the earth?" (ibid., 1:xxxvii–xxxviii, emphasis in original).

14. "Indian Eloquence," *Knickerbocker; or New York Monthly Magazine* 7.4 (April 1836): 385.

15. Edward G. Gray, *New World Babel: Languages and Nations in Early America* (Princeton: Princeton University Press, 1999), 7. Gray suggests further that Du Ponceau's position on this score reflected "his Romantic desire to make an exceptional American literary contribution. In the study of American Indian speech, he believed he found the one way for his countrymen to make that contribution. By suggesting that a people's language was a fixed, ancient cultural endowment, over which that people had little control, Du Ponceau also foreshadowed the Romantic idea that language, nation, and race were indistinct" (7).

16. See Sean P. Harvey, "'Must Not Their Languages Be Savage and Barbarous Like Them?': Philology, Indian Removal, and Race Science," *Journal of the Early Republic* 30 (Winter 2010): 505–32.

17. Du Ponceau, "Report," *APS Transactions*, 1:xxvii, xix.

18. Catherine II, Empress of Russia, "Letter to Zimmerman," May 9, 1785, in John Pickering, *An Essay on a Uniform Orthography for the Indian Languages of North America* (Cambridge: Cambridge University Press; Hilliard and Metcalf, 1820), 4.

19. The inaugural efforts of Catherine the Great and Peter Pallas were widely cited by such figures as Barton, Du Ponceau, Pickering, and Gallatin. For an excellent account of Washington's efforts on her behalf, see Gray, *New World Babel*, 112–14.

20. Of these, the *Mithridates, oder Allgemeine Sprachkunde* of J. C. Adelung and F. Adelung was perhaps most often cited by American Indian philologists as being the most significant and pathbreaking due to its unprecedented comprehensiveness of scope. See, for example, Du Ponceau's "Report," *APS Transactions*, 1:xix.

21. For more on Jefferson's obsession with Indian languages as key artifacts of Indian eloquence and important forms of historical documentation, see Gray, *New World Babel*, esp. 118–23; for additional discussion of Jefferson's championing of eloquence in Indian speech, particularly as embodied by Chief Logan's Address, see Steven Conn, *History's Shadow: Native Americans and Historical Consciousness in the Nineteenth Century* (Chicago: University of Chicago Press, 2004), 8–9, 83–84.

22. Lyle Campbell and William J. Poser offer a thorough rebuttal to the oft-repeated claim that Jones's findings were groundbreaking; placing Jones's work in a long history of inquiries into Indo-European languages, Campbell and Poser contextualize Jones in terms of his key predecessors dating to the twelfth century and argue that his method bore little resemblance to the "comparative method" that arose subsequent to him. See their *Language Classification: History and Method* (Cambridge: Cambridge University Press, 2008), 32–47. On the American reception of Jones, see Gray, *New World Babel*, 116–17.

23. For a rich and comprehensive history of the development of historical and comparative linguistics, see Campbell and Poser, *Language Classification*; on the development of ethnological study of Indian languages, see Conn, *History's Shadow*, 79–115.

24. John Pickering to Jeremiah N. Reynolds, July 30, 1836, in Michael Mackert, "Horatio Hale and the Great Exploring Expedition," *Anthropological Linguistics* 36.1 (1994): 3.

25. Samuel F. Haven, *Archæology of the United States. Or, Sketches Historical and Bibliographical, of the Progress of Information and Opinion Respecting Vestiges of Antiquity in the United States*, Smithsonian Contributions to Knowledge No. 3 (Philadelphia: T. K. and P. G. Collins, 1856), 54.

26. Friedrich Schlegel, "On the Indian Language, Literature, and Philosophy" (1808), in *The Aesthetic and Miscellaneous Works of Frederick von Schlegel*, trans. E. J. Millington (London: Henry G. Bohn, 1860), 439. The "comparative" of the comparative method speaks not only to a focus on grammar, rather than vocabulary, as a basis for discussion; more specifically, it refers also to a style of analysis that has a diachronic dimension. As Henry M. Hoenigswald put it, "to a process whereby original features can be separated from recent ones and where the aim of classification is subordinated to the aim of reconstruction" (Hoenigswald, "On the History of the Comparative Method," *Anthropological Linguistics* 5.1 [January 1963]: 2). On the significance of philology to German Orientalism, and the role of comparative grammar in the development of German ethnology, see Tuska Benes, "Comparative Linguistics as Ethnology: In Search of Indo-Germans in Central Asia, 1770–1830," *Comparative Studies of South Asia, Africa, and the Middle East* 24.2 (2004): 117–32. Benes's discussion of Schlegel begins on page 122; see also Campbell and Poser, *Language Classification*, esp. 48–73.

27. Peter S. Du Ponceau to Thomas Jefferson, February 17, 1817, Historical and Literary Committee Letterbook, vol. 1, [56], p. 58, VIII.5, APS Archives, American Philosophical Society, Philadelphia. This letter is also remarkable for the joy Du Ponceau conveys in describing the poetry of polysynthetic grammar: "You will be pleased to hear, that our Committee have particularly turned their attention to the languages of our Indian nations and that many curious & interesting facts have been the result of their enquiries.

For instance, it has been observed, that no nation elsewhere can combine so many ideas together in one word by means of a most admirable combination of Grammatical forms, by which they can write almost all the parts of speech into one which is the verb, & with them may be very properly denominated verbum χάι ξσχήμ. 'For it is truly the word of words.' What would not Anacreon, or Tibullus have given to have been able in their amatory poems to say in one single word 'O thou who makest me happy!' This is done in the language of the Delawares by means of the vocative inflexion of the participle of a compound verb. The word is *Wulamalesohatian*! From *Wulamalsin* to be happy, from which are formed a variety of verbs, including by means of slight alterations & inflexions the ideas of the pronouns both governing & governed, & all the other accessory ideas which are found in the participle above mentioned, which is regularly declined thro' all its cases as the verbs are conjugated thro' their moods & Tenses, those multiform compound parts of speech, in which there are fewer irregularities than in any other language; are peculiar to the Indian nations, are found with few variations in all their idioms thro' the Continent from north to South, & disappear in the adjacent Countries of Asia & Europe. I am preparing a communication to the Society on this interesting subject; the Study of languages has been too long confined to mere 'word hunting' for the sake of finding affinities of sound. Perhaps a comparison of the Grammatical forms of the different nations may produce more successful results."

28. Christian Charles Josias Bunsen, *Outlines of the Philosophy of Universal History, Applied to Language and Religion*, 2 vols. (London: Longman, Green, and Longman, 1854), 1:50.

29. Barton obtained his copy of Pallas's *Vocabularia Comparativa* from Joseph Priestley in the spring of 1796, citing it as the "great work that has enabled me to extend my inquiries, and to arrive at some degree of certainty on the subject." The work was dedicated to Jefferson, as vice president of the United States and president of the American Philosophical Society, in honor of his elevation of the study of American Indian languages to national attention (Barton, *New Views on the Origins and Nations of America* [Philadelphia: John Bioren, 1797], xxiii).

30. As Gallatin writes: "The selection of the words was necessarily controlled by the materials. Those and no others could be admitted, but such as were found in a number of the existing vocabularies, sufficient for the purpose intended. Some words of inferior importance were introduced, only because they were common to almost all the vocabularies; and many have been omitted, because they were to be found only for a few dialects" (Gallatin, "A Synopsis of the Indian Tribes within the United States East of the Rocky Mountains, and in the British and Russian Possessions in North America," *Archæologica Americana, Transactions and Collections of the American Antiquarian Society*, vol. 2 [Cambridge: Harvard University Press, 1836], 2).

31. My thanks to Cristobal Silva, who first suggested the latter implication to me.

32. Gallatin proceeded by assembling four comparative groupings. The first number, consisting of fifty-three tribes, included the comparison of 180 common words (a number, he notes, that reduced by more than half the number that could be obtained for some of

the languages); the second number compared fifty-three words across sixteen additional tribes; the third consisted of roughly the same number, across four additional tribes; his final grouping contained seventeen miscellaneous vocabularies that were too scanty to accommodate to any common form (see Gallatin, "Synopsis," 2).

33. Thomas Jefferson, *Notes on the State of Virginia*, in *Thomas Jefferson: Writings*, ed. Merrill D. Peterson (New York: Library of America, 1984), 227.

34. See, for example, John Pickering, *Remarks on the Indian Languages of America, From the Encyclopedia Americana*, vol. 6 (1831; Philadelphia: Carey and Lea, 1836), 584–85. For a helpful and more thorough discussion of Jefferson's missteps on this score, see Gray, *New World Babel*, esp. 127–28.

35. Henry Rowe Schoolcraft, *The Literary Voyager or Muzzeniegun*, ed. Philip B. Mason (East Lansing: Michigan State University Press, 1962), 47.

36. [John Pickering,] "Languages of the American Indian," *North American Review* 9.24 (June 1819): 183.

37. Linda F. Wiener, "Of Phonetics and Genetics: A Comparison of Classification in Linguistic and Organic Systems," *Biological Metaphor and Cladistic Classification: An Interdisciplinary Perspective*, ed. Henry M. Hoenigswald and Linda F. Wiener (Philadelphia: University of Pennsylvania Press, 1987), 219. See also Thomas Paul Bonfiglio, *Mother Tongues and Nations: The Invention of the Native Speaker* (New York: Walter de Gruyter, 2010), esp. 185–217.

38. Bonfiglio, *Mother Tongues and Nations*, 217.

39. This is not to suggest, of course, that the lowest ranks of a biological taxonomy are anything other than a synchronic "freezing" of evolutionary types and subtypes at an arbitrary historical moment; evolution is not teleological, but open-endedly processual. My point, rather, is that the divergent timelines proper to the evolution of linguistic vs. anatomical properties is such as to make anatomical-style taxonomies of language relatively unstable.

40. Henry Rowe Schoolcraft, *Algic Researches, Comprising Inquiries Respecting the Mental Characteristics of the North American Indians, First Series, Indian Tales and Legends*, vol. 1 (New York: Harper and Brothers, 1839), 9. Here, he offers a direct indictment of a previous generation of linguistic collectors, as persons, "profoundly ignorant of the grammatical principles of the languages they spoke, and incapable of discriminating the fabulous from the true in the histories they related.... The result was, then as now, that they comprehended the scope and genius of none of the languages they spoke. Whoever will submit to the labour of a critical examination into the subject, will soon become satisfied that the mediums of communication he is compelled to use are jargons, and not languages. It is impossible not to attribute to this imperfect state of oral translation, a considerable share of the errors and misunderstandings which have characterized our intercourse, political and commercial, with the tribes" (10–11).

41. Ibid., 17–18.

42. Although Blumenbach ultimately privileges the reliability of skeletal evidence over that of skin color in his project of producing racial classification (in a manner that

anticipates the more rigid anatomical hierarchies of Georges Cuvier and Samuel George Morton), he also finds—to his evident disappointment and frustration—that cranial structures betray phenomenal variations as well, and thus may not embody the unmistakable "truth" of race in the manner hoped: "It might have been expected that a more careful anatomical investigation of genuine skulls of different nations would throw a good deal of light upon the study of the variety of mankind; because when stripped of the soft and changeable parts they exhibit the firm and stable foundation of the head, and can be conveniently handled and examined, and considered under different aspects and compared together. It is clear from a comparison of this kind that the forms of skulls take all sorts of license in individuals, just as the colour of skins and other varieties of the same kind, one running as it were into the other by all sorts of shades, gradually and insensibly: but that still, in general, there is in them a constancy of characteristics that cannot be denied, and is indeed remarkable, which has a great deal to do with the racial habit, and which answers most accurately to the nations and their peculiar physiognomy" (Blumenbach, *On the Natural History of Mankind*, 3rd ed., trans. Thomas Bendyshe. in *The Anthropological Treatises of Johann Friedrich Blumenbach* [London: Longman, Green, Longman, Roberts & Green, 1865], 234–35). For a helpful discussion of Blumenbach in the context of race theory in the early national period of the United States, see Bruce R. Dain, *A Hideous Monster of the Mind* (Cambridge: Harvard University Press, 2002), esp. 58–77. On the development of craniology, and particularly its legacy in the United States among the cohort surrounding Samuel George Morton in Philadelphia, see Ann Fabian, *The Skull Collectors: Race, Science, and America's Unburied Dead* (Chicago: University of Chicago Press, 2010).

43. [Louis Ferdinand] Alfred Maury, "On the Distribution and Classification of Tongues—Their Relation to the Geographical Distribution of Races; and on the Inductions Which May Be Drawn from These Relations," in *Indigenous Races of the Earth; Or, New Chapters of Ethnological Enquiry; Including Monographs on Special Departments of Philology, Iconography, Cranioscopy, Palæontology, Pathology, Archæology, Comparative Geography, and Natural History*, ed. Josiah C. Nott and George R. Gliddon (Philadelphia: Lippincott; London: Trübner, 1857), 25–26, emphasis in original.

44. Ibid., 34, 28–29.

45. [Robert Walsh, Peter S. Du Ponceau, Samuel Brown, Thomas Cooper, and R. M. Patterson], "Topics of Inquiry Respecting the Indians," enclosure of Robert Walsh to J. C. Calhoun, March 30, 1819, MsComm. to APS [45], p. 381, Lot III, APS Archives, 1, American Philosophical Society, Philadelphia.

46. Peter S. Du Ponceau to Thomas Jefferson, July 12, 1820, Literary and Historical Committee Letterbook, vol. 2, p. 32, VIII.5, APS Archives, American Philosophical Society, Philadelphia.

47. Du Ponceau, "Report," xxxvii.

48. Alexander von Humboldt, *Personal Narrative of Travels to the Equinoctal Regions of the New Continent, during the Years 1799–1804*, trans. Helen Maria Williams, vol. 3 (London: Longman, Hurst, Rees, Orme, and Brown; J. Murray; M. Colburn: 1818), 245–46. James Cowles Pritchard—president of the Ethnological Society of London, Fellow of

the Royal Society, and devoted student of Blumenbach, draws a connection between this passage and his strong endorsement of Du Ponceau's theory of polysynthesis, which, he writes, "developed and confirmed... and in a surprising manner extended" the work of Humboldt and Johann Vater (Pritchard, "General Survey of the Aboriginal People of America," *Researches into the Physical History of Mankind*, 3rd ed., 5 vols. [London: Sherwood, Gilbert, and Piper, 1847], 5:304–5).

49. Peter Stephen Du Ponceau, "Notebooks on Philology," 9 vols., 6:78, Mss.410.D92, Box 2, Peter S. Du Ponceau Papers, American Philosophical Society, Philadelphia. The passage appears in Humboldt's *Personal Narrative*, trans. Helen Maria Williams, vol. 6, pt. 1 (London: Longman et al.: 1826), 362.

50. Richard F. Burton, *The City of Saints, and Across the Rocky Mountains to California* (New York: Harper and Brothers, 1862), 121–22.

51. William Wadden Turner to John Russell Bartlett, November 5, 1849, Box 3, Correspondence: 1847–1849, John Russell Bartlett Papers, John Carter Brown Library, Providence, RI, emphasis in original.

52. Louis Agassiz to Josiah C. Nott and George Gliddon, February 1, 1857, in J. C. Nott and Geo. R. Gliddon, *Indigenous Races of the Earth; Or, New Chapters on Ethnological Enquiry; Including Monographs on Special Departments of Philology, Iconography, Cranioscopy, Paleontology, Pathology, Archaeology, Comparative Geography, and Natural History: Contributed by Alfred Maury, Francis Pulszky, and J. Aitken Meigs, M.D., (With Communications from Prof. Jos. Leidy, M. D., and Prof .L. Agassiz, L.L.D.) resenting Fresh Investigations, Documents, and Materials; by J.C. Nott, M.D., and Geo. R. Gliddon, Authors of "Types of Mankind"* (Philadelphia: Lippincott; London: Trübner, 1857).

53. Samuel George Morton to John Russell Bartlett, January 28, 1847, Box 3, Correspondence: 1847–1849, John Russell Bartlett Papers, John Carter Brown Library, Providence, RI.

54. Edmund Spenser, *Poetical Works*, ed. J. C. Smith and E. de Selincourt (London, 1912), qtd. in Steven F. Walker, "'Poetry is/is not a cure for love': The Conflict of Theocritean and Petrarchan *Topoi* in the *Shepheardes Calender*," *Studies in Philology* 76.4 (Autumn 1979): 353.

55. I am grateful to Mac Test for our conversation about the significance of this allusion.

56. Du Ponceau, "The Translator's Preface," *A Grammar of the Language of the Lenni Lenape or Delaware Indians*," trans. Du Ponceau, *Transactions of the American Philosophical Society*, vol. 3, n.s. (Philadelphia: APS–James, Kay, Jun & Co., 1830), 75.

57. Pickering, "An Essay on a Uniform Orthography for the Indian Languages of North America," 5–6.

58. *APS Transactions*, 1:382.

59. Trumbull, "On the Best Method for Studying North American Languages," 63.

60. Lora Romero, *Home Fronts: Domesticity and Its Critics in the Antebellum United States* (Durham: Duke University Press, 1997), 44.

61. Du Ponceau, "The Translator's Preface," 70–71.

NOTES TO CHAPTER 2

1. Titian Ramsay Peale, "Diary" (1819), Mss. Film 694, American Philosophical Society, Philadelphia.

2. Calhoun's instructions are reprinted in the "Preliminary Notice" of Edwin James's official chronicle of the expedition, *Account of an Expedition from Pittsburgh to the Rocky Mountains, Performed in the Years 1819 and '20, by Order of The Hon. J. C. Calhoun, Sec'y of War; Under the Command of Major Stephen H. Long. From the Notes of Major Long, Mr. T. Say, and Other Gentlemen of the Exploring Party*, 2 vols. (Philadelphia: Carey and Lea, 1823), 1:3–4. In February 1820, while the expedition was encamped at Council Bluffs, Iowa, Calhoun scaled back his original orders: the initial goal of exploring from the Missouri northwest, as far as the 49th parallel, was abandoned; thereafter, the expedition pursued its exploration west to the Rockies, and southwest toward the headwaters of the Red River. By order of Major Long, the zoologist Thomas Say assumed primary responsibility for ethnological documentation, including medical and linguistic matters, at this time (1:421–23).

3. "Topics of Inquiry Respecting the Indians," enclosure of Robert Walsh to J. C. Calhoun, March 30, 1819, MsComm. to APS [45], Lot III, 1, APS Archives, American Philosophical Society, Philadelphia. The committee that assembled the questionnaire included Walsh, Peter S. Du Ponceau, Samuel Brown, Thomas Cooper, and R. M. Patterson.

4. As Laura Dassow Walls recounts in her extraordinary book *The Passage to Cosmos*, Jefferson and Gallatin enlisted the expertise of the Baron Alexander von Humboldt to assess the contested region of Texas—the United States wished to assert the boundary north of the Rio Grande, and New Spain claimed the region north to the Red River—even as the Lewis and Clark Expedition explored the northwestern reaches of the Louisiana Purchase (Walls, *The Passage to Cosmos: Alexander von Humboldt and the Shaping of America* [Chicago: University of Chicago Press, 2009], 99–107, esp. 104).

5. Understandably, the failure of these expeditions has overshadowed their scientific and ethnographic intentions, but these efforts were seriously conceived. Jefferson's secret instructions for the Freeman-Custis Expedition mirror those for the Lewis and Clark Expedition (it was conceived as the historically famous expedition's southern counterpart). See Dan Flores, ed., *Jefferson & Southwestern Exploration: The Freeman-Custis Expedition of 1806* (Norman: University of Oklahoma Press, 1984).

6. Thomas Jefferson to Meriwether Lewis, June 20, 1803, in *Letters of the Lewis and Clark Expedition, With Related Documents, 1783–1854*, 2 vols., ed. Donald Dean Jackson (Urbana: University of Illinois Press, 1978), 1:62. Lewis's instruction on the correct use of Jefferson's skeletal vocabulary forms almost certainly came from Jefferson himself. Although Lewis devoted significant time to training in topics of natural history and surveying with members of the American Philosophical Society (on topics such as botanical and animal specimen collecting and labeling, compass and sextant use, and so on), he did not appear to have received special training in linguistics in Philadelphia. Among those consulted were Caspar Wistar, Andrew Ellicott, Benjamin Rush, and Robert Patterson.

Lewis did consult extensively with Benjamin Smith Barton, who was an authority on Indian languages, on techniques of natural specimen collection and may have discussed linguistics with him. On Lewis's training in Philadelphia prior to the expedition, see Paul Russell Cutright, *Contributions of Philadelphia to Lewis and Clark History* (Philadelphia: Lewis and Clark Trail Heritage Foundation, 2001), 1–19.

7. "Topics of Inquiry Respecting the Indians," 381–82.

8. "The Exploring Party," *New York Globe* 1.5 (May 1819): 267–68.

9. Qtd. in William Goetzmann, *Exploration and Empire: The Explorer and the Scientist in the Winning of the American West* (1966; Austin: Texas State Historical Association, 2000), 304.

10. Victor Turner, "From a Planning Meeting for the World Conference on Ritual and Performance," qtd. in Taylor, *The Archive and the Repertoire*, 280.

11. Stephanie LeMenager, *Manifest and Other Destinies: Territorial Fictions of the Nineteenth-Century United States* (Lincoln: University of Nebraska Press, 2004), 45, 42, 44. I take inspiration from LeMenager's work but disagree with her assessment that Calhoun's recommendation that the Long Expedition avail themselves of Jefferson's instructions for Meriwether Lewis "betrays, again, just how little thinking about the fabled 'American desert' had been done since the start of the nineteenth century" (42). This assessment underestimates, in my view, the more forwardly militaristic posture of the expedition and does not consider the archival materials I discuss here, which document an approach to philology (if not "the fabled 'American desert'" itself) that had undergone a profound evolution since the voyage of Lewis and Clark.

12. For a discussion of the history of the expedition's unfavorable historical reception, see Roger L. Nichols and Patrick L. Halley, *Stephen Long and American Frontier Exploration* (Newark: University of Delaware Press, 1980), 16–18. Cf. Goetzmann, *Exploration and Empire*, 58–64; and Goetzmann, *New Lands, New Men: America and the Second Great Age of Discovery* (1986; Austin: Texas State Historical Association, 1995), 120–26. Thomas Say's skillful notation of the flora and fauna discovered on the expedition (including the coyote) were in fact quite significant, forming the basis of his seminal work *American Entomology: Descriptions of the Insects of North America*, 3 vols. (Philadelphia, 1824–28). Important also were Edwin James's observations on the geology of the southern plains. The expedition was also the first Euro-American party to summit Pike's Peak, and their surveyorship of the region resulted in a map that was authoritative for another twenty years, the "Map of Arkansa and Other Territories of the United States," published in Carey & Lea's *A Complete Historical, Chronological and Geographical American Atlas*, in 1822.

13. This result may reflect, in part, confusion about the vocabulary forms to be used. The Historical and Literary Committee's instructions state that "MR. Jefferson's excellent skeleton of vocabulary requires only to be filled up. It is presumed the Expedition have it. If not, a copy can be given them" ("Topics of Inquiry Respecting the Indians," 381). Internal evidence suggests that the Jefferson vocabulary forms were not provided in the end. The standard Jefferson vocabulary form held then in the APS collections consists of 282 words; the comparative vocabulary assembled by the Long Expedition (of the Otoes,

Konza, Omaha, Sioux, Atsina (Gros Ventre), Pawnee, and Cherokee) consists of 154 words, including many not found in the Jefferson skeleton (Thomas Say and John Dougherty, "Vocabularies of Indian Languages," in James, *Account of an Expedition*, 2:lix–lxxxviii).

14. "Indian Language of Signs," in James, *Account of an Expedition*, 1:378–94.

15. Jeffrey E. Davis, *Hand Talk: Sign Language among American Indian Nations* (Cambridge: Cambridge University Press, 2010), 7, 23, 123.

16. Álvar Núñez Cabeza de Vaca, *Álvar Núñez Cabeza de Vaca: His Account, His Life, and the Expedition of Pánfilo de Narváez*, trans. and ed. Rowena Adorno and Patrick Charles Pautz, 3 vols. (Lincoln: University of Nebraska Press, 1999), 1:233.

17. Meriwether Lewis, "August 14, 1805," in *The Lewis and Clark Journals: An American Epic of Discovery*, ed. Gary Moulton (Lincoln: University of Nebraska Press, 2003), 178.

18. For Lewis's account of Sacagawea's role in translating for the Shoshone (including the affecting scene of her reunion with her brother, Cameahwait), see ibid., 185–86. On the difficulty of "relying on limbs rather than larynx" in the use of sign languages in cross-cultural encounters on the eastern seaboard, see James Axtell, "Babel of Tongues: Communicating with the Indians in Eastern North America," in *The Language Encounter in the Americas, 1492–1800*, ed. Edward G. Gray and Norman Fiering (New York: Berghahn, 2000), 18–27, 18.

19. Larzer Ziff, *Writing in the New Nation: Prose, Print, and Politics in the Early United States* (New Haven: Yale University Press, 1991), 171.

20. Ibid., 170, 172. Other literary scholars who have devoted focused attention to sign language include David Murray, who offers a Derridean reading of PISL in conjunction with other nineteenth-century accounts of Indian languages and writing systems, highlighting contradictions that are produced by binary assumptions (primitive and civilized, simple and complex, natural and abstract) on an evolutionary model of linguistic development. See Murray, *Forked Tongues: Speech, Writing and Representation in North American Indian Texts* (Bloomington: Indiana University Press, 1991), chap. 2, esp. 15–23. Gerald Vizenor amplifies Ziff's important recognition that the supersession of sign language by interpreted speech inaugurates a process of literary annihilation and suggests that "sign language and postindian literatures are simulations of survivance" (Vizenor, *Manifest Manners: Narratives of Postindian Survivance* [Lincoln: University of Nebraska Press, 1999], 78). Cheryl Walker also builds on Ziff's observation (Walker, *Indian Nation: Native American Literature and Nineteenth-Century Nationalisms* [Durham: Duke University Press, 1997], 13). Birgit Brander Rasmussen explores Indian Sign Language in the context of nonalphabetic Native writing systems, drawing out connections posited by Garrick Mallery between sign language and Native pictographic writing (Rasmussen, *Queequeg's Coffin*, 35–38, 59–61). Most recently, Kay Yandell has offered a rich and valuable reading of *Pretty-shield, Medicine Woman of the Crows*, a signed Native autobiography conveyed by Pretty Shield to Frank Linderman alternately via Plains Hand Talk and through the aid of an interpreter. Positioning Plains Hand Talk as a classic element of the "moccasin telegraph system," Yandell approaches sign language as a transcultural rather than

translational medium, "an undertheorized yet productive conduit for the flow of cultural, political, and linguistic negotiations" across the frontier in a host of historical and literary scenarios. Like Murray, Yandell draws substantively on Derrida to explore Plains Hand Talk as a communicative system; ultimately, her reading offers an important reorientation to the critical discourse on Native autobiography inaugurated by such figures as Arnold Krupat and H. David Brumble III (Yandell, "The Moccasin Telegraph: Sign-Talk, Autobiography, and *Pretty-shield, Medicine Woman of the Crows,*" *American Literature* 84.3 [September 2012]: 534).

21. Ziff attributes his understanding of PISL to the seminal midcentury linguist A. L. Kroeber's 1972 foreword to the Hague edition of Garick Mallery's *Sign Language among North American Indians* and quotes the following passage: "Speech consists overwhelmingly of elements wholly without transparent or inherent resemblance of symbol to signification, but the sign language elements overwhelmingly do show such connection between gesture and meaning." From this, Ziff claims that "Plains Indian sign language is almost totally pantomimic" and further infers that, "since the signs are not grounded in words, those who use them recognize the limits of what they can express and thus of the understanding they can achieve" (170). However, neither of these claims follows from Kroeber's assertion of an overwhelming incidence of "connection" between gesture and meaning, and both are in fact incorrect. In pointing this out, I do not mean to subject Ziff to undue criticism; indeed, his inferences faithfully reflect long-established historical patterns of misrecognition where PISL is concerned, which are only now slowly being corrected in lay understandings. Compared to oral languages, PISL does indeed have a higher ratio of "natural" or pantomimic signs (the analogy in oral languages would be onomatopoeia) to arbitrary, or conventional signs (though the incidence of signs in PISL containing arbitrary elements is greater than those classified as *purely* pantomimic; most of PISL's more than thirteen thousand documented signs contain pantomimic and conventional elements). This difference, though, should not be taken as proof of PISL's lesser linguistic complexity or expressive power. Nor should it be surprising. As Jeffrey Davis has pointed out, signed language is "much more fit . . . for icon representation than speech is. . . . One could say that sign languages are more iconic (visual really) simply because they can be" (Davis, *Hand Talk,* 190–91).

22. George Augustus Frederick Ruxton, *Adventures in Mexico and the Rocky Mountains* (London: John Murray, 1847), 292–93.

23. George Frederick Ruxton, *Life in the Far West,* ed. LeRoy R. Hafen (1849; Norman: University of Oklahoma Press, 1951), 4. Ruxton places these terms, which he also footnotes as originating in "the Indian figurative language," in the mouth of a character named Killbuck, a fictionalized representation of a trapper Ruxton encountered on his travels in the Rockies two years prior to the book's simultaneous publication in London and Philadelphia. LeRoy Hafen presents compelling circumstantial evidence that the individual depicted was probably John S. Smith, a leading trader with the Cheyenne in the upper Arkansas (240–44).

24. I should hasten to point out that, in comparing Lewis's impressions of Indian Sign Language with those of Ruxton, I do not mean to suggest that their respective experiences

of Indian Sign Language were interchangeable—nor, for that matter, that they encountered precisely the same language. Linguists have identified numerous regional and tribal signed dialects and multiple dialect groups in North America. In his seminal work from 1960, LaMont West distinguished between two major dialect groups: a North Central Plains dialect (in all probability the dialect encountered by both Lewis and Ruxton) ; and a Far Northern Plains dialect, which had currency in what is now Alberta, Saskatchewan, Manitoba, and British Columbia (summarized in Davis, *Hand Talk* , 99). The most comprehensive assessment of historical linguistic relatedness among North American signed languages was undertaken by Jeffrey E. Davis, who finds a greater than 90 percent lexical similarity among available PISL varieties and suggests "that these are dialects of the same language, and that the core lexicon of PISL has been transmitted and remained resilient for at least the past two hundred years" (131; see 99–132 for a full discussion of his comparative methodology).

25. [Edward Everett], Review of *Account of an Expedition from Pittsburgh to the Rocky Mountains . . .* , *North American Review* 7.2 (April 1823): 262.

26. [Lewis Cass], Review of *Manners and Customs of Several Indian Tribes, located west of the Mississippi . . .* , *North American Review* 22.50 (January 1826): 61. Cass reserved special scorn for Long's 1826 expedition into the Upper Mississippi Valley, which "should serve as a warning to future travelers, passing rapidly through the interior, against committing themselves by the discussion of questions affecting our aborigines, for a full consideration of which, much time, tedious and laborious investigations, and highly favorable opportunities, are essentially requisite. It is not every man, who has lost sight of the flag staff of an interior post, or who has seen a buffalo or a muskrat, that can add anything valuable to the immense stock of materials, which has been accumulating for more than three centuries" (61).

27. John Heckewelder, *An Account of the History, Manners, and Customs of the Indian Natives who once inhabited Pennsylvania and the Neighbouring States*, in *Transactions of the Historical & Literary Committee of the American Philosophical Society*, vol. 1 (Philadelphia: Abraham Small, 1819), 116.

28. Ibid. It is worth noting here that Heckewelder and Cass are both speaking of sign language use among the Delaware—a tribe not thought to be fluent in PISL but rather users of a less-well documented variant of American Indian Sign Language (AISL).

29. William Dunbar, "On the Language of Signs among certain North American Indians" (1801), *Transactions of the American Philosophical Society* 6.1 (Philadelphia: C. and A. Conrad, 1809), 1–8; Thomas Jefferson, *Notes on the State of Virginia*, in *Thomas Jefferson: Writings*, ed. Merrill D. Peterson (New York: Library of America, 1984), 227.

30. Serious and sustained attention to Indian Sign Languages begins with Garrick Mallery, who borrowed heavily from William Tylor's ideas on the universal "gesture language," and who worked under John Wesley Powell at the Smithsonian Institution. Mallery's *Sign Language among North American Indians*, originally published in 1881 in the *First Annual Report of the Bureau of Ethnology*, is the pioneering text; all who have worked on Indian Sign Languages since remain significantly in his debt. Prior to the

twentieth-century works of major linguists such as William Stokoe, Alfred Kroeber, C. F. Voeglin, LaMont West, Allan Taylor, Brenda Farnell, and (especially) Jeffrey E. Davis, the major early accounts include also William Philo Clark, *The Indian Sign Language* (Philadelphia: L. R. Hamersley, & Co., 1885); and William Tomkins, *Universal Indian Sign Language of the Plains Indians of North America* (1926; New York: Dover, 1969). See also Thomas S. Sebok, *The Sign & Its Masters* (Austin: University of Texas Press, 1979), 128–67.

31. For a detailed rebuttal of the most common misconceptions about sign languages in the early nineteenth century (specifically that sign languages are pictorial; that they are universal; that they lack abstraction; and that they are primitive), see Harlan Lane, *When the Mind Hears: A History of the Deaf* (New York: Random House–Vintage, 1989), 212–13.

32. On the origins and spread of PISL, see Allan R. Taylor, "The Plains Indian Sign Language," in *Atlas of Languages of Intercultural Communication in the Pacific, Asia, and the Americas*, ed. Stephen A. Wurm, Peter Mühlhäusler, and Darrell T. Tyron (Berlin: Walter de Gruyter, 1996), 1241–42; J. Davis, *Hand Talk*, 19–21; Brenda Farnell, *Do You See What I Mean? Plains Indian Sign Talk and the Embodiment of Action* (Austin: University of Texas Press, 1995), 33–38; and Naomi S. Baron, *Speech, Writing and Sign: A Functional View of Linguistic Representation* (Bloomington: Indiana University Press, 1981), 224–32. For a dissenting view of this (otherwise widely countenanced) origin hypothesis, see William J. Samarin, "Demythologizing Plains Indian Sign Language History," *International Journal of American Linguistics* 53.1 (January 1987): 65–73. On the process of ethnogenesis in the Southwest, see Gary Clayton Anderson, *The Indian Southwest, 1580–1830: Ethnogenesis and Reinvention* (Norman: University of Oklahoma Press, 1999), 3–5.

33. Farnell, *Do You See What I Mean?*, 2–8.

34. Laura Murray, "Vocabularies of Native American Languages: A Literary and Historical Approach to an Elusive Genre," American Quarterly 53.4 (December 2001): 590–623.

35. The literature on gesture is vast and dates to antiquity. Distinguishing between gesture and sign remains an active area of debate in linguistics, philosophy of mind, and (in particular) in the emergent field of gesture studies. For a concise overview by a leading figure, see Adam Kendon, "Gesture," *Annual Review of Anthropology* 26 (1997): 109–28; on the origins of the divide between "sign" (as a linguistic unit) and "gesture" (as a "paralinguistic" designation), see Adam Kendon, "Some Reflections on the Relationship between 'Gesture' and 'Sign,'" *Gesture* 8.3 (2008): 348–66; see also Robert A. Yelle, "The Rhetoric of Gesture in Cross-Cultural Perspective," *Gesture* 6.2 (2006): 223–40; and Baron, *Speech, Writing, and Sign*, 201–14. On the semantic and cognitive aspects of spontaneous gesture, see David McNeill, *Hand and Mind: What Gestures Reveal about Thought* (Chicago: University of Chicago Press, 1992). Brenda Farnell joins Kendon in finding "that the modality of manual gestures is as fundamental as the vocal modality as an instrument for the representation of meaning," and in her book on Plains Sign Talk among the Assiniboine juxtaposes "vocal gestures" (that is, for oral speech) with "manual gestures in order to place

"these two types of semiotic practice on more equal theoretical ground" (Farnell, *Do You See What I Mean?*, 21–22; on pointing as a linguistic component of PISL, 157–63).

36. James, *Account of an Expedition*, 1:379.

37. William Philo Clark, "Fight," *The Indian Sign Language, with Brief Explanatory Notes of the Gestures Taught Deaf-Mutes in our Institutions for Their Instruction, and a Description of Some of the Peculiar Laws, Customs, Myths, Superstitions, Ways of Living, Code of Peace, and War Signals of Our Aborigines* (1885; Lincoln: University of Nebraska Press, 1982), 172.

38. Examples of free root morphemes in English include words like "art" and "dodge" and can be combined with other morphemes (bound or free) to become other words that may change their grammatical or semantic type. (Art + *s*) pluralizes the noun; (Art + *y*) results in an adjective. Both of these root morphemes are polysemous, in that they are singular forms that carry multiple meanings. The compound (dodge + ball) indicates the former's etymology in a value-neutral act of physical evasion; when combined with the bound morpheme "-*er*" its pejorative semantic extension to concepts of deceit and dishonesty is readily apparent, as in the phrase, "artful dodger." Morphemes are further divisible into phonemes—a term, despite its common association with sound, is also used to describe the finite hand shapes employed in sign languages. In her analysis of PISL, Brenda Farnell prefers the term "kineme" to phoneme," which she defines as "a unit of movement, or a shape of the hand, for example, that provides a constituent part of a sign recognized by native speakers as making a difference in meaning" (47). For a helpful overview of morphology, phonology, and syntax in PISL, see Davis, *Hand Talk*, 130–70; on PISL morphology in conjunction with Peircean tripartite semiotics, see Farnell, *Do You See What I Mean?*, 41–57.

39. Edwin James, *Account of an Expedition*, 1:381, 384. It is perhaps worth noting that, in an apparent concession to conservative sexual mores in Great Britain, the entry for "copulation" is elided from the 1823 London edition.

40. Ibid., 1:381.

41. Garrick Mallery, *Sign Language among North American Indians Compared with That among Other Peoples and Deaf-Mutes. First Annual Report of the Bureau of Ethnology to the Secretary of the Smithsonian Institution, 1879–'80, by J. W. Powell, Director* (Washington, DC: Government Printing Office, 1881), 354, emphasis in original. Brian Hochman discusses this passage from Mallery in the context of the emergence of new media technologies of visual representation at the end of the nineteenth century and offers a compelling and highly suggestive comparison of Mallery's serial presentation of visual depictions of signs to the serial motion photography of Eadweard J. Muybridge (Hochman, "Writing Motion: The Life and Work of Garrick Mallery," address at Media Evolution and Language Technologies, C19: The Society of Nineteenth-Century Americanists 2nd Biennial Conference, Berkeley City Club, April 14, 2012.

42. "Topics of Inquiry Respecting the Indians," 372.

43. On the relationship of speech to Indian embodiment and gesture and their extraordinary powers of combined articulation in Cooper's Leather-Stocking novels, see Ruttenburg, *Democratic Personality*, 312–16.

44. Pauline Moffitt Watts, "Pictures, Gestures, Hieroglyphics: 'Mute Eloquence' in Sixteenth-Century Mexico," in *The Language Encounter in the Americas, 1492–1800*, ed. Edward G. Gray and Norman S. Fiering (New York and Oxford: Berghahn, 2000), 85–86.

45. Jay Fliegelman, *Declaring Independence: Jefferson, Natural Language, & the Culture of Performance* (Stanford: Stanford University Press, 1993), 2. For a useful book-length treatment of American Indian oratory and eloquence in a host of contexts, including its performative and gestural aspects, see William M. Clements, *Oratory in Native North America* (Tucson: University of Arizona Press, 2002), esp. 103–23. For an illuminating and valuable discussion of Iroquois oratory and republicanism in the eighteenth century, see Sandra M. Gustafson, *Eloquence Is Power: Oratory & Performance in Early America* (Chapel Hill: University of North Carolina Press, 2000), 111–39; on gesture, in particular, see 118.

46. For an influential treatment of the eighteenth-century play of texts that figured forms of virtual embodiment in the public sphere, see Michael Warner, *The Letters of the Republic: Publication and the Public Sphere in Eighteenth-Century America* (Cambridge: Harvard University Press, 1990). In a distinct but related vein, see also Christopher Looby's influential discussion of Federal-era textual responses to linguistic pluralism and its perceived threats to national legitimacy in *Voicing America: Language, Literary Form, and the Origins of the United States* (Chicago: University of Chicago Press, 1996), 203–65, and passim; see also Jill Lepore's discussion of Noah Webster's quest for a national language in *A is for America: Letters and Other Characters in the Newly United States* (New York: Random House-Vintage, 2002), 15–41. On the spectral and spectacular forms of democratic sovereignty embodied in popular voice, see Ruttenburg, *Democratic Personality*. On language as "the costume of thought," see Fliegelman, *Declaring Independence*, 35, 39.

47. Fliegelman, *Declaring Independence*, 43.

48. Edwin James, *Account of an Expedition from Pittsburgh to the Rocky Mountains*, 1:395.

49. Ibid., 1:397.

50. Ibid., 2:210. This and the following episode, both describing the descent of the Arkansas River, are indicated internally to have been written by Thomas Say (173).

51. Ibid., 2:211.

52. Ibid., 2:186.

53. Caleb Atwater, *Remarks Made on a Tour to Prairie du Chien; thence to Washington City, in 1829* (Columbus, OH: Isaac N. Whiting, 1831), 119–21. For another gloss on this speech, see Conn, *History's Shadow*, 86. "Driven by emotion and 'enthusiasm,' the Indian body itself becomes eloquent," Conn writes. "The achievement of Indian eloquence might not raise the estimation of all Indians, but it had the force to make individual Indian speakers into real men." I agree in large part with Conn's discussion of Indian eloquence here and elsewhere; I would add only here that in producing "real men," the vehicle of Indian eloquence does not transcend race, but produces particular and distinctive types of men that embody divergent racial qualities.

54. Ezra Tawil, *The Making of Racial Sentiment: Slavery and the Birth of the Frontier Romance* (New York: Cambridge University Press, 2006), 50; on Native Americans as deficient in sentiment, see 104–8.

55. Atwater, *Remarks Made on a Tour to Prairie du Chien* 122–23.

56. Ibid., 123.

57. Ibid.

58. Thomas Jefferson, *Notes on the State of Virginia* (1784), in *Writings*, ed. Merrill D. Peterson (New York: Library of America, 1984), 184. For reference, I will reproduce Jefferson's rendition of Logan's brief speech from *Notes* here: "I appeal to any white man to say, if ever he entered Logan's cabin hungry, and he gave him not meat; if ever he came cold and naked, and he clothed him not. During the course of the last long and bloody war, Logan remained idle in his cabin, an advocate for peace. Such was my love for the whites, that my countrymen pointed as they passed, and said, 'Logan is the friend of white men.' I had even thought to have lived with you, but for the injuries of one man. Col. Cresap, the last spring, in cold blood, and unprovoked, murdered all the relations of Logan, not sparing even my women and children. There runs not a drop of my blood in the veins of any living creature. This called on me for revenge. I have sought it: I have killed many: I have fully glutted my vengeance. For my country, I rejoice at the beams of peace. But do not harbor a thought that mine is the joy of fear. Logan never felt fear. He will not turn on his heel to save his life. Who is there to mourn for Logan?—Not one" (188–89).

59. Qtd. in Antonello Gerbi, *The Dispute of the New World: The History of a Polemic, 1750–1900*, trans. Jeremy Moyle (Pittsburgh: University of Pittsburgh Press, 2010), 6. As Steven Conn has pointed out, it is striking that Jefferson presents Logan's speech in Query VI, a chapter titled "Productions Mineral, Vegetable and Animal," rather than in Query XI, "Aborigines": "Jefferson used the story of Logan's eloquence as the culmination of his description of Indians as objects of natural historical interest, a discussion that includes, among other things, a meditation on body hair. Working, as it were, from the corpus inward, Jefferson moves to a consideration of the Indian's mental capacities" (Conn, *History's Shadow*, 84). See also Ezra Tawil's *The Making of Racial Sentiment*, which provides valuable insight into this passage (62–65).

60. Atwater, *Remarks Made on a Tour to Prairie du Chien*, 81.

61. Samuel Akerly, "Observations on the Language of Signs, read before the New-York Lyceum of Natural History, on the 23d of June, 1823," *American Journal of Science and Arts* 8.2 (January 1824): 350.

62. Thomas Reid, *An Inquiry into the Human Mind, on the Principles of Common Sense*, 3rd ed. (London: Cadell, Longman, Kincaid, and Bell, 1769), 72. On natural language, including a discussion of Reid and Jefferson, see Fliegelman, *Declaring Independence*, 44–51; on natural or universal language, Native Americans, and deaf education, see Lane, *When the Mind Hears*, 281–83; and Lepore, *A is for American*, 91–110. On the theory of the primacy of gesture as pioneered by Condillac and developed by manualists in the nineteenth century and further connections between deafness, race, and American Indian Sign Language (focusing particularly on Mallery), see Douglas C. Baynton, *Forbidden*

Signs: American Culture and the Campaign Against Sign Language (Chicago: University of Chicago Press, 1998), esp. 36–55.

63. Reid, *An Inquiry into the Human Mind*, 75.

64. Ibid., 76.

65. Ibid.

66. Immanuel Kant, *Anthropology, History, and Education. The Cambridge Edition of the Works of Immanuel Kant*, ed. Günter Zöller and Robert B. Louden, trans. Mary Gregor, Paul Guyer, et al. (Cambridge: Cambridge University Press, 2007), 270–71.

67. To be sure, Akerly's particular approach was problematic—combining an unorthodox inventory of signs that borrowed from several sources, including Plains Indian Sign Language (though I should point out that this tally did not appear to include any that could have been supplied by John Dunn Hunter, discussed below) and some invented on the fly as substitute for English words. The lack of trained teachers of the deaf in the 1820s at the New-York Institution led to a public accounting of his methods (or lack thereof) before the New York State Senate and to the eventual resignations of Akerly and Mitchill in 1829 (see Lane, *When the Mind Hears*, 215–40).

68. T. H. Gallaudet, "On the Natural Language of Signs; and its Value and Uses in the Instruction of the Deaf and Dumb," *American Annals of the Deaf and Dumb, conducted by the Instructors of the American Asylum*, vol. 1 (Hartford: n.p., 1848), 79. Gallaudet discusses the Long Expedition's sign language findings on page 59.

69. Reid, *An Inquiry into the Human Mind*, 75–76.

70. Peter Stephen Du Ponceau, "Notebooks on Philology," 9 vols., 3:3, Mss.410.D92, Box 2, Peter S. Du Ponceau Papers, American Philosophical Society, Philadelphia.

71. Ralph Waldo Emerson, *Nature* (1836), in *Essays and Lectures* (New York: Library of America, 1983), 20, 22, 20.

72. Ralph Waldo Emerson, "Experience," (1843), in *Essays and Lectures* (New York: Library of America, 1983), 485.

73. Peter Stephen Du Ponceau, "Notebooks on Philology," 9 vols., 7:60–61, Mss.410. D92, Box 2, Peter S. Du Ponceau Papers, American Philosophical Society, Philadelphia.

74. Peter Stephen Du Ponceau, "Notebooks on Philology," 9 vols., 3:48, Mss.410.D92, Box 2, Peter S. Du Ponceau Papers, American Philosophical Society, Philadelphia.

75. Robert Allen Warrior, *The People and the Word: Reading Native Non-Fiction* (Minneapolis: University of Minnesota Press, 2005), 182. Hillary E. Wyss and Stephanie Fitzgerald have championed Warrior's figure of "intellectual trade routes" recently in a special joint edition of *Early American Literature* and *American Literary History* devoted to a rethinking of early American literary studies (Wyss and Fitzgerald, "Land and Literacy: The Textualities of Native Studies," *American Literary History* 22.2 [Summer 2010]: 271–79).

76. Warrior, *The People and the Word*, 182–83.

77. Ibid., 182.

78. Akerly, "Observations on the Language of Signs," 350.

NOTES TO CHAPTER 3

1. Information about Hunter's life through the end of his schooling is culled from the *Memoirs*; about his visit with Jefferson, only scanty details are known. In his *Curiosities of Human Nature*, Samuel Goodrich records the by then common understanding that, following his trek across the Alleghenies, "Hunter paid a visit to Mr. Jefferson, who received him kindly, and, taking a strong interest in his welfare, gave him letters of introduction to several persons at Washington. Hunter went thither, and, passing on, came to Philadelphia, and at last to New York, everywhere exciting a lively interest, by the remarkable character of his story, and the manner in which he related it." In a letter to Jefferson dated July 20, 1823, I. J. Chapman mentions the "favourable testimony which not only Mr. Randolph and you yourself had towards [Hunter]"; another letter, from the Philadelphian Elliot Cresson, reports firsthand Jefferson's confidence in the authenticity of Hunter's story despite questions that had been raised about it (Samuel Goodrich, *Curiosity of Human Nature: by the Author of Peter Parley's Tales* [Boston: Bradbury, Soden & Co., 1844], 243; Richard Drinnon, *White Savage: The Case of John Dunn Hunter* [New York: Schocken, 1972], 113–14).

2. Six editions of Hunter's autobiography were published in the 1820s, in four different countries. The first edition was published in Philadelphia, in a title that emphasized Hunter's ethnological observations rather than the account of his captivity: *Manners and Customs of Several Indian Tribes Located West of the Mississippi; Including Some Accounts of the Soil, Climate, and Vegetable Productions, and the Indian Materia Medica: To Which is Prefixed the History of the Author's Life during a Residence of Several Years among Them* (Philadelphia: J. Maxwell, 1823). Two enlarged British editions shortly followed in 1823 and 1824, published by Longman, Hurst, Rees, Orme, Brown, and Green under the title *Memoirs of a Captivity among the Indians of North America from Childhood to the Age of Nineteen: With Anecdotes Descriptive of Their Manners and Customs. To Which is Added, Some Account of the Soil, Climate, and Vegetable Productions of the Territory Westward of the Mississippi*. German and Dutch editions appeared in 1824; a Swedish edition followed in 1826. My discussion of the text here relies on Richard Drinnon's excellent 1973 edition for Schocken Books, which reproduces the 1824 London edition (significant for its inclusion of Hunter's 1823 pamphlet *Reflections on the Different States and Conditions of Society; With the Outlines of a Plan to Ameliorate the Circumstances of the Indians of North America*. Quotations from the text are from this edition and are cited parenthetically.

3. Richard Drinnon's, *White Savage: The Case of John Dunn Hunter* (1972) presents some impressive historical detective work; I find his claims largely convincing, and in what follows I make substantive use of Drinnon's documentary trail concerning Hunter's life subsequent to the events depicted in the autobiography. Contemporary scholars who discuss Hunter have treated the question of his veracity with understandable circumspection.

4. Drinnon makes no mention of Hunter's multiple visits to the New-York Institution for the Deaf and Dumb in 1822 (nor have I seen this discussed elsewhere). Although my own arguments concerning Hunter do not finally turn on the veracity of his life story as

he represented it in all of its detail (I am as much interested in what the record does not, and perhaps cannot, reveal than in what it may prove), I do think that (for reasons I will explore in greater detail below) Hunter's visits to the New-York Institution lend further credence to, rather than detract from, his claims of having lived for significant a significant period among tribes west of the Mississippi.

5. Matt Cohen, *The Networked Wilderness: Communicating in Early New England* (Minneapolis: University of Minnesota Press, 2010), 11, 25.

6. Taylor, *The Archive and the Repertoire*, 34.

7. LeMenager, *Manifest and Other Destinies*, 24; Eric J. Sundquist, *Empire and Slavery in American Literature, 1820–1865* (Oxford: University Press of Mississippi, 2006), 22–25.

8. The principle of linguistic relativity has its roots in nineteenth-century German philology, particularly the work of Wilhelm von Humboldt. Although strains of this theory appear in Humboldt's writings as early as 1812, Konrad Koerner suggests that Humboldt's concept of a linguistic *Weltanschauung* crystallized following his exchanges with John Pickering and Peter Du Ponceau on Native American languages. In an 1827 paper, Humboldt offered his most influential expression of that theory in the following terms: "Die Sprache ist durchaus kein blosses Verständingungsmittel, sondern der Abdruck des Geistes und der Weltansicht des Redenden ["Language is by no means a mere means of communication, but the imprint of mind and the world-view of the speaker"] (qtd. in Koerner, "Wilhelm von Humboldt and North American Ethnolinguistics: Boas [1894]—Hymes [1961]," in *North American Contributions to the History of Linguistics*, ed. Francis P. Dinneen and Koerner [Amsterdam: John Benjamins, 1990], 116). For more on the relationship of Humboldt's *Weltansicht* hypothesis to the work of Sapir and Whorf (and its prior legacy in Kantian thought), see James William Underhill, *Humboldt, Worldview, and Language* (Edinburgh: Edinburgh University Press), esp. 53–58. Although widely felt, the twentieth-century legacy of the Whorf-Sapir hypothesis has been contested thoroughly and frequently (though it is now making something of a comeback). For a helpful and widely cited, though by now somewhat dated, overview, see Paul Kay and Willett Kempton, "What Is the Sapir-Whorf Hypothesis?," *American Anthropologist* 86.1 (March 1984): 65–79.

9. *Monthly Review* 102 (November 1823): 243, rpt. in Drinnon, *White Savage*, 5.

10. Homi Bhabha, "Of Mimicry and Man," in *The Location of Culture* (London: Routledge, 1994), 87, 89, emphases in original.

11. For an excellent and thought-provoking discussion of John Neal's obsession with Hunter and his own style of play with authorial costume, see Jonathan Elmer, "John Neal and John Dunn Hunter," in *John Neal and Nineteenth-Century American Literature and Culture*, ed. Edward Watts and David Carlson (Lanham, MD: Bucknell University Press, 2011), 145–57.

12. In addition to his discussion of sign language in the "Considerations on the Physical and Moral Condition of the Indians," Hunter refers to the use of sign language on four occasions within the *Memoirs* proper: on the westward trek of his party to the Pacific Ocean, "high up the [Platte] river, or among the mountains," where Hunter and his party

encountered some tribes "with whom we were obliged to communicate wholly by signs" (39); in communication with a party of English traders, with whom, "by signs, we made them understand our apprehensions of the hostile Sioux, which were settled lower down, on the Missouri" (54); in conversation with Watkins (64); and, at greatest length, in his account of Tecumseh's speech before the Osage (28).

13. William Philo Clark, *The Indian Sign Language, with Brief Explanatory Notes of the Gestures Taught Deaf-Mutes in Our Institutions for their Instruction, and a Description of some of the Peculiar Laws, Customs, Myths, Superstitions, Ways of Living, Code of Peace and War Signals of Our Aborigines* (1885; Lincoln: University of Nebraska Press, 1982), "Day," 142; "Wind," 406; "God," 247.

14. Pierre Bourdieu, *Outline of a Theory of Practice*, trans. Richard Nice (Cambridge: Cambridge University Press, 1977), 80.

15. Ibid., 79.

16. Cyrus Redding, *Personal Reminiscences of Eminent Men*, 3 vols. (London: Saunders, Otley, & Co., 1867), 3:50, 46.

17. Qtd. in Henry Stuart Foote, *Texas and the Texans; Or, Advance of the Anglo-Americans to the South-West; Including a History of Leading Events in Mexico, from the Conquest by Fernando Cortes to the Termination of the Texan Revolution*, 2 vols. (Philadelphia: Thomas, Cowperthwait & Co., 1841), 1:245.

18. John Sugden, "Early Pan-Indianism; Tecumseh's Tour of the Indian Country, 1811–1812," *American Indian Quarterly* 10.4 (Autumn 1986): 273–74. See also Sugden's biography, *Tecumseh: A Life* (New York: Henry Holt, 1999), which is the best and most-well sourced treatment of Tecumseh's life and political career.

19. Given the significance and semantic weight Hunter accords to Tecumseh's use of gesture, it is tempting to infer that Tecumseh was employing one version of American Indian Sign Language in his speech before the Osage—either Plains Indian Sign Language (which was practiced by the Osages, with which Hunter was familiar, and which Tecumseh had certainly encountered in numerous locations), or a regional variant more widely in use in the Great Lakes region and Ohio Valley. Although I think this inference is likely accurate, Hunter does not specify Tecumseh's use of gesture as such in this moment, and I therefore refrain from characterizing it in those terms here. Nevertheless, I do think the weight of evidence suggests that Tecumseh was not only knowledgeable of sign language but used it routinely as a component of his oratory, which I discuss below.

20. Although questions have persisted about Hunter's documentation of Tecumseh's speech—early critics, assuming Hunter to be an imposter, questioned whether it happened at all; more legitimate questions remain about the accuracy of the transcription given the span of years that passed between its delivery and Hunter's book—the text of the speech has been reprinted with some frequency. Contemporary sources that reproduce it typically affirm its authenticity and make no mention of controversy. See George McMichael and James S. Leonard, eds., *The Longman Anthology of American Literature*, 10th ed. (Boston: Longman-Pearson, 2011), 1:711–13; and Howard Zinn and Anthony Arnove, eds., *Voices of a People's History of the United States*, 2nd ed. (New York: Seven Stories, 2009), 133–35.

The most recent editions of *The Norton Anthology of American Literature* reproduce the speech but note carefully its problems of authentication. William M. Clements is perhaps the most thorough recent skeptic of Hunter's account of Tecumseh's speech, questioning its detail and repeating the oft-rehearsed (though incorrect) claim that no evidence exists that Tecumseh visited the Osage. Clements's arguments are thoughtful and worth taking seriously, though I disagree with his conclusions. In particular, I think he underestimates the mnemonic function that embodied speech and performance served in recording events, stories, and orations—elements that Hunter emphasizes above the *verbatim* content of the speech itself (see Clements, *Oratory in Native North America* [Tucson: University of Arizona Press, 2002], 53–59).

21. Shawnee and Osage belong to separate language families (Shawnee is an Algonquian language; Osage is a Siouan language). Tecumseh was multilingual (he spoke Shawnee, Muskogee, and some English), but no evidence suggests that he spoke Osage. His Pan-Indianist diplomacy also entailed the work of oral interpreters. Accompanying Tecumseh on his southern tour of 1811–12 was Seekaboo, a Muskogee kinsman who spoke Shawnee, Muskogee, Choctaw, English, and is reported to have been conversant in Spanish, French, and the Mobilian trade language as well. See Sugden, *Tecumseh: A Life*, 237–51; and Glenn Tucker, *Tecumseh: A Vision of Glory* (New York: Bobbs-Merrill, 1956), 16–17. On the use of sign language and other trade languages in in the Southeast, see J. Leitch Wright, *The Only Land They Knew: The Tragic Story of the American Indians in the Old South* (New York: Free Press–Macmillan, 1981), 286.

22. Brooks, *The Common Pot*, 2.

23. See Sean P. Harvey, "'Must Not Their Languages Be Savage and Barbarous Like Them?': Philology, Indian Removal, and Race Science," *Journal of the Early Republic* 30 (Winter 2010): 505–32.

24. Maureen Konkle, *Writing Indian Nations: Native Intellectuals and the Politics of Historiography, 1827–1863* (Chapel Hill: University of North Carolina Press, 2004), 1–41; for a comprehensive history of the treaty system, see Francis Paul Prucha, *American Indian Treaties: The History of a Political Anomaly* (Berkeley: University of California Press, 1994). For a valuable perspective on the problems of spatial representation that the "homogenizing image" of treaties with the Comanche created through the 1850s, see Mark Rifkin, *Manifesting America: The Imperial Construction of U.S. National Space* (New York: Oxford University Press, 2009), esp. 130–38.

25. Although the name of Tecumseh is popularly synonymous with Pan-Indian resistance in the Northwest Territory today, the movement he and his brother led may be understood more fully as a culmination of a long legacy of Pan-Indian resistance and tribal confederation that stretched from Kentucky, Ohio, and New York into the more distant precincts of the Great Lakes region. The advent of the Western Indian Confederacy is tied to the Great Council at Fort Detroit in 1785 and eventually included participation of the Shawnees, the Six Nations of the Iroquois, the Wyandots (Hurons), Miamis, Ojibwes, Delawares, Ottawas, Potawatomis, Kickapoo, Kaskaskia, and some Cherokees; their resolution was to defend in common the Ohio River boundary established by the 1768 Fort

Stanwix treaty negotiated with the British. Historians typically correlate its dissolution with the Battle of Fallen Timbers, which ended the Northwest Indian War. On the origins and development of Pan-Indian movements in the eighteenth century through the time of Tecumseh's and Tenskwatawa's Confederacy, see Gregory Evans Dowd, *A Spirited Resistance: The North American Indian Struggle for Unity, 1745–1815* (Baltimore: Johns Hopkins University Press, 1992); on the political history of the Confederacy, see Richard White, *The Middle Ground: Indians, Empires, and Republics in the Great Lakes Region, 1650–1815* (New York: Cambridge University Press, 1991), 413–68, esp. 441–45 for Joseph Brant's central role in articulating a common sense of mission; and Colin G. Calloway, *One Vast Winter Count: The Native American West before Lewis and Clark* (Lincoln: University of Nebraska Press, 2003), 367–426; on the long history of Shawnee confederation and political action prior to, and including the Northwestern Confederation, and continuing through the history of Tecumseh and Tenskwatawa, see Calloway, *The Shawnees and the War for America* (New York: Penguin, 2007); for important discussion of Tenskwatawa's religious movement, which too often has been overshadowed by Tecumseh, see R. David Edmunds, *The Shawnee Prophet* (Lincoln: University of Nebraska Press, 1983); see also Edmunds, *Tecumseh and the Quest for Indian Leadership* (Boston: Little, Brown, 1984). For rich and comprehensively researched discussion of the above history in the context of Tecumseh's life, see John Sugden's authoritative biography, *Tecumseh: A Life*.

26. Walter D. Mignolo, *Local Histories/Global Designs: Coloniality, Subaltern Knowledges, and Border Thinking* (Princeton: Princeton University Press, 2000), 221. To clarify lest I be misunderstood, I am not making a historical claim about U.S. strategies for designating territories considered desirable for annexation through the treaty system. Those strategies reflected regional geopolitical and commercial aims and often began with the identification of areas desirable for the establishment of riverine transportation corridors, buffer zones against lands held by Indians perceived as hostile, and their exploitable natural resources (for mining, farming, and so on). Those priorities often entailed the marking of lines on maps that had nothing to do with Indian tribal identity or linguistic identity and frequently encompassed multiple Native claims to ownership. In these scenarios, in which desired land cessions corresponded to multiple Native land claims, William Henry Harrison was particularly adept in developing tactics for playing off Native peoples against one another through tactics of separate and secret negotiation, often levying annuities, livestock, and promises of favor in a manner designed to inflame jealousy and hostility between different Native peoples; in these scenarios, oral linguistic difference provided a highly eligible pretext to establish points of division. For discussion of Harrison's highly effective career in Indian treaty negotiation, see Robert M. Owens, *Mr. Jefferson's Hammer: William Henry Harrison and the Origins of American Indian Policy* (Norman: University of Oklahoma Press, 2007).

27. Konkle is particularly cogent on the supposed "problem" with the term "Indian nations" and deserves quoting at length here: "It is sometimes objected that an 'Indian nation'—a phrase that became common in Anglo-American legal discourse by the mid-eighteenth century—is not really 'Indian' because it is a product of colonization and

settlement, an argument that reifies culture as the only real freedom for native peoples. The effects of Eurocentrism are a condition of modernity—in most societies around the world, they cannot be escaped. As the historian Arif Dirlik points out, to posit that colonized or indigenous peoples are at their most authentic when they are least effected by Eurocentrism is to deny their experience in time. It is also often maintained in literary criticism, historiography, and popular discourse that Indian nations do not have that much real power or autonomy relative to the United States and never really did, which implies that to speak of Indian nations' political authority is deluded if not absurd. But relative size and power does not stop Andorra and Lichtenstein, for example, from being considered sovereign nations" (Konkle, *Writing Indian Nations*, 6).

28. Mignolo, *Local Histories/Global Designs*, 13.

29. In characterizing the "middle ground," Richard White takes care to differentiate his understanding of the complex cultural processes of exchange at work in a scenario of "accommodation" from the more common term "acculturation"; his important insights deserve echoing here: "As commonly used, *acculturation* describes a process in which one group becomes more like another by borrowing discrete cultural traits. Acculturation proceeds under conditions in which a dominant group is largely able to dictate correct behavior to a subordinate group. The process of accommodation described in this book certainly involves cultural change, but it takes place on what I call the middle ground. The middle ground is the place in between: in between cultures, peoples, and in between empires and the nonstate world of villages. It is a place where many of the North American subjects and allies lived. It is the area between the historical foreground of European invasion and occupation and the background of Indian defeat and retreat" (White, *The Middle Ground: Indians, Empires, and Republics in the Great Lakes Region, 1600–1815* [Cambridge: Cambridge University Press, 1991], x).

30. Versions of American Indian Sign Language (AISL) were practiced across all regions of North America historically; Plains Indian Sign Language (PISL) was the most widely practiced variant of these and is best documented among tribes west of the Mississippi (though, as I have mentioned already, Algonquian speakers, including the Shawnee, were documented as practitioners). However, the precise genetic relationship of dialects of AISL that may have been practiced in the Great Lakes region (and, particularly, areas farther northeast) to PISL is not clear. Nevertheless, it is reasonable to conclude that any non-PISL variants of AISL (in the Great Lakes region or elsewhere) would have had a high level of compatibility with PISL. In the first place, as Davis has demonstrated in the largest comparative analysis to date, historical documentations of PISL have between 80 and 92 percent lexical similarity. By contrast, consider that PISL and American Sign Language (ASL), which are not genetically related, evince approximately 50 percent lexical similarity. Second, because the Great Lakes region bordered closely areas in which PISL was in wide use, some degree of lexical borrowing was certainly present. See Jeffrey E. Davis, "Discourse Features of American Indian Sign Language," in *Discourse in Signed Languages*, ed. Cynthia B. Roy (Washington, DC: Gallaudet University Press, 2011), 179–217, esp. 190–94.

31. Isaac Galland, "Language," *Chronicles of the North American Savages* 1.1 (May 1835): 9, emphasis in original.

32. I am extremely grateful to Stephen Warren for his expertise and generosity in corresponding with me on this question, and who suggested that most Shawnee knew, and spoke, these languages. For more on historical patterns of contact among the Shawnee and their history of sociopolitical organization in the nineteenth century, see Warren's excellent book, *The Shawnees and Their Neighbors, 1795–1870* (Champaign: University of Illinois Press, 2009); a forthcoming book from Warren promises to shed new light on the extent of the precontact travels and relations of the Shawnee. Colin Calloway offers this helpful short history of the extent of Shawnee relations: "The people who emerged into history as the Shawnees were members of the Algonquian language family. They were culturally and linguistically related to other Algonquian-speaking peoples like the Delawares, Miamis, Kickapoos, Illinois, and Sauks and Foxes, although not necessarily allied with them. In intertribal diplomacy, Shawnees addressed the Delawares as grandfathers, the Wyandots and Iroquois as uncles or elder brothers, and other tribes as younger brothers" (Calloway, *The Shawnees and the War for America*, 4).

33. I am deeply indebted to Colin Calloway for his communication with me on this subject and for his valuable cautions with respect to the degree such questions can, and cannot, be answered.

34. In addition to the Shawnee, Jeffrey E. Davis has gathered evidence of the use of PISL among the Sauk, Kickapoo, Meskwaki (Fox), Ojibwe, and Wyandot-Huron (Davis, *Hand Talk*, 7–8); see also Allan R. Taylor, "The Plains Indian Sign Language," in *Atlas of Languages of Intercultural Communication in the Pacific, Asia, and the Americas*, ed. Stephen A. Wurm, Peter Mühlhäusler, and Darrel T. Tryon (The Hague: Mouton de Gruyter, 1996), 1242, who also places it with the Shawnees, Wyandots, and Kickapoos, as well as Cherokees and Delawares. Other evidence suggests that PISL was regionally present as well. For example, George Drouillard was hired by the Lewis and Clark expedition for his proficiency in PISL; Drouillard, whose father was a French Canadian Indian trader and his mother, a Shawnee, was born in Detroit.

35. Atwater, *Remarks Made on a Tour to Prairie du Chien*, 119–22.

36. The wording of this passage is the original and differs in punctuation and syntax from the version quoted most frequently, that being Benjamin Drake's 1841 *Life of Tecumseh*. Drake enlisted Ruddell as a firsthand source of information about Tecumseh and received a lengthy letter in response that contains the passage as quoted. The letter was reproduced in its entirety by George E. Lankford in his article about Ruddell's captivity (Lankford, "Losing the Past: Draper and the Ruddell Indian Captivity," *Arkansas Historical Quarterly* 49.3 [Autumn 1990]: 214–39). Ruddell's letter, dated January 17, 1822, is reproduced on pages 222–28; the passage quoted is on page 228.

37. Henry R[owe] Schoolcraft, *Travels in the Central Portions of the Mississippi: Comprising Observations on its Mineral Geography, Internal Resources, and Aboriginal Population* (New York: Collins and Hannay, 1825), 140.

38. Qtd. in Benjamin Drake, *Life of Tecumseh, and of his Brother, the Prophet; with a Historical Sketch of the Shawnoe Indians* (Cincinnati: E. Morgan, 1841), 97.

39. Heckewelder, *An Account of the History, Manners, and Customs, of the Indian Natives*, 1:292; [John Richardson], "A Canadian Campaign, By a British Officer," *Albion, A Journal of News, Politics, and Literature* (April 28, 1827), 5.

40. Attributed to Stokoe by Jeffrey Davis, "Discourse Features of American Indian Sign Language," 200.

41. On PISL as a language of prestige, and its recognized role in public oratory, see Davis, "Discourse Features of American Indian Sign Language," 206–7; Allan R. Taylor, "Nonspeech Communication Systems," in *Languages*, ed. Ives Goddard, vol. 17 of *Handbook of North American Indians*, ed. William C. Sturtevant (Washington, DC: Smithsonian Institution, 1996), 276–78; Taylor, "The Plains Indian Sign Language," 1243; and W. C. Vanderwerth, *Indian Oratory: Famous Speeches by Noted Chieftains* (Norman: University of Oklahoma Press, 1971), 9.

42. On "gesticulation" as ill-modulated gesture, see Watts, "Pictures, Gestures, Hieroglyphics," 85–86.

43. This was the observation of Colonel William Stanley Hatch, who witnessed Tecumseh's oratory and manner of speech in several settings (*A Chapter of the History of the War of 1812 in the Northwest. Embracing the Surrender of the Northwestern Army and Fort, at Detroit, August 16, 1812; with a Description and Biographical Sketch of the Celebrated Indian Chief Tecumseh* [Cincinnati: Miami Printing and Publishing, 1872], 116; Glenn Tucker, *Tecumseh: Vision of Glory* (New York: Bobbs-Merrill, 1956], 83).

44. John Richardson, *Tecumseh; Or, The Warrior of the West: A Poem, in Four Cantos* (1828; Ottawa, Canada: Golden Dog, 1978). For a reading of Richardson's poem in the context of other literature on Tecumseh, see Sayre, *The Indian Chief as Tragic Hero*, 268–302, esp. 289–92.

45. "Tecumseh's Speech to Governor Harrison 20th August 1810," enclosure of William Henry Harrison to William Eustis, August 22, 1810, in *Messages and Letters of William Henry Harrison*, ed. Logan Esarey, 2 vols. (Indianapolis: Indiana Historical Association, 1922), 1:465.

46. Moses Dawson, *A Historical Narrative of the Civil and Military Services of Major-General William H. Harrison, and a Vindication of his Character and Conduct as a Statesman, a Citizen, and a Soldier, with a Detail of his Negotiations and Wars with the Indians, until the Final Overthrow of the Celebrated Chief Tecumseh, and his Brother the Prophet* (Cincinnati: M. Dawson, 1821), 156. For a valuable reading of this episode that explores many of the themes of language and Indian political divisibility I examine here, see Sean P. Harvey, *Native Tongues: Colonialism and Race from Encounter to the Reservation*, 74–76.

47. Ibid., 156–57, 159. Cf. Benjamin Drake, *Life of Tecumseh, and of his Brother, the Prophet; with a Historical Sketch of the Shawnoe Indians* (Cincinnati: E. Morgan, 1841), 127. Drake's language is very close to Dawson's in a corollary passage describing this exchange and relies substantively on Dawson throughout in his more even-handed narration of the meeting at Vincennes.

48. William Henry Harrison to William Eustis, August 22, 1810, in *Messages and Letters of William Henry Harrison*, ed. Logan Esarey, 2 vols. (Indianapolis: Indiana Historical Association, 1922), 1:461.

49. Although he does not label this interjection as sign language, Robert B. McAfee, who later served under Harrison and was promoted to general during the War of 1812, also characterizes Tecumseh's manual interjection as a form of signaling: "As soon as it was interpreted in Shawnoese, Tecumseh interrupted the interpreter and said that it was all false, and giving a signal to his warriors, they seized their tomahawks and war clubs and sprang upon their feet" (McAfee, *History of the Late War in the Western Country* [1816; rpt., Bowling Green, OH: Historical Publications Co., 1919], 22). McAfee was not, however, present at Vincennes; in his account of events he did not witness during this campaign, including the meeting at Vincennes, he relies on interviews with Harrison, Croghan, and Todd, and on the diary of Eleazar D. Wood, builder of Fort Meigs.

50. Galland, "Language," 9. For rich discussion of these issues, see Sean P. Harvey, *Native Tongues*, esp. 71–79.

51. Charles Taylor, "The Politics of Recognition," *Multiculturalism: Examining the Politics of Recognition*, ed. Amy Gutmann (Princeton: Princeton University Press, 1994), 25–73.

52. Ibid.

53. Dawson, *A Historical Narrative of the Civil and Military Services of Major-General William H. Harrison*, 159.

54. Sugden, *Tecumseh: A Life*, 201. Another recent scholar glosses over the crucial linguistic play of this episode entirely, stating only that "the peace council was about to become a bloodbath." See Adam Jortner, *The Gods of Prophetstown: The Battle of Tippecanoe and the Holy War for the American Frontier* (New York: Oxford University Press, 2012), 174.

55. To be sure, the negotiations that unfolded between Tecumseh and Harrison over the succeeding days revised and rhetorically recalibrated the power relations between them in various ways and largely to Harrison's ultimate benefit. My point is not to document their relationship widely or to characterize it comprehensively but rather to use a signature episode between them as an opportunity to revisit the archival record and reassess the linguistic basis of Native resistance.

56. Dawson, *A Historical Narrative of the Civil and Military Services of Major-General William H. Harrison*, 159.

57. *The Life of Major-General William Henry Harrison: Comprising a Brief Account of His Important Civil and Military Services, and an Accurate Description of the Council at Vincennes with Tecumseh, as well as the Victories of Tippecanoe, Fort Meigs and the Thames* (Philadelphia: Grigg & Elliot, and T.K. & P.G. Collins, 1840), 25.

58. Ibid., 23.

NOTES TO CHAPTER 4

1. Epigraph: Manuel Mier y Terán, Diary, June 3, 1828, in *Texas by Terán: The Diary Kept by General Manuel de Mier y Terán on his 1828 Inspection of Texas*, ed. Jack Jackson, trans. John Wheat (Austin: University of Texas Press, 2000), 81.

2. Warrior, *The People and the Word*, 182.

3. Drake, *Life of Tecumseh*, 132.

4. Rasmussen, *Queequeg's Coffin*, 8, see esp. 52–58, in which she discusses an exchange of wampum initiated by the Haudenosaunee diplomat, Kiotseaeton, with the French on the St. Lawrence River in 1645, an episode recorded in the *Jesuit Relations*. Recognizing wampum as "part of a narrative and documentary tradition that the Haudenosaunee have used for generations," Rasmussen uses the term "writing" for both alphabetic script and wampum, "to claim the authority of that term for both forms of inscription. The term 'Pen-and-Ink Work,'"—a term she borrows from a contemporaneous Haudenosaunee observer—"displaces the hegemonic power of the word 'writing' (too easily equated solely with alphabetism) and marks alphabetic script as one of many kinds of writing at play in the conflict between Europe and the Americas" (50, 53). Germaine Warkentin also discusses this episode in an influential essay that brings history of the book studies to bear on indigenous literacies for Canadian First Nations (Warkentin, "In Search of 'The Word of the Other': Aboriginal Sign Systems and the History of the Book in Canada," *Book History* 2 [1999]: 1–27). Matt Cohen's work on this front has been inspirational; on wampum, as one element of the spectrum of Native communication practices, see *The Networked Wilderness*, 1–28; also groundbreaking, also inspirational, are Lisa Brooks and Phillip H. Round on these topics. See Round, *Removable Type*, 11, 13, 18, 72, 111, and passim; and Brooks, *The Common Pot*, esp. 54–64.

5. John Tanner, *A Narrative of the Captivity and Adventures of John Tanner, (U.S. Interpreter at the Saut de Ste. Marie,) during Thirty Years Residence among the Indians in the Interior of North America*, ed. Edwin James (New York: G. & C. & H. Carvill, 1830), 156–57. As Tanner reports, Tenskwatawa's reception was mixed. Many followed, threw away their medicine bags, and accepted his message; others, including Tanner himself, rejected him. For a valuable assessment of Tenskwatawa's complex legacy in the North, see Timothy D. Willig's excellent *Restoring the Chain of Friendship: British Policy and the Indians of the Great Lakes, 1783–1815* (Lincoln: University of Nebraska Press, 2008), esp. 243–72. On Tanner's autobiography more generally, Gordon Sayre makes a valuable contribution in which he contextualizes nineteenth-century racial identity not in terms of phylogeny but rather systems of kinship relations (Sayre, "Abridging between Two Worlds: John Tanner as American Indian Autobiographer," *American Literary History* 11.3 [Autumn 1999]: 480–99).

6. Thomas L. McKenney and James Hall, *History of the Indian Tribes of North America, with Biographical Sketches and Anecdotes of the Principal Chiefs, 1833–44*, 2 vols. (Philadelphia: D. Rice, 1872), 1:63–64. In this section, McKenney and Hall misidentify the Creek as Seminole.

7. Sayre, *The Indian Chief as Tragic Hero*, 258–59.

8. Theron A. Nunez Jr., "Creek Nativism and the Creek War of 1813–14," *Ethnohistory* 5.1 (Winter 1958): 8.

9. George Stiggins, "A Historical Narration of the Genealogy, Traditions and Downfall of the Ipsocaga or Creek Tribe of Indians, Written by One of the Tribe," in Theron A.

Nunez Jr., "Creek Nativism and the Creek War of 1813–14, Part 2" [Stiggins Narrative, continued], *Ethnohistory* 5.2 (Spring 1958): 147; emphases and irregular punctuation in text; on Stiggins's "Narration" and its emphasis on the processes of civil polity among the Muskogee, see Round, *Removable Type*, 119; on Stiggins's background and tribal affiliations, see Sayre, *The Indian Chief as Tragic Hero*, 220–21.

10. Stiggins, "A Historical Narration," 150.

11. McKenney and Hall, *History of the Indian Tribes of North America, with Biographical Sketches and Anecdotes of the Principal Chiefs*, 64–65.

12. Richard White, *The Middle Ground: Indians, Empires, and Republics in the Great Lakes Region, 1600–1815* (Cambridge: Cambridge University Press, 1991), 518. White emphasizes the importance of the Rebecca Galloway legend in Tecumseh's posthumous reinvention; for Canadians, he achieved the status of a founding national hero. For more on the assimilation and mythical recasting of Tecumseh's significance and legacy, see Sugden, *Tecumseh: A Life*, 391–401; Sayre, *The Indian Chief as Tragic Hero*, 268–302; and Terry Rugeley, "Savage and Statesman: Changing Historical Interpretations of Tecumseh," *Indiana Magazine of History* 55 (December 1999): 289–311. See also Dowd, *A Spirited Resistance*, 196–99.

13. See Gordon Sayre's chapter on Tecumseh in *The Indian Chief as Tragic Hero*, esp. 280–86, for an extremely thoughtful and valuable discussion of this particular legacy of Tecumseh for William Henry Harrison.

14. McKenney and Hall, *History of the Indian Tribes of North America, with Biographical Sketches and Anecdotes of the Principal Chiefs*, 64, 65.

15. Ibid., 63, 66, 67.

16. For a brilliant and important reading of *Life of Black Hawk* that discusses these concerns in light of Native claims of territoriality in contest with the treaty system, see Mark Rifkin, *Manifesting America: The Imperial Construction of U.S. National Space* (New York: Oxford University Press, 2009), 75–108.

17. Black Hawk, *Life of Black Hawk, or Mà-ka-tai-me-she-kià-kiàk, Dictated by Himself*, ed. J. Gerald Kennedy (New York: Penguin Classics, 2008), 21, emphasis in original.

18. Ibid., 56, 62, 61, emphasis in original. Mark Rifkin also reads this as a pointed echo of the mode of Pan-Indian organization emblematized by Tecumseh and Tenskwatawa. See Rifkin, *Manifesting America*, 103–5. See also Dowd, *A Spirited Resistance*, 191–202.

19. Rifkin, *Manifesting America*, 81.

20. I borrow the phrase "non-native oral device" from Cheryl Walker, *Indian Nation: Native American Literature and Nineteenth-Century Nationalisms* (Durham: Duke University Press, 1997), 73. Eric Cheyfitz, "The (Post)Colonial Construction of Indian Country: U.S. American Indian Literatures and Federal Indian Law," in *The Columbia Guide to American Indian Literatures of the United States Since 1945* (New York: Columbia University Press, 2006), 89.

21. See Gordon Whittaker, "The Sauk Language: A First Look," *Papers of the Twenty-Seventh Algonquian Conference*, ed. David Pentland (Winnipeg: University of Manitoba Press, 1998), 397, qtd. in Arnold Krupat, "Patterson's *Life*; Black Hawk's Story; Native American Elegy," *American Literary History* 22.3 (Fall 2010): 543.

22. Black Hawk, *Life of Black Hawk*, 6.

23. In his reading of title page images of Black Hawk in 1834 and 1836 editions of the *Life*, Phillip Round perceives a similar form of ideological work. The 1834 Boston edition depicts Black Hawk in a buttoned military coat and hair closely cropped in a three-quarter profile typical of formal sittings for military officers: "Although a prisoner of war, he appears totally assimilated into the system that imprisons him." By contrast, the 1836 London edition—produced in a space and ideological climate very distant from a U.S. national agenda—includes a portrait of him as a warrior in full regalia, with roach hairstyle and peace medallion, in an attitude that emphasizes both his cultural difference and political independence. "This portrait underscores those elements of the composite narrative that [contemporary reviewer William] Snelling found most compelling—Black Hawk's honor and perhaps 'the gall fermenting in his veins'" (Round, *Removable Type*, 184, 162).

24. [Lewis Cass], Review of *Manners and Customs of Several Indian Tribes, located west of the Mississippi . . .*, *North American Review* 22.50 (January 1826): 101.

25. Cass's assignment of "peculiar malignity" to the *Quarterly Review* is contained in a letter to Jared Sparks, editor of the *North American Review*, on July 30, 1825; the second statement is from a letter Cass wrote to Thomas McKenney on the same day. Both are quoted from Drinnon, *White Savage*, 65, 64. Drinnon's account of Cass's campaign against Hunter is comprehensive, and his refutation of Cass's principal claims against Hunter is persuasive (61–94).

26. [Cass], Review of *Manners and Customs*, 108.

27. Ibid., 101, 97.

28. Elmer, "John Neal and John Dunn Hunter," 149.

29. [Robert Walsh], "Tanner's Indian Narrative," *American Quarterly Review* 8 (September 1830): 113; Sayre, "Abridging between Two Worlds: John Tanner as American Indian Autobiographer," *American Literary History* 11.3 (Autumn 1999): 480–99, 486.

30. See Drinnon, *White Savage*, 121–52.

31. Sayre, "Abridging between Two Worlds," 486.

32. Drinnon, *White Savage*, 155–62.

33. [John Dunn Hunter], *Reflections on the Different States and Conditions of Society; with the Outlines of a Plan to Ameliorate the Circumstances of the Indians of North America* (London: J. R. Lake, 1823), 13, 14.

34. Hunter, *Reflections on the Different States and Conditions of Society*, 8–9.

35. Ibid., 16.

36. See David J. Weber, *The Mexican Frontier, 1821–1846: The American Southwest under Mexico* (Albuquerque: University of New Mexico Press, 1982), 166; for more detailed figures, see Jack Jackson, ed., *Texas by Terán: The Diary Kept by General Manuel de Mier y Terán on his 1828 Inspection of Texas*, trans. John Wheat (Austin: University of Texas Press, 2000), 206–7n47. On the "Americanization" of the northern Mexico borderlands between Independence and the U.S.-Mexico War, and the breakdown of Mexican relations with Native Americans during the same period, see David J. Weber, *Myth and the History of the History of the Hispanic Southwest* (Albuquerque: University of New Mexico Press, 1988), 105–32.

Also highly recommended is Andrés Reséndez, *Changing National Identities at the Frontier: Texas and New Mexico, 1800-1850* (Cambridge: Cambridge University Press, 2004).

37. Joseph Chambers Clopper, "J. C. Clopper's Journal and Book of Memoranda for 1828," *Quarterly of the Texas State Historical Association* 13 (July 1909): 44-80, 71.

38. David J. Weber, for example, discusses it only briefly and exclusively in terms of Anglo-Americans in his seminal book *The Mexican Frontier, 1821-1846*, denoting it "The Edwards fiasco"; Stuart Reid discusses it at greater length and includes mention of Hunter but ignores the central role of the Cherokee; Andres Reséndez includes valuable discussion of the Cherokee in his treatment of the Fredonian affair but, strangely, makes no mention of Hunter whatsoever (Weber, *The Mexican Frontier, 1821-1846*, 166-67; Stuart Reid, *The Secret War for Texas* [College Station: Texas A&M University Press, 2007], 21-25; Andrés Reséndez, *Changing National Identities at the Frontier: Texas and New Mexico, 1800-1850* [Cambridge: Cambridge University Press, 2005], 36-45).

39. Dianna Everett, *The Texas Cherokees: A People between Two Fires, 1819-1840* (Norman: University of Oklahoma Press, 1990), 23. For another discussion of the Fredonian Rebellion from the standpoint of the Cherokee that includes discussion of Hunter, see Mary Whatley Clarke, *Chief Bowles and the Texas Cherokees* (Norman: University of Oklahoma Press, 1971), 3-50. On Hunter, which unfortunately includes several erroneous statements concerning his life and the controversy surrounding his identity, see 30-36.

40. Pekka Hämäläinen, *The Comanche Empire* (New Haven: Yale University Press, 2008), 152; Everett, *The Texas Cherokees*, 25-26; Weber, *The Mexican Frontier*, 161-76; on the Comanche threat specifically, see 89, 114-15.

41. Ernest William Winkler, "The Cherokee Indians in Texas," *Quarterly of the Texas State Association* 7.2 (October 1903): 95-103.

42. Qtd. in Everett, *The Texas Cherokees*, 34; Drinnon, *White Savage*, 182.

43. Qtd. in Everett, *The Texas Cherokees*, 36.

44. This grant request was protested vigorously by U.S. Minister Joel Roberts Poinsett, who worked against the cause of Indian confederation in Texas as a potential obstacle to U.S. expansionist designs; Poinsett also feared that Hunter intended to enlist British intervention in the territory—another prospect he was eager to avoid. See Drinnon, *White Savage*, 184-89.

45. Winkler, "The Cherokee Indians in Texas," 129-30.

46. Report of Peter Ellis Bean to Stephen Austin, typography true to source, qtd. in Drinnon, *White Savage*, 196.

47. The Fredonian Declaration of Independence, December 21, 1826, in *Documents of Texas History*, ed. Ernest Wallace, David M. Vigness, and George B. Ward, 2nd ed. (Austin: State House Press, 1994), 60.

48. Ibid.

49. Ibid.

50. Benjamin W. Edwards to Aylett C. Buckner, December 26, 1826, in Frank Johnson, *A History of Texas and Texans* (Chicago: American Historical Society, 1914), 1: 36-37, emphasis in original.

51. Ibid., 1:37.

52. Benjamin W. Edwards to the Inhabitants of Austin's Colony, January 16, 1827, in Henry Stuart Foote, *Texas and the Texans; Or, Advance of the Anglo-Americans to the South-West; Including a History of Leading Events in Mexico, from the Conquest by Fernando Cortes to the Termination of the Texan Revolution*, 2 vols. (Philadelphia: Thomas, Cowperthwait & Co., 1841), 1:260; Benjamin W. Edwards and Herman B. Mayo to the Citizens of the United States of North America, n.d., in Foote, *Texas and the Texans*, 272–73.

53. James Kerr to Stephen Austin, January 24, 1827, qtd. in Reid, *The Secret War for Texas*, 24; see also Drinnon, *White Savage*, 209–10, 223–24.

54. Drinnon, *White Savage*, 184–92, 209.

55. See Peter Ellis Bean to Manuel de Mier y Terán, July 11, 1828, in *Texas by Terán*, ed. Jackson, 106–7.

56. Stephen Austin to the Inhabitants of the District of Victoria, January 22, 1827, in Frank Johnson, *A History of Texas and Texans* (Chicago: American Historical Society, 1914), 1:40–41.

57. Stephen Austin to John Dunn Hunter, January 4, 1827, in Johnson, *A History of Texas and Texans*, 42–43.

58. Qtd. in Foote, *Texas and the Texans*, 1:245.

59. *Travels in the Interior Parts of America; Communicating Discoveries Made in Exploring the Missouri, Red River and Washita, by Captains Lewis and Clark, Doctor Sibley, and Mr. Dunbar; with a Statistical Account of the Countries Adjacent. As Laid Before the Senate, by the President of the United States. In February, 1806, and Never Before Published in Great Britain* (London: Richard Phillips, 1807), 45–48.

60. Manuel de Mier y Terán to President Guadalupe Victoria, March 28, 1828, in *Texas by Terán*, 34.

61. In the surname Mier y Terán, "Mier" is the patronym; under ordinary naming conventions, "Mier" would be used to designate his name as a customary abbreviation of surname. However, in the vast majority of secondary sources that discuss Manuel de Mier y Terán, it is "Terán" that is used as the lone surname. In keeping with that tradition, I use "Terán" here.

62. Mier y Terán, Diary, June 3, 1828, *Texas by Terán*, 76. In his diary around this time, Terán provides further corroboration that PISL was in use locally, including Native peoples located traditionally east of the Mississippi. Two days earlier, the arrival of the Comisión de Límites in Nacogdoches was met on the outskirts of town by two Kickapoos on horseback, who signed "friend" in greeting (73).

63. Ibid., 80.

64. Ibid.

65. Virgil, *The Aeneid*, trans. Allen Mandelbaum (New York: Bantam Classic, 1981), 23–24.

66. *Texas by Terán*, 92.

67. Ibid., 77.

68. Ibid., 98.

69. Ibid., 31–32.

70. See, for example, Jean-Louis Berlandier, *The Indians of Texas in 1830*, ed. John C. Ewers, trans. Patricia Reading Leclercq (Washington: Smithsonian Institution Press, 1969), 33–37.

71. José María Sánchez, "A Trip to Texas in 1828," trans. Carlos E. Casteneda, *Southwestern Historical Quarterly* 29.4 (April 1926): 262, 271, cf. *Texas by Téran*, 56–57.

72. Sánchez, A Trip to Texas in 1828," 267.

NOTES TO CHAPTER 5

1. John Russell Bartlett, *Personal Narrative of Explorations and Incidents in Texas, New Mexico, California, Sonora, and Chihuahua, Connected with the United States and Mexican Boundary Commission During the Years 1850, 1851, 1852, 1853*. (1854; Chicago: Rio Grande Press, 1965), 78. All subsequent references are to this edition and are cited parenthetically.

2. My use of the term, "marvelous possessions," of course, is intended to evoke Stephen Greenblatt, *Marvelous Possessions: The Wonder of the New World* (Chicago: University of Chicago Press, 1992).

3. Goetzmann, *Exploration and Empire*, 261.

4. *Autobiography of John Russell Bartlett*, ed. Jerry E. Mueller (Providence: John Carter Brown Library, 2005), 21–31. Jerry Mueller deserves much credit for sparking new interest in Bartlett. In addition to the excellent notes he provides for this first-published edition of Bartlett's *Autobiography*, Mueller has also established a valuable visual bibliography of the artwork produced by the Boundary Commission. See *An Annotated Guide to the Artwork of the United States Boundary Commission, 1850–1853*(Las Cruces, NM: Gem Enterprises, 2000).

5. *Transactions of the American Ethnological Society*, vol. 1 (New York: Bartlett and Welford; London: Wiley and Putnam, 1845), vi–viii.

6. On the development of ethnology in the United States, including tensions between linguists and anatomists, see Reginald Horsman, *Race and Manifest Destiny: The Origins of American Racial Anglo-Saxonism* (Cambridge: Harvard University Press, 1981); Robert Bieder, *Science Encounters the Indian, 1820–1880: The Early Years of American Ethnology* (Norman: University of Oklahoma Press, 1986); and Ann Fabian, *The Skull Collectors: Race, Science, and America's Unburied Dead* (Chicago: University of Chicago Press, 2010). Among literary scholars, Carolyn Karcher and Samuel Otter have been particularly influential in assessing the impacts of Morton and his circle on the works of Herman Melville, and his own preoccupations with race-making (Karcher, "Melville's 'The Gees': A Forgotten Satire on Scientific Racism," *American Quarterly* 27.4 [October 1975]: 421–42; Otter, *Melville's Anatomies* [Berkeley: University of California Press, 1999], esp. 102–72).

7. For an excellent discussion of Gallatin's work on Indian languages, see Bieder, *Science Encounters the Indian*, 18–54; see also Conn, *History's Shadow*, 96–99. For additional background on the development of ethnological linguistics, see Gray, *New World Babel*;

on the impact of ethnological linguistics on federal Indian policy in the 1820s–1830s, see Sean Harvey, "'Must Not Their Languages be Savage and Barbarous Like Them?': Philology, Indian Removal, and Race Science," *Journal of the Early American Republic* 30.4 (Winter 2010): 505–32.

8. At that time, Gallatin's understanding was that the War Department, having a material interest in the results of his linguistic researches, would sponsor its publication; owing, however, to the decade-long protraction of Gallatin's writing schedule, the "Synopsis" was published, in redacted form, at the invitation of the American Antiquarian Society (Albert Gallatin to W. L. Marcy, March 12, 1846, in *The Writings of Albert Gallatin*, 3 vols. [Philadelphia: Lippincott, 1879], 2:625–2).

9. The most famous of these, certainly, were the first two expeditions of John C. Frémont (also a Corresponding Member of the AES). See his *Report of the Exploring Expedition to the Rocky Mountains in 1842 and to Oregon and Northern California in 1843-'44* (Washington: Blair and Rives, 1845). The classic, and truly indispensable, study of the Corps of Topographical Engineers remains William Goetzmann, *Army Exploration in the American West, 1803–1863* (New Haven: Yale University Press, 1959).

10. John Russell Bartlett, *The Progress of Ethnology: An Account of Recent Archæological, Philological and Geographical Researches in Various Parts of the Globe, Tending to Elucidate the Physical History of Man* (New York: Bartlett & Welford, 1847), 3.

11. "Preface," *Transactions of the American Ethnological Society*, 1:ix.

12. Albert Gallatin to W. L. Marcy, March 12, 1846, in *The Writings of Albert Gallatin*, 626.

13. Ibid., 627.

14. John Russell Bartlett to Caleb Cushing, n.d., in *Chronicles of the Gringos: The U.S. Army in the Mexican War, 1846–48, Accounts of Eyewitnesses & Combatants*, ed. George Winston Smith and Charles Judah (Albuquerque: University of New Mexico Press, 1968), 407, hereafter cited parenthetically. In addition to Marcy, Gallatin had also written to Winfield Scott and John C. Frémont. William H. Prescott, member of the American Ethnological Society and author of the best-selling *Conquest of Mexico*, also wrote to Cushing in an effort to acquire Mexican manuscripts and rare imprints (see ibid., 406–7).

15. For an excellent history of the naval expedition that resulted in Hale's work, see Barry Alan Joyce, *The Shaping of American Ethnology: The Wilkes Exploring Expedition, 1838–1842* (Lincoln: University of Nebraska Press, 2001).

16. Albert Gallatin, "Notes on the Semi-Civilized Nations of Mexico, Yucatan, and Central America" *Transactions of the American Ethnological Society*, vol. 1 (New York: Bartlett and Welford, 1845), 1–49.

17. Albert Gallatin, "A Synopsis of the Indian Tribes of North America," *Archæologia Americana, Transactions and Collections of the American Antiquarian Society*, vol. 2 (Cambridge: Harvard University Press, 1836), 3–4. Gallatin's eight "great families" were subdivided into twenty-eight lesser families. By 1848, with the addition of vocabularies and grammars provided by Hale and others, Gallatin would revise upward his estimate of lesser indigenous language families to thirty-two; even within this enlarged sample,

Gallatin found underlying grammatical structures to be consonant. See Gallatin, "Hale's Indians of North-West America, with an Introduction" (1848), xcvii–xcx.

18. Nor had many of these sources been widely available prior to the mid-nineteenth century. In the 1830s and 1840s, Henri Compans-Tournaux, the former French charge d'affaires in Brazil, had single-handedly excavated, indexed, and published scores of military and missionary accounts dating to the fifteenth century, including the Casteñeda account of the 1540–42 Coronado expedition into New Mexico used by Gallatin.

19. Albert Gallatin to William H. Emory, October 1, 1847, in Emory, *Notes of a Military Reconnaissance from Fort Leavenworth, in Missouri, to San Diego, in California, Including Parts of the Arkansas, Del Norte, and Gila River* (1848), 129, emphasis in original.

20. [E. G. Squier,] "New Mexico and California," *American Review: A Whig Journal Devoted to Politics* 2.5 (November 1848): 504.

21. Bartlett, *Autobiography*, 35; cf. Goetzmann, *Army Exploration in the American West, 1803–1863*, 168–69.

22. John Russell Bartlett to Evert Duyckinck, January 12, 1850, Box 1, Duyckinck Family Papers, New York Public Library. This comparison to Alexander von Humboldt indicates the truly magisterial scale of Bartlett's ambitions. From Bartlett's point of view, the more recent contributions of E. G. Squier approached this level of significance as well. Squier had approached Bartlett in 1846, in order to find an audience for the exhibition of artifacts he and Edwin Hamilton Davis had excavated in the burial mounds and tumuli in the vicinity of Chillicothe, Ohio. Following the initial sponsorship of Gallatin, who offered to pay for the publication of the Squier/Davis manuscript, Joseph Henry of the Smithsonian collaborated with Samuel F. Haven, librarian of the American Antiquarian Society, to publish Squier and Davis's *Ancient Monuments of the Mississippi Valley*, as the first volume of the Smithsonian "Contributions to Knowledge" series. Having energetically promoted Squier's work in his own *Progress of Ethnology* (1847), Bartlett in retrospect would gauge Squier's work as "the most valuable contribution, by far, that had yet been made to American Archaeology" (Bartlett, *Autobiography*, 32). For important recent discussions of the impact of Humboldt's example in nineteenth-century America, see Aaron Sachs, *The Humboldt Current: Nineteenth-Century Exploration and the Roots of American Environmentalism* (New York: Viking-Penguin, 2006); and Walls, *The Passage to Cosmos*; a seminal discussion of Humboldt remains Mary Louise Pratt's "Alexander von Humboldt and the Reinvention of América," chapter 6 of her *Imperial Eyes*, 109–40. For an insightful and well-researched account of Squier and his impacts on American ethnological research, see Terry A. Barnhart, *Ephraim George Squier and the Development of American Anthropology* (Lincoln: University of Nebraska Press, 2005). Discussion of Squier's and Davis's negotiations with Bartlett, the American Ethnological Society, the American Antiquarian Society, and the Smithsonian is found in chapters 2–3 (30–69).

23. Bartlett, *Autobiography*, 38.

24. Henry Rowe Schoolcraft to John Russell Bartlett, June 24, 1850, microfilm, Reel 1:26, The Mexican Boundary Commission Papers of John Russell Bartlett, 1850–1853, John Carter Brown Library, Providence, RI.

25. Schoolcraft's appropriation request appears to have been unavailing in the form initially proposed. However, after consulting with Colonel James D. Graham about the details of outfitting such a scientific survey in the Gila/Colorado watershed, Bartlett also submitted an itemized program to Thomas Ewing at the somewhat more modest proposed cost of $19,100. This was to include $1,500 for the position of "ethnologist, philologist, and historiographer," ostensibly to be filled by Bartlett himself (*Report of the Secretary of the Interior made in compliance with a resolution of the Senate calling for information in relation to the commission appointed to mark and run the boundary between the United States and Mexico*, 32nd Cong., 1st sess., 1852. Sen. Ex. Doc. 119, 13). In fact, as the debate over Bartlett's tenure as commissioner played out in Congress, the question of Bartlett's authorization to draw on public monies to pursue his personal research agenda would prove to be highly controversial.

26. Charles C. Rafn to John Russell Bartlett, October 2, 1850, microfilm, Reel 12 (B4):2, The Mexican Boundary Commission Papers of John Russell Bartlett, 1850–1853, John Carter Brown Library, Providence, RI. Bartlett would honor the latter half of Rafn's request by proposing for membership Colonel William Bliss, the brilliant young charge d'affaires under Zachary Taylor during the U.S.-Mexico War who was fluent in eight languages and in whose honor the present army base in El Paso is named.

27. James Edward Alexander to John Russell Bartlett, October 2, 1851, microfilm, Reel 12 (B4):4, The Mexican Boundary Commission Papers of John Russell Bartlett, 1850–1853, John Carter Brown Library, Providence, RI.

28. Bartlett, "Personal Narrative or Journal of J. R. Bartlett, while commissioner on the part of the United States, to survey and research the Boundary Line between the United States and Mexico, under the Treaty of Guadalupe Hidalgo, August 13, 1850 to December 6, 1853," Mexican Boundary Commission Original Journal, p. 100, John Russell Bartlett Papers, John Carter Brown Library, Providence, RI. Bartlett elects not to mention the detail of the sarsaparilla bottle in the published *Personal Narrative*.

29. Treaty of Guadalupe-Hidalgo, 1848, in *U.S.-Mexico Borderlands: Historical and Contemporary Perspectives*, ed. Oscar J. Martínez (Wilmington, DE: Scholarly Resources, 1996), 23.

30. Goetzmann, *Exploration and Empire*, 261–65. For the fullest recent account of the Boundary Commission, including elucidation of these details concerning the controversy surrounding the Bartlett/Condé compromise, see Joseph Richard Werne, *The Imaginary Line: A History of the United States and Mexican Boundary Survey, 1848–1857* (Fort Worth: Texas Christian University Press, 2007); for additional treatments of the Boundary Survey, see Robert V. Hine, *Bartlett's West: Drawing the Mexican Boundary* (New Haven: Yale University Press, 1968); Harry P. Hewitt, "The Mexican Boundary Survey Team: Pedro García Conde in California," *Western Historical Quarterly* 20.2 (1990): 171–96; Paula Rebert, *La Gran Linea: Mapping the United States-Mexico Boundary, 1849–1857* (Austin: University of Texas Press, 2001); and Dawn Hall, *Drawing the Borderline: Artist-Explorers of the U.S.-Mexico Boundary Survey* (Albuquerque: Albuquerque Museum, 1996). For a recent discussion enlarging on Hewitt that focuses on the work of the Mexican delegation, enlisting

important archival material from Mexico, see Paula Rebert, "*Trabajos Desconocidos, Ingenieros Olvidadas:* Unknown Works and Forgotten Engineers of the Mexican Boundary Commission," in *Mapping and Empire: Soldier-Engineers on the Southwestern Frontier,* ed. Dennis Reinhartz and Gerald D. Saxon (Austin: University of Texas Press, 2005), 156–84.

31. This point is documented in Goetzmann, *Exploration and Empire,* 263.

32. John Russell Bartlett to Samuel F. Haven, AAS Archives, Box 10, American Antiquarian Society, Worcester, MA.

33. The best and most comprehensive source on the life of Mangas Coloradas is Edwin R. Sweeney's biography *Mangas Coloradas: Chief of the Chiricahua Apaches* (Norman: University of Oklahoma Press, 1998); see, in particular, 227–49 for a discussion of Mangas's encounters with Bartlett.

34. Alex Hunt, "Mapping the Terrain, Making the Earth: William Emory and the Writing of the U.S./Mexico Border," in *American Literary Geographies: Spatial Practice and Cultural Production, 1500–1900,* ed. Martin Brückner and Hsuan L. Hsu (Newark: University of Delaware Press, 2007), 128.

35. John Cremony, *Life among the Apaches* (1868; New York: Indian Head Books, 1991), 176–77.

36. Brian DeLay has written a groundbreaking history of Indian raids and counter-raids across the borderlands during this period; see his *War of a Thousand Deserts: Indian Raids and the U.S.-Mexican War* (New Haven: Yale University Press, 2008). DeLay takes particular note of article 11 of the Treaty of Guadalupe-Hidalgo (see esp. 294–303), which I also discuss below.

37. A vivid firsthand account of the capture of Mangas Coloradas is provided by Daniel Ellis Conner, *Joseph Reddeford Walker and the Arizona Adventure,* ed. Donald J. Berthrong and Odessa Davenport (Norman: University of Oklahoma Press, 1956), 35–42; on the capture and death of Mangas Coloradas, see Edwin R. Sweeney, *Mangas Coloradas: Chief of the Chiricahua Apaches* (Norman: University of Oklahoma Press, 1998), 441–65; cf. Dee Brown, *Bury My Heart at Wounded Knee* (1971; New York: Macmillan, 2001), 194–99.

38. Orson Squire Fowler, "The Phrenology of Mangas Colorado, Or Red Sleeve," in *Human Science or Phrenology* (San Francisco: A. L. Bancroft, 1873), 1195–96. See also Daniel Thrapp, *Encyclopedia of Frontier Biography,* vol. 2 (Lincoln: University of Nebraska Press, 1991), 935–36.

39. Cremony, *Life among the Apaches,* 60; cf. Bartlett, *Personal Narrative,* 1:311.

40. Treaty of Guadalupe-Hidalgo, 26–27.

41. Speaking of his own contact with the Apache of this region while accompanying the expedition of General Stephen Watts Kearny during the U.S.-Mexico War, William H. Emory reported on a similar slippage of legal customs between the United States and American Indians vis-à-vis their shared enmity toward Mexico. One unnamed Apache chief (in all probability, this was Mangas Coloradas, who told Bartlett he remembered Kearny from their previous trek through his country) offered this observation to Kearny: "You have taken New Mexico, and will soon take California; go, then, and take Chihuahua,

Durango and Sonora. We will help you. You fight for land; we care nothing for land; we fight for the laws of Montezuma and for food. The Mexicans are rascals; we hate and will kill them all" (Emory, *Notes on a Military Reconnaissance*, 60).

42. Bartlett's early affection for Cooper is noted in William Gammell, *Life and Services of the Hon. John Russell Bartlett. A Paper Read before the Rhode Island Historical Society, November 2, 1886* (Providence: Providence Press Company, 1886), 4.

43. See Amy S. Greenberg, *Manifest Manhood and the Antebellum American Empire* (New York: Cambridge University Press, 2005), esp. 1–17; and Amy Kaplan, *The Anarchy of Empire in the Making of U.S. Culture* (Cambridge: Harvard University Press, 2002), esp. her introduction and chapter 1.

NOTES TO INDIAN PASSPORTS

1. Epigraph: Oliver O. Howard, "Causes of the Piute and Bannock War," *Overland Monthly* 9.53 (May 1887): 497.

2. Qtd. in Danielle Tisinger, "Textual Performance and the Western Frontier: Sarah Winnemucca Hopkins's *Life among the Piutes: Their Wrongs and Claims*. *Western American Literature* 37.2 (Summer 2002): 173.

3. Sarah Winnemucca Hopkins, *Life among the Piutes: Their Wrongs and Claims*, ed. Mary Peabody Mann (1883; Reno: University of Nevada Press, 1994), 2. All subsequent references are to this edition and are cited parenthetically.

4. Andrew S. McClure, "Sarah Winnemucca: [Post]Indian Princess and Voice of the Paiutes" *MELUS* 24.2 (Summer 1999): 29–51.

5. Randolph B. Marcy, *The Prairie Traveler. A Hand-Book for Overland Expeditions* (1859; Old Saybrook, CT: Globe Pequot–Applewood, 1986), 215, 216.

6. Julius Froebel, *Seven Years' Travel in Central America, Northern Mexico, and the Far West of the United States* (London: Richard Bentley, 1859), 265–66.

7. Ibid., 265.

8. Taylor, *The Archive and the Repertoire*, 28.

9. Gerald Vizenor's conception of "survivance" entails not only modes of survival and resistance (as the compound word suggests) but speaks more specifically of strategies of perseverance that sustain traditional forms of agency in a manner that evokes the character of sovereignty I have explored here: "Survivance is an active sense of presence, the continuance of native stories, not a mere reaction, or a survivable name. Native survivance stories are renunciations of dominance, tragedy, and victimry. Survivance means the right of succession or reversion of an estate, and in that sense, the estate of native survivancy" (Vizenor, "Preface," *Manifest Manners: Narratives of Postindian Survivance* (Lincoln: University of Nebraska Press, 1999), vii). Roach, *Cities of the Dead*, 26.

10. Jace Weaver, Craig S. Womack, and Robert Warrior, *American Indian Literary Nationalism* (Albuquerque: University of New Mexico Press, 2006), 70.

Index

Account of an Expedition from Pittsburgh to the Rocky Mountains (James), 58, 61–62, 70, 85–86, 199n2, 200n13, 205n39

Adams-Onís Transcontinental Treaty (1819), 13, 54, 137

Adelung, Johann and Frederick, 27; *Mithridates*, 193n20

Aeneid, The (Virgil), 114, 139–40

affect, and racial embodiment, 45–46, 47–49, 70–75, 94–95, 173–75, 176, 206n53, 207n58, 207n59

Agassiz, Louis, 40–41

Akerley, Samuel, 13, 75–78, 81, 83, 208n67

Algonquian linguistic group, 7, 30, 101, 106, 212n21, 214n30, 215n32

American Antiquarian Society (AAS), 5, 18, 28, 29, 149, 224n8, 225n22

American Ethnological Society (AES), 4, 5, 14, 15–16, 20, 147, 149–55, 224n14, 225n22; collaborations with War Department, 151–53; collaboration with Smithsonian, 225n22; membership of, 149–50, 159, 224n9, 224n14

American Indian Sign Languages (AISL): and intertribal political alliances, 85; misrecognized as sublinguistic, 103; Native multilingualism and, 101–2, 3, 214n30; prevalence of, 3; unclassified by linguists, 3, 103; treatment in Americanist cultural studies, 60, 61, 62, 80, 201n20. *See also* networks; Plains Indian Sign Language; Tecumseh

American Philosophical Society (APS), 5, 6–7, 13, 18, 20–21, 23, 25, 26, 31, 37, 38, 62–63, 68–69, 125, 126, 150, 195n29, 199n3, 199n6, 200n13; aligned against John Dunn Hunter, 126; institutional collaboration with War Department, 51, 52–57, 78, 150; *Transactions*, 21, 31, 54

Apaches, 15, 154–55, 180, 227n37, 227n41; languages of, 155, 164; Lipans, 145–48; Mimbreño band, 164–65, 166–72, 173, 175. *See also* Chipota; Dalgadito; Mangas Coloradas; Ponce

archives, 3, 11, 14, 57, 80, 81, 98–99, 100, 105–13, 187n5

Arkansas River, 13, 54, 58, 69, 71, 85, 86, 120, 137, 202n22

Arkansas Territory, 58, 123, 127, 128

Army Corps of Topographical Engineers, 150, 153, 224n9

Athapaskan language family, 164

Atwater, Caleb, 73–75, 102, 206n53

Austin, Stephen F.: Austin's Colony and, 132, 133, 141, 142; Fredonian Rebellion and, 129, 132, 134, 135–36, 142

Bakhtin, Mikhail, 52

Bannock War (1878), 177, 178, 182

Bartlett & Welford, 15, 16, 156

Bartlett, John Russell, 5–7, 14–16, 17, 18, 39, 41–42, 143, 145–76; American Ethnological Society and, 5, 14, 15–16, 20, 148–53, 163–65; *Autobiography of John Russell Bartlett*, 6, 156; Bartlett & Welford bookstore, 15, 16; compromise with Condé on "initial point" of southern New Mexico boundary, 5, 159–63; *Dictionary of Americanisms*, 6–7, 148; ethnological activities of, 5–6, 17–18, 41–42, 43, 145–47, 156–58, 164–65, 169, 171–72, 226n25; literary sentimentalism of, 172–76; negotiations with Apache concerning Mexican captives, 167–72; *Personal Narrative of Explorations and Incidents in Texas, New Mexico, California, Sonora, and Chihuahua*, 5–6, 14–15, 146–48, 16263, 165–76; *Progress of Ethnology*, 151, 225n21; pursuit of boundary commissioner appointment, 155–59, 226n25; regard for J. F. Cooper, 171

Barton, Benjamin Smith, 7, 28, 54, 195n29, 200n6

Bean, Peter Ellis, 134, 222n55; report to Stephen Austin on Fredonians of, 131, 221n46

Benton, Thomas Hart, 150, 157

Bhabha, Homi, 90

Black Hawk, 120–24, 134; *Life of Black Hawk*, 120–24, *122*, 219n16, 219m18, 220n23; production of the "Ne-Ka-Na-Wen" (Dedication) and, 121–23, *122*; and Tenskwatawa, 120

Blumenbach, Johann Gottfried von, 34–35, 196n42, 197n46

"border gnosis" (Mignolo), 10–11, 100

borderlands, 3–11, 82, 84–85, 100, 113, 114–43, 188n10, 188n13, 189n21, 213n26; Northwest Territory-Canada, 82, 98, 100–102, 114, 135–36; U.S./ Mexico and U.S./New Spain, 13, 14, 15, 17, 54–57, 79–80, 85, 115, 128, 129, 140–43, 147–48, 157, 159, 163–76, 178, 181, 220n36, 226n30, 227n36

Bourdieu, Pierre, *Outline of a Theory of Practice*, 93–94

Bowen, J. T., 109, 110, 111, 112

Brant, Joseph, 100, 212n25

Brooks, Lisa, 99, 190n24, 218n4

Buffon, Georges-Louis Leclerc, Comte de, 4, 31, 74–75, 149

Bunsen, Christian C. J., 28

Bureau of Ethnology, 15, 203n10

Burton, Sir Richard, 39

Byrd, Jodi A., 9, 189n18, 190n24

Cabeza de Vaca, Álvar Nuñez, 58–59

Caddoes, 69, 128, 138, 139. See also Dehahuit

Calhoun, John C., 52, 130, 156, 199n2

calumet (also "peace pipe"), 52, 55, 71, 97, 98

California, 150, 155, 156, 157, 161, 164, 167, 178, 227n41

Calloway, Colin G., 212n25, 215n32, 215n33

Cameahwait, 59, 201n18

captivity narratives, 4, 7, 13, 81, 83, 87, 89, 92, 115–17, 209n2. See also Indian captivity

Canada, 14, 51, 82, 98, 113, 114–15, 218n4, 219n12

Cass, Lewis, 25, 61–62, 145, 149; on John Dunn Hunter, 14, 83, 119, 124–26, 220n25; on Long Expedition, 203n26; on *Quarterly Review*, 124–25, 220n25; on PISL on as evidence of poverty of Native oral speech, 61–62, 203n28; on Tecumseh, 124–26

Catherine II (empress of Russia), 26–27, 193n19

Cherokees (western), involuntary migration into Texas (1819–1820), 128,

129; and Comanches, 129, 221n40; role in Fredonian Rebellion, 129–34, 220n38, 221n39; language of, 201; as users of PISL, 215n34
Chinese language, 23, 192n11; written script compared to PISL, 62–63, 68
Chipota, 145–46, 172, 177
Clark, William, 14, 27, 52, 71, 149; on John Dunn Hunter, 83, 125, 126; on the necessity of Indian Removal, 125; and Tenskwatawa, 115. *See also* Lewis and Clark Expedition
Clopper, J. C., 128–29
Cohen, Matt, 84, 115, 190n24, 218n4
Comanches, 56, 69, 71, 72, 142, 179–80, 212n24; Comancheria, 129, 221n40; language of 72–73
Comisión de Límites, 85, 137–44, 222n62; and Fredonian Rebellion, 85, 137; compared with Long Expedition, 137. *See also* Terán, Manuel de Mier y
Compans-Tournaux, Henri, 225n18
comparative anatomy, and linguistics, 7, 18, 28, 32, 34–40, 196n42
Condé, Pedro Garcia, 159–60, 162, 168, 172, 226n30. *See also* United States and Mexico Boundary Commission
Conn, Steven, 194n21, 194n23, 206n53, 207n59
Cooper, James Fenimore, 12, 18–25, 44–51, 148, 171, 191n6. *See also* Pioneers, *The*
Coronado, Francisco Vásquez de, 154, 225n18
Council at Vincennes: Gen. Harrison and Tecumseh (Bowen), 109–11, *110*
craniology, 35, 196n42
Cremony, John, on Mangas Coloradas, 166; and rescue of Aredia and Trinfan, 167–68; as interpreter 170, 171; and reunion of Inez Gonzalez with family, 174
Cushing, Caleb, 153, 224n14
Cuvier, Georges, 34–35

Dalgadito, 164, 168, 170–71
Davis, Jeffrey E., 202n20, 202n23, 203n30, 204n34, 205n39, 214n30, 215n34, 216n41
deafness, 75–77; as analogue to "natural" condition of Native peoples, 76–77; supposed as barrier to reason, 76
degeneracy, 31, 35, 43, 74–75, 136, 149
Dehahuit, 138–39, 140
Deleuze, Gilles, and Félix Guattari, *A Thousand Plateaus*, 9, 79, 189n16, 189n18
Detroit, 118, 212n25, 215n34; Battle of, 105, 216n43
diaspora of Native peoples into Texas, 5, 14, 82, 128–29, 131. *See also* Indian Removal
dialect, 6, 45, 65, 129; and language, 20, 29–31, 34, 41, 43, 149, 154, 192n11, 195n30, 196n40, 203n24, 214n30
Dictionary of Americanisms (Bartlett), 6, 148
Disturnell Map (1847), 147, 160–61, 165; depicted, *161*
Doña Ana, New Mexico, 159, 160, 161, 162, 163
Drinnon, Richard, 83, 124, 126, 209n3, 209n4, 220n25, 221n44
Drouillard, George, 59, 215n34
Du Ponceau, Peter Stephen, 5–7, 12, 15, 17, 25, 30, 31–32, 36–37, 40, 42–44, 58, 83, 96, 192n11, 193n13, 193n15, 199n3, 210n8; correspondence with Heckewelder, 21, 25–26, 54; declaration of Hunter as incompetent in Osage, 126–27; and etymological and comparative methods, 28–29, 31–32, 42–43, 55; philological notebooks of, 17, 36, 77–79; and polysynthesis, 23–24, 26, 39, 55, 192n10, 194n27, 197n48; on superiority of speech to writing for evidence of mind, 51
Dunbar, William, 62–63, 136–37, 203n29

Duwali (also "Bowles," "Bowl"), 129, 134, 221n39
Duyckinck, Evert, 5, 15, 16, 157

Edwards, Benjamin: role in Fredonian Rebellion of, 129, 131, 132–33, 221, 221n38; signatory of Fredonian Treaty of Union, League and Confederation, 131
Edwards, Haden: role in Fredonian Rebellion of, 129, 134, 221n38; *empresario* grant of, 82, 130–31; signatory of Fredonian Treaty of Union, League and Confederation, 131
El Paso del Norte, 160, 164
Eliot, John, 4, 29
eloquence, 24–25, 47, 95, 96, 101, 102–4, 136, 184, 194n21, 206n45, 206n53, 207n59; and polysynthetic languages, 26, 42–43, 192n10, 193n13, 194n27; and racial embodiment, 47, 70–74. *See also* gesture; oratory
embodied speech. *See* American Indian Sign Languages; deafness; gesture; oratory; Plains Indian Sign Language
Emerson, Ralph Waldo, 78
Emory, William, 3, 153, 154–55, 158, 165, 227n41
empresarios, 14, 82, 130–31, 134, 135, 137, 141–42; Colonization Laws (Mexico) and, 129
empire, U.S., 85; and narrative of westward expansionism, 55–56, 85, 125–26; iconography of, 52–54, 146–47, 220n23; as intellectual activity, 4–5, 151; as representational project, 8, 79–80, 151, 163–66
environmentalism, as theory of evolutionary development, 149
Ethnological Society of London, 60, 159, 197n48
ethnology, 2–4, 40, 5, 223n6, 225n22;

"American School" of, 40, 223n6; as decentralized amateur field, 4, 5, 6, 15, 39, 147, 148–49, 151–52, 158; as imperial discipline 4, 52–54, 56, 151; tensions between anatomists and linguists and, 39–42, 223n6
Eustis, Wiliam, 106, 107
Ewing, Thomas, 157, 158, 226n25

Farnell, Brenda, 63–64, 203n30, 204n32, 204n35, 205n38
Fields, Richard, 129–31, 133, 134–35, 136; assassination of, 134; Crittenden on, 130; signatory of Fredonian Treaty of Union, League and Confederation, 131
Fliegelman, Jay, 70, 206n45, 206n46, 207n62
Fort Wayne Treaty (1809), 105
Foucault, Michel, 8–9
Fowler, Orson Squire, 167
Fredonian Republic. *See* Red and White Republic of Fredonia
Fredonian Treaty of Union, League and Confederation, 131–33, 135, 136; as modeled on Declaration of Independence, 131; territorial designations of, 131; pact of mutual defense of, 132; as transgression of U.S. racial constitutionalism, 132–33. *See also* Red and White Republic of Fredonia
Freeman-Custis Expedition, 54, 199n5
Frémont, John C., 1, 3, 156, 177, 178, 179, 181, 224n9, 224n14
Froebel, Julius, 180–81

Gadsden Purchase, 5. *See also* "initial point" of New Mexico southern boundary
Galland, Isaac, 101, 215n31, 217n50
Gallatin, Albert, 5, 12, 15–16, 20, 39, 40, 43, 148–49, 151–55, 158, 164, 175, 195n5,

225n22; and Hale's "Indians of North-West America," 153–55, 224n17; on indigenous languages of Mexico, 153–54, 225n18; linguistic collaborations with War Department, 150–53, 224n8, 224n14; "Notes on the Semi-Civilized Nations of Mexico, Yucatan, and Central America," 151; "A Synopsis of the Indian Tribes of North America," 29, 30, 149–50, 195n30, 195n32, 224n17
Gallaudet, Thomas, 13, 75–78
Garrard, Lewis Hector, 1–3
Genl. Harrison & Tecumseh (Chapin), 111, *112*
gesture, 57, 63, 64–68, 82, 94–95, 96–97, 98–99, 101–4, 111, 114, 138, 168, 204n35; denied as speech, 103–5, 106–13; and embodied speech, 136, 202n20, 203n30, 205n43, 206n45, 211n19, 216n40; and gesticulation, 70–72, 73–75, 95, 103–7, 109, 206n44, 216n42; Stokoe on, 103, 216n40; universality of, 75–76, 103, 203n30, 207n62
Ghost Dance Religion, 98
Gila River, 148, 153, 156, 164, 167, 172
Gliddon, George, and Josiah C. Nott: *Indigenous Races of the Earth*, 35; *Types of Mankind*, 40–41
Gonzales, Inez, 166, 170, 172–76
Gray, Edward, 25, 187n7, 193n15, 194n21
"Great American Desert, The," 13, 57, 137
Great Britain, 104–5, 120, 124–25, 130, 154, 205n39; alliance with Tecumseh, 98, 103, 105, 108–9, 114, 212n25; and Red Stick War, 117; rumored alliance with Fredonians, 134, 221n44

Hale, Horatio, 153, 224n15, 224n17
Hämäläinen, Pekka, and Samuel Truett, 9–10, 189n21
Harrison, William Henry: 1840 presidential campaign of, 95, 135–36; confrontation with Tecumseh at Vincennes, 105–13, *110*, *112*, 115, 216n46, 217n49, 217n55; importance of Tecumseh to later political career and, 118–19, 219n12, 219n13; negotiating tactics with Native peoples and, 213; and Tenskwatawa, 109
Haven, Samuel F., 28, 225n22
Heckewelder, John, 18, 20–21, 23, 25, 26, 38, 43, 44, 54, 62, 103, 126, 191n7, 192n11, 203n28
Heintzelman, Samuel P., 17
History of the Indian Tribes of North America, with Biographical Sketches and Anecdotes of the Principal Chiefs, 1833-44 (McKenney and Hall), 117–20, 218n6
History, Manners, and Customs of the Indian Nations (Heckewelder), 20, 21, 26, 54
Hoowaneka (Little Elk), 74–75
Howard, Oliver O., 177, 178, 181, 182
Humboldt, Baron Alexander von, 4, 5, 17, 28, 36, 56, 86, 149, 157, 159
Hunter, John Dunn, 13–14, 81–82, 209n1; agrarian scheme for Quapaws, 127–29; assassination of, 134; authorial identity and, 86–90, 209n2, 210n11; captivity and upbringing among Osage, 85–90; and embodied discourse, 93–95; knowledge of Plains Indian Sign Language and, 81, 92–93, 210n12; as possible imposter, 13–14, 81–82, 83–84, 91, 95, 124–27; publication and reception of works and, 90–91, 124–27, 209n2; role in Fredonian Rebellion of, 112–13, 114, 127–28, 130–36, 143–44; as signatory of Fredonian Treaty of Union, League and Confederation, 131; Tecumseh and, 95–99, 128, 130, 134, 135–36, 211n9, 211n20; travel to London, 127

234   Index

Indian agency system, 27, 29, 55, 71, 117, 146, 150, 152, 178, 182
Indian captivity, 15, 86–87, 102, 115–16, 133, 148, 166–76, 215n36
"Indian Eloquence" (*Knickerbocker*), 24–25
"Indian Language of Signs" (*Account of an Expedition*), 61, 65, 68–69, 103
"Indian passports," 146–47, 172, 177–78; as figure for appendix of *Life among the Piutes*, 178, 182–83, 185; as figure of survivance, 185, 228n9; as informal system for territorialization of Native lands and peoples in western borderlands, 177–78, 179–82; as "ludicrous reverse of the passport system of the Old World," 180–81; as reiterative colonial scenario, 181–82
Indian Removal, federal policy of, 7, 11, 14, 73, 84, 125, 128, 140, 181
"Indian Sign," 145, 146, 175
indigenous populations of North America, theorized origins of, 12, 19, 20, 25, 26, 27, 30–31, 36, 40, 42, 44, 51, 55, 149, 154. *See also* Native Peoples of North America
Indo-European languages, 27, 194n22, 194n26
"initial point" of New Mexico southern boundary, negotiated by Bartlett and Condé, 159–64, *161*, 165, 226n28, 226n30
"intellectual trade routes" (Warrior), 5, 80–81, 113, 114, 208n75
interracial speech acts, 12, 19, 44–47, 94–95
Iturbide, Augustín (emperor of Mexico), 129, 132, 137

Jackson, Andrew, 73, 119
Jefferson, Thomas, 21, 27, 28, 29–30, 31, 33, 36, 37, 38, 40, 43, 55, 62, 63, 74, 83, 107, 127, 128, 149, 157, 194n21, 194n27, 195n29, 196n34, 199n4, 199n5, 199n6, 200n11, 207n59, 209n1
Jones, Sir William, 12, 27–28, 194n22

Kant, Immanuel, 76
Konkle, Maureen, 99–100, 190n24, 212n24, 213n27

Laceechnesharu (Knife Chief), 71
Lamarckianism, 50
language, as artifact, 2, 43, 64, 68, 194n21; inadequacy of, 143, 166, 172–75; natural vs. artificial, 76–77, 207n62. *See also* dialect; language encounter; linguistics; Native American languages
language encounter: scenarios of: 1–3, 47–49, 59, 64–74, 104–5, 138–39, 200n13; PISL and, 63–65. *See also* oratory; *Pioneers, The* (Cooper)
Last of the Mohicans, The (Cooper, also *LOTM*), 12, 19–20, 23–25, 49–51
Latin, 27, 88, 114, 139
Latour, Bruno, 9
Leclaire, Antoine, 121, 123
LeMenager, Stephanie, 58, 84–85, 188n13, 200n11
Lenni Lenape (Delaware), 20, 46, 47, 49, 51, 96, 128, 130, 138, 212n25, 215n32, 215n34; language of, 18, 21, 22, 26, 44, 61, 155, 195n27, 203n28. *See also Last of the Mohicans, The* (Cooper); *Pioneers, The* (Cooper)
Lewis and Clark Expedition, 8, 27, 52, 54–55, 58, 59–60, 92, 150, 199n4, 199n5, 200n11, 215n34
Lewis, Meriwether, 27, 55, 59–60, 61, 199n6, 201n18, 203n24. *See also* Lewis and Clark Expedition
lexicography, 5, 6–7, 148; practices of lexical collection, 1–3, 5–6, 17–18, 64–69

Life among the Apaches (Cremony), 166–68
Life among the Piutes: Their Wrongs and Claims (Winnemucca), 177–85; as "ethnoautobiography," 178; and protocols of literary authentication, 177–78; as "outbreak of American Indian in human literature," 178; relays between text and scenarios of theatrical performance, 177–78, 183–85
Life of Black Hawk, or Mà-ka-tai-me-she-kià-kiàk (Black Hawk and Patterson), 120–24, *122*, 219n16, 219m18, 220n23
linguistics: comparative method, 33, 194n22, 194n23, 194n26; and/as epistemology, 2, 10, 11–12, 19, 20, 32, 43, 44, 56, 57, 64, 68–69, 88, 93, 107, 125, 150, 152; etymological, 28–31, 40–41, 194n23, 195n30, 195n32, 196n40; ideology, 42; lexical variation and, 12, 28–29, 33, 42, 43, 63, 101, 203n24, 214n30; and linguistic diversity, 33–34; linguistic genealogy and classification, 32–34, 195n32, 196n37, 196n39; linguistic relativity, principle of, 89, 210n8; morphology, 25, 42, 57, 64, 65, 205n38; phonology, 19, 34, 42, 43, 205n38; "promiscuous words," 58; syntax, 34, 42, 55, 57, 58, 63, 69, 100, 205n38. *See also* ethnology; philology
Linnaeus and Linnaean classification, 31, 32, 34–35, 88
literacies: alphabetic, 21–22, 84, 87, 88, 90–91, 115, 180, 182; alphabetic illiteracy, 21–22, 121, 179–81; indigenous non-alphabetic, 115–18, 92–93, 201n20, 218n4
Literary Voyager; Or, Muzzenigun, 30–31
Local Histories/Global Designs: Coloniality, Subaltern Knowledges and Border Thinking (Mignolo), 10–11, 100, 189n22, 190n23, 213n26
"locus of enunciation" (Mignolo), 11, 100

Logan, 74–75, 194n21, 207n58, 207n59
Long Exploring Expedition, 8, 51–58, 61–63, 76, 84–85, 137, 150, 200n11, 200n12, 200n13
Long, Maj. Stephen Harriman, 51, 52, 58, 137, 199n2, 203n18. *See also* Long Exploring Expedition
Louisiana Purchase, 27, 54, 199n4

Mallery, Garrick, 66, 67, 68, 201n20, 202n20, 203n30, 205n41, 207n62
Mangas Coloradas (also "Mangus Colorado," "Red Sleeve," "Red Sleeves"), 164–65, 166–72, 175, 180–81, 227n33, 227n41; Bartlett's estimation of, 164–65, 171–72; capture and death of, 167, 227n37; decapitation and phrenological examination of, 167; "Indian passport" of, 180–81; reputation of, 166–67; negotiations with Bartlett concerning Mexican captives, 167–72
manifest destiny, 9–10, 165, 176
Mann, Mary Peabody, 178, 183
Marcy, Randolph, 179–80, 181
Marcy, William L., 151–53, 155, 224n8, 224n14
Maury, Louis Ferdinand Alfred, 35–36, 40
Mayo, Herman B., on John Dunn Hunter, 95, 136; as signatory of Fredonian Treaty of Union, League and Confederation, 131
McKenney, Thomas L., and James Hall, 117–20, 218n6, 220n25
Melville, Herman, 167, 223n6
Mexican Revolution (1821), 128, 137
Mexico City, 5, 54, 134, 153
Mignolo, Walter D., 10–11, 100, 189n22, 189n23, 190n24
Missouri River, 1, 52, 69, 164, 199n2, 210n12
monogenesis, 27, 36, 40, 149, 154, 175

236 *Index*

Monroe, James, 52
Monthly Review (London), 90–91, 94
Morton, Samuel George, 40, 158, 196n42, 223n6; on philology as "broken reed," 41–42
Murray, Laura, 64, 197n5, 201n21

Nacogdoches, 13, 82, 129, 130, 131, 132, 134, 137, 139, 141, 142, 222n62
Narrative of the Captivity and Adventures of John Tanner (Tanner and James), 116, 218n5
Native American languages, 2, 3–4, 6–7, 10, 11–13, 14, 17–51, 54–57, 58–72, 75–82, 84–85, 99–101, 114, 121–23, 126, 129, 135–37, 139, 149–50, 152–56, 183–84, 187n5, 185n7, 191n7, 192n10, 192n11, 193n13, 193n15, 194n21, 194n27, 195n29, 195n30, 195n32, 196n40, 199n6, 200n13, 201n18, 201n20, 202n22, 202n23, 203n30, 204n32, 207n62, 210n8, 212n21, 214n30, 215n32, 215n34, 216n41, 223n7, 224n17. See also American Indian Sign Languages; eloquence, linguistics; Native linguistic diversity; physiognomy; Plains Indian Sign Language; polysynthesis
"Native intellectual sovereignty" (Warrior, Weaver, and Womack), 178, 185
Native linguistic diversity, 23–24, 33–34, 36, 39, 43, 59, 100–102; as argument against Native political union, 100, 105–8, 135–36; as argument for antiquity of Native American origins, 29–30; and Fredonian Republic, 136–37
Native Peoples of North America: Apalaches, 58; Arapahoes, 69, 71; Assiniboines, Farnell on PISL and, 204n35; Atsinas (Gros Ventre), 200n13; Bannocks, 182; Chickasaws, 9, 96, 130; Choctaws, 95, 128 (language of, 212n21); Coco Maricopas, 17 (language of, 154–55); Dakotas, language of, 39; Illinois peoples, 155, 215n32; Illinois trade language, 101; Iowas, 96, 102; Iroquois, Six Nations of (also "Haudenosaunee"; collectively Mohawks, Oneidas, Senecas, Cayugas, Onondagas, and Tuscaroras), 20, 33, 46, 115, 206n45, 212n25, 215n32, 218n4 (Iroquoian languages, 26, 36); Kickapoos, 85, 96, 128, 130, 138, 212n25, 215n32 (as speakers of PISL, 102, 215n34, 222n62); Kiowas, 56, 69, 71; Konzas, 56, 70, 200n13; Massachusetts, language of, 29; Mayans, 151 (language of, 154); Meskwakis (also "Fox"), 96, 121 (language of, 215n32; as speakers of PISL, 101, 102, 215n34); Mexicas, language of (Nahuatl), 154; Miamis, 100, 105, 106, 128, 212n25, 215n32; Missourias, 102 (language of, 38, 106, 108); Mohawks, 20, 100; Muskogees (Creek), 5, 95 101, 117–19, 212n21, 218n6, 218n9; Narragansetts, language of, 29; Natchez peoples, 117; Navajos, 164, 165, 166 (blankets of, 165); Nottoways, language of, 36; Ojibwes (also "Chippewa"), 30, 73, 102, 115, 116, 120, 212n25, 215n34; Omahas, 56, 200n13; Otoes, 56, 86, 102 (vocabulary of, 200n13); Otomis, language of, 154; Ottawas, 73, 120, 212n25; Piankeshaws, 130; Pimas, 154; Piñals, 172; Potawatomis, 73, 86, 96, 105, 106, 107, 108, 120, 130, 212n25; Quapaws, 127, 128, 130; Shoshones, 59, 201n18; Sioux, 96, 210n12 (vocabulary of, 200n13); Winnebagos, 73–75, 102, 120; Wyandots (Huron, also "Wyandotte"), 20, 33, 212n25, 215n32 (language of, 108; use of

PISL by, 215n34). *See also* Apaches; Comanches; Osages; Sauks; Shawnees
Neal, John, 83, 91, 210n11
networks, 4, 5, 6–8, 10, 11, 79, 80–82, 114–37, 150–53, 183; indigenous, 4, 11, 13, 84–85, 112–13; of learned societies, 4, 16, 20, 52–57, 158–59, 225n22, 226n22; semiotic, 10–11, 93, 106, 114–18, 120. *See also* "intellectual trade routes"
New Madrid earthquakes (1811–1812), 95, 98, 117–18, 119
New Mexico, 5, 16, 54, 148, 150, 153, 154, 156, 157, 164, 166, 167, 225n18, 227n41; disputed southern boundary of, 159–63, *161, 162*
New York, NY, 3, 4, 5, 6, 15, 16, 20, 75, 81, 82, 83, 126, 147, 148–49, 156, 167
New York Globe, 8, 56, 79
New-York Historical Society, 148, 158
New-York Institution for the Deaf and Dumb, 75, 81, 82, 83, 209n4
North American Review, 61, 124 191n6, 191n7, 203n26, 220n25
Notes on the State of Virginia (Jefferson), 29, 203n29, 207n58

O'Fallon, Benjamin, 71
onomatopoeia, 202n20
oratory, 13, 14, 23, 24–25, 64, 70–71, 73–76, 92, 96, 101–5, 119, 123, 206n45, 206n46, 211n19, 211n20; PISL and, 216n41. *See also* affect, and racial embodiment; eloquence; Tecumseh
orthography, 12, 30, 31, 44, 55, 58, 64, 121
Osages, 13, 56, 69, 85–86, 88, 95–99, 102, 114, 124, 128; language of, 88, 90, 92, 96–97, 126, 212n21

Pallas, Peter, 26–27, 28, 193n19
Pan-Indianism, 5, 13, 14, 82, 85, 95–113, 115–24, 125–26, 128, 130, 131, 134–35, 136–37, 211n18, 212n21, 212n25, 219n18; linguistic arguments for and against, 104–9, 135–36; media and multilingualism of, 105–9. *See also* Black Hawk; Fields, Richard; Hunter, John Dunn; Tecumseh; Tenskwatawa
Patterson, John A., 121, 122, 123
Patterson, Robert, 199n3, 199n6
Pawnees, 56, 69, 71, 85, 86, 200n13
peace medallions, 52, 54–55, 71, 111, 220n23
Peale, Titian Ramsay, 52, 53
performance, 1–3, 7, 50, 57, 62, 63–64, 79, 84, 93, 100, 104–5, 109, 146–47, 159–60, 177, 180–81, 183–85, 190n24, 206n45, 211n20; and pantomime, 1, 3, 13, 60–61, 65, 93, 109, 170–71, 181, 202n20; racial, 90–91, 94–95, 136, 140, 170–71
Personal Narrative of Explorations and Incidents in Texas, New Mexico, California, Sonora, and Chihuahua (Bartlett), 5–6, 14–15, 146–48, 162–63, 165–76
personhood: authorial, 86–90, 209n2, 210n11; "Indian passports" and, 176–82; national 165–66, 175–76; racial, 72–75, 89–91, 126–27, 133
philology, 7, 8, 25, 42, 43, 77, 149, 151, 194n26, 210n8; as "broken reed" (Morton), 41–42; of race, 12, 18–19, 26–42, 69, 149, 151, 175, 197n43, 200n11; "Universal philology," 42. *See also* linguistics
phrenology, 167
physiognomy, 35–37, 196n42
Pickering, John, 6, 27, 30, 31–32, 33, 43, 55, 210n8
Pike, Zebulon, 54
Pioneers, The (Cooper), 12, 21–23, 44–49, 191n6
Piutes, 177–78, 182–84; story of tribal name, origins of, 177, 183–84
Plains Indian Sign Language (PISL, also

"Plains Sign Talk," "Plains Hand Talk"), 2–3, 12–13, 57–82, 139, 204n31, 208n67; archive and, 3, 11, 14, 57, 80; ASL and, 214n30; Cabeza de Vaca and, 59; as challenge to existing linguistic epistemologies, 68–69; challenges of representation of, 64–68; and cognition, 69; and deaf education, 75–77, 207n62, 208n67, 208n68; as documented on Lewis and Clark expedition, 59–61, 201n18, 203n24; as documented by Long Expedition, 51, 58, 61–62, 65–69, 70–73, 75–77; geographical range of, 63, 100–101, 136–37, 214n30; as haunting presence of language encounter scenarios, 57, 63–64; historical study of, 203n30; as imagined key to Indian interiority, 70–74; as indication of poverty of Native oral speech, 60–61; as indigenous communicative network, 14, 63, 81–82, 85, 136–37; John Dunn Hunter and, 81, 92–93, 210n12; as lingua franca, 63, 69, 103; mnemonic function of, 63–64, 211n20; morphology of, 205n38; origins and spread of, 63, 204n32; as pantomime, 60–61, 202n20; as language of prestige, 216n43; Tecumseh and, 101–13, 211n19; as variant of AISL, 203n24, 203n28, 211n19; as writing, 68. *See also* American Indian Sign Language; gesture; linguistics
Plan of Iguala (1821), 133
Poe, Edgar Allan, 58, 148
Poinsett, Joel Roberts, 134, 221n44
Polk, James, 148, 152–53, 156
polygenesis, 27, 35–36, 40
polysynthesis, 7, 23–24, 26, 34, 39, 43, 55, 194n27, 198n48; and agglutination, 23, 192n10
Ponce, 164, 168, 170–71
Prairie Traveler, The (Marcy), 179–80

primitivism, 75–77
Pritchard, James Cowles, 149, 197n48
Procter, Henry, 103, 105
Progress of Ethnology (Bartlett), 151, 225n21
prophecy, 98, 100, 114, 115–16, 118, 120
public spheres, 82, 125–26, 178, 185, 206n46

Rafn, Charles C., 158, 159, 226n26
Rasmussen, Birgit Brander, 115, 190n24, 201n20, 218n4
Red and White Republic of Fredonia (also "Fredonian Rebellion", "Fredonian Republic"), 13, 14, 81, 83, 85, 95, 112, 127–37, 138, 139, 144; "Agents of the Committee of Independence" of, 131; "Committee of Red People" 131; in historiography, 221n38, 221n39; John Dunn Hunter's role in, 112–13, 114, 127–28, 130–36, 143–44; millennialist echoes of, 129, 133–34; PISL and, 136–37; racial underpinnings of, 127–36; slavery and, 133; troubling national hybrid as, 132; as "unnatural," 135–36; U.S. revolutionary rhetoric of, 131, 132–33; U.S.-style rights-based constitutionalism and, 132–33
Red River, 58, 120, 131, 199n4; in Fredonian Treaty, 131; as southern U.S. boundary following Louisiana Purchase, 54, 129, 199n2
Red Stick War, 117–19
Redding, Cyrus, 94–95, 127
Reid, Thomas, 75–77, 207n62
Remarks Made on a Tour to Prairie du Chien; thence to Washington City, in 1829 (Atwater), 73–76, 206n53, 215n35
Richardson, John, 105, 216n39, 216n44
Rifkin, Mark, 9, 121, 188n13, 190n24, 212n24, 219n16, 219n18

Rio Grande: as southwestern boundary of Fredonian Republic, 131; as U.S./Mexico Boundary following Treaty of Guadalupe-Hidalgo (1848), 152, 159–62, 199n4
Rocky Mountains, 1, 29, 40, 54, 60, 86, 61, 69, 150, 152, 154, 164, 195n30, 199n2, 202n22
Round, Phillip H., 115, 190n24, 218n4, 220n23
Ruddell, Stephen, recollections of Tecumseh, 102, 103–4, 215n36
Ruttenburg, Nancy, 192n2, 205n43
Ruxton, George A. F., 60–61, 202n22, 203n24

Sabine River, 128; as U.S.-Mexico international boundary, 137
Sacagawea, 59, 201n18
San Antonio de Bexar, 128–29, 130, 137, 141, 142
Sánchez, José Maria, 141; romantic sentimentalism of, 143–44. *See also* Comisión de Límites
Santa Rita Copper Mines (New Mexico), 163–64, 167; depicted, *162*
Sauks (also "Sacs"), 96, 101, 102, 120–21; language of, 121–23, 215n32, 219n21; oral speech as phonetically represented, *122*; as speakers of PISL, 101, 102, 215n34
Say, Thomas, 58, 65, 71, 72–73, 206n50
Say-do-carah ("conquerors,"), 177, 183–85; as name for Piutes, story of, 177, 183–84
Sayre, Gordon, 117, 126, 190n24, 216n44, 218n5, 218n8, 219n12, 219n13
Schlegel, Friedrich, 12, 27–28, 31, 50, 96, 194n26
Schoolcraft, Henry Rowe, 12, 39, 40, 43, 83, 102, 104, 125, 148, 196n40; coinages of "Algic" and "Ostic," 33–34; disdain for "word hunters," 30–32; support of Bartlett, 157–58, 226n25
Senaco, 179–80
Seven Years' Travel in Central America, Northern Mexico, and the Far West of the United States (Froebel), 180–81
Shawnees, 13, 82, 96, 98, 100, 115, 128, 130, 138, 212n25; language of, 104–5, 106, 108, 212n21; multilingualism of, 101–2, 214n30, 215n32, 215n34
Shepheardes Calendar (Spenser), 41–42
Smithsonian Institution, 15, 66, 67, 203n30, 225n22
sovereignty, 3, 80, 99, 135, 168, 169, 178, 180–81, 182, 183, 185, 206n46, 213n28, 228n9
Sparks, Jared, 83, 124, 220n25
spatiality: indigenous space and spatiality, 3, 9–11, 51, 82, 114–18, 120–21, 125, 131, 138, 181–82, 184–85, 189n18, 219n16; Mexican space and spatiality, 128–29, 137–40, 141–43, 160–63, 168–70, 172–75, 220n36; "spatial turn" in Americanist scholarship, 188n10; U.S. national space and spatiality, 3–5, 6–7, 9–11, 13, 14, 51, 52–58, 72–73, 78–79, 85, 99–101, 115, 125, 126, 137, 160–63, 165–66, 168–70, 175–76, 179–82, 199n2, 199n4, 212n24, 221n44. *See also* borderlands; networks
Speech acts and racial classification, 89–91, 128–29, 138, 172–76
Squier, Ephraim G., 4, 5, 151, 155, 157, 158, 225n22
Stephens, John Lloyd, 148, 151
Stiggins, George, 117–18, 218n9
Stokoe, William, 103, 203n30, 216n40
Sugden, John, 95–96, 108, 211n18

Tanner, John, 115–17; *A Narrative of the Captivity and Adventures of John Tanner* (Tanner and James), 116, 218n5

Tarrarecawao (Long Hair), 71
Taylor, Charles, and 1990s Québécois debate, 107
Taylor, Diana, 2, 3, 84, 100, 181
Taylor, Zachary, 148, 152, 156, 161, 226n27
Tecumseh (also "Te-cum-seh," "Tecumpseh," "Tecumthé"), 5, 13–14, 126; attacked by Cass, 124–26, 128, 130, 134, 144; confrontation with Harrison at Vincennes, 105–13, *110, 112*, 115, 216n46, 217n49, 217n54, 217n55; likely knowledge of sign language of, 101–5; and Pan-Indian movements, 85, 99–100, 114–20, 126, 135–36, 212n25; posthumous reputation of, 117–20, 219n12, 219n13; and Shawnee multilingualism, 100–102, 104–105, 212n21; speech before the Osage, 82, 86, 95–99, 211n19, 211n20. *See also* eloquence; Harrison, William Henry; Hunter, John Dunn; oratory; Pan-Indianism; Red Stick War
Tejanos, 128, 130, 142–43
Tenskwatawa (The Prophet), 100, 212n25, 218n5; and Black Hawk, 120; religious edicts of, 116; as symbol of confederated Native resistance, 114–15, 119–20, 212n25, 218n5, 219n18; and wampum use as bodily surrogacy, 116–17
Terán, Manuel de Mier y, 114, 137–42, 222n61; comparison of Native peoples and Anglo-Americans to, 141–43; conference with Dehahuit and, 138, 140; Fredonian Rebellion and, 137, 138; on Mexican Tejanos, 141, 142–43; observations of PISL and, 139, 222n62; pessimism about Mexican control of Texas about, 138–40; policy recommendations of, 140; quotation of Virgil and, 114, 139–40; racial characteristics of Native peoples and, 138, 140–41; reception of Native emissaries of in Nacogdoches of, 138. *See also* Comisión de Límites
Texas, 5, 13, 14, 54, 59, 81, 83, 85, 112, 114, 120, 123, 128–44, 145–47, 157, 160–61, 177, 179–80, 199n4; Anglo-American squatters within, 128, 130, 132, 137. *See also empresarios*
Tower of Babel, 36
transcontinental railroad, 157, 162
translation, 18, 20–21, 43, 44, 47, 49, 51, 59, 93–94, 106–13, 121, 123, 171, 196n40, 201n18, 201n20; depicted, *110*
Treaty of Guadalupe-Hidalgo (1848), 5, 15, 145, 160, 166, 172; Article 5, 145, 156, 160; Article 11, 168, 172, 227n36
treaty system, 2, 73, 99–100, 105, 121, 135–36, 190n24, 212n24, 212n25, 213n26, 219n16; and codification of "Indian nations," 99–100, 213n27; and linguistic divisibility of Native peoples, 99, 100, 106–8, 212n23
Truckee, 177–79, 181, 182–83; etymology of name, 177, 181; and "rag friend" conferred by Frémont, 178–79, 181, 185
Trumbull, John, 18, 47
Turner, William Wadden, 16, 39, 158

United States and Mexico Boundary Commission (1850–1857), 4, 5–6, 14, 145–48, 155–76, 226n25, 226n30. *See also* Bartlett, John Russell; Condé, Pedro Garcia
U.S.-Mexico War, 1, 3, 4, 5, 14–15, 150, 151, 152, 156, 161, 167, 179, 188n13, 226n26, 226n41

Vater, Johann, 27, 198n48
Victoria, Guadalupe (Mexican General and president), 130, 134, 137, 141
Vizenor, Gerald: on sign language, 201n20; and survivance, 185, 228n9

vocabulary collection, 1–3, 6–7, 17–18, 26–27, 64, 200n13; American Indian Sign Languages and, 3, 64–69; nonstandard orthographies and, 12, 30–31, 43–44, 55; problems of translation and, 1–3, 17–18
vocabulary forms ("skeletons"), 8, 36, 37, 38, 200n13
"Vocabulary of Indian Languages" (*Account of an Expedition*), 69
Vocabulary; Or, Collection of Words and Phrases which have supposed to be peculiar to the United States (Pickering), 6–7
Volney, Constantin-François Chasseboef, Comte de, 38

Wabokieshiek, 120, 123
Wah-To-Yah and the Taos Trail (Garrard), 1–3
Walsh, Robert, 52, 126, 197n45, 199n3
wampum, 93, 106, 114, 115, 118, 120; as form of personal surrogacy, 116–17; as writing, 218n4
War Department, collaboration with learned institutions on ethnological programs of, 5, 13, 14, 15, 55–57, 78, 147, 149–54, 183, 224n8
Warrior, Robert Allen, 5, 80–81, 114–15, 178, 185, 190n24, 208n75
Watts, Pauline Moffitt, 70, 206n44
Weaver, Jace, and Craig S. Womack, 178, 185
Welford, Charles, 16, 148, 156
Weller, John B., 156, 161
Western Engineer, 52, 53, 54
White, Richard, 100–101, 118–19, 212n25, 214n29, 219n12
Whorf-Sapir hypothesis, 210n8
Williams, Roger 4, 29
Winamek, 107, 109
Winnemucca, Sarah (Thoctmetony),177–85; as author of *Life Among the Piutes*, 177–79; literacy and liminality of, 178, 182–83; and Native intellectual sovereignty, 185; and survivance, 185, 228n9; theatrical performance and textuality, 184–85

Ziff, Larzer, 59–60, 61, 80, 201n20
Zeisberger, David, 44, 51, 192n10

About the Author

Robert Lawrence Gunn is Associate Professor of English at the University of Texas at El Paso.